Your Future Home

WITHDRAWN FROM
GVSU LIBRARIES

Reprint of the 1923 edition with an introduction by Lisa D. Schrenk

The American Institute of Architects Press
Washington, D.C.

NA
7205
.Y69
1992

The American Institute of Architects Press
1735 New York Avenue, N.W.
Washington, D.C. 20006-5292

Introduction copyright 1992 by The American Institute of Architects
All rights reserved
Printed in the United States of America
96 95 94 93 92   5 4 3 2 1

First published in 1923 by Weyerhaeuser Forest Products, St. Paul, Minnesota

Library of Congress Cataloging-in-Publication Data

Your future home/the Architects' Small House Service Bureau of the
    United States, Inc.
        p. cm.
        "Reprint of the 1923 edition with an introduction by Lisa D.
    Schrenk."
        ISBN 1-55835-041-1
        1. Small houses—United States—Designs and plans.
    I. Architects' Small House Service Bureau of the United States.
    NA7205.Y69   1992
    728'.37'0223—dc20   92-23511
                                               CIP

Design by Market Sights, Washington, D.C.
Printed by John D. Lucas Printing Company, Baltimore, Md.

410892

Contents

vii   Introduction to the reprint edition:

        The Work of the Architects' Small House Service Bureau,

        by Lisa D. Schrenk

7   Introduction to the 1923 edition

11   Some fundamental hints on financing the building of a home

12   How to select a plan to suit your needs

14   How to read and understand plans

15   Portfolio of house plans

154   What the Architects' Small House Service Bureau has to offer

The SMALL HOME

FINANCING — PLANNING   BUILDING

Published Monthly by

The Architects' Small House Service Bureau
of the United States, Inc.

National Headquarters

1200 2nd Ave. South

MINNEAPOLIS · · · MINNESOTA

Regional Offices
✛✛✛

NEW YORK
BOSTON
CHICAGO
SEATTLE
INDIANAPOLIS
MINNEAPOLIS
MILWAUKEE
ST. LOUIS
PITTSBURGH
DENVER

The Work of the Architects' Small House Service Bureau

After World War I, a group of Minnesota architects created the Architects' Small House Service Bureau, an organization they hoped would provide quality small house designs that could be constructed at reasonable cost. Between its foundation in 1919 and dissolution in 1942, the Bureau became a national organization endorsed by the American Institute of Architects that provided designs and educational services for the small house builder.[1]

During World War I federal government restrictions on the building industry had drastically reduced house construction, causing a postwar housing shortage that was compounded by sharply rising building costs.[2] By 1921 an estimated 1.24 million housing units were needed to meet a shortage that Senator James Wadsworth proclaimed of "dangerous proportions."[3] In addition to a lack of housing, Secretary of Commerce Herbert Hoover reported that 30 percent of the existing units were "below American ideals of decent family life."[4]

One way to provide designs that could fill the pressing need for low-cost housing was to sell plans through the mail. Such services were not new. A complete mail-order plan service was begun by George Palliser in the 1870s. His offerings, expanding on earlier builders' guides and plan books, provided architectural designs and details in book form to be copied by builders. Palliser also offered designs, advice, and alterations for individual buyers through the mail.[5] This mail-order service, with more detailed plans and specifications than the plan books, was intended to provide the architectural services needed for a small house, taking the place of a local architect.

The concept of the mail-order plan service grew rapidly, along with middle-class demand for reasonably priced houses. By the start of the twentieth century, a wide variety of designers were advertising plan books in magazines and home builders' bulletins.[6] Building associations, product manufacturers, lumber dealers, and newly formed home service organizations provided mail-order designs. Companies such as Aladdin and Sears Roebuck provided building materials as well as designs.[7]

As demand for these services grew, a power struggle emerged among architects, plan book writers, and builders. Each hoped to capture the expanding market for construction of single-family homes and influence national housing standards.[8] Architects, feeling threatened, spoke out against "cheap" plan book

In 1922 the Architects' Small House Service Bureau began publishing ten to fifteen designs per issue in *The Small House*. The monthly journal also featured educational articles on architectural styles and financing and building a home.

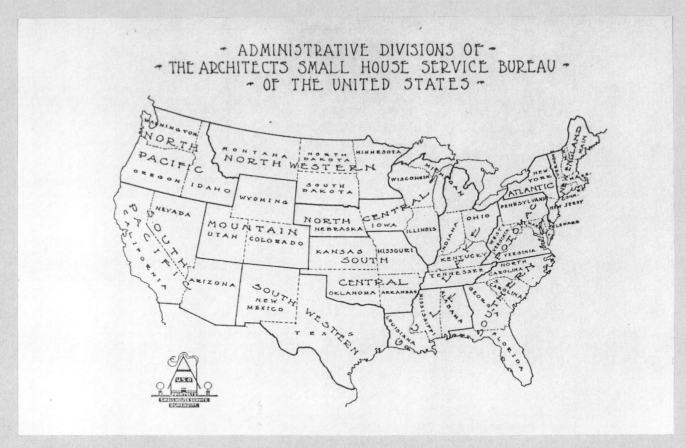

designers who claimed to be architects, arguing that an architect's professional mastery of the principles of design and construction produced better houses.[9] In truth, architects occasionally produced bad designs and the quality of plan book designs varied widely.

In 1919 several Minnesota architects assembled to address the postwar housing shortage and discuss how to combat the rash of poorly designed houses being constructed in Minneapolis and across the country. Their collaboration resulted in the development of the Architects' Small House Service Bureau, which Carl A. Gage, Beaver Wade Day, Frederick Mann, and Roy Childs Jones founded to serve the small home builder.[10] Other local architects involved later included Edwin H. Hewitt, Robert T. Jones, Rollin C. Chapman, and former Prairie School architects William Gray Purcell and John Van Bergen.

With the creation of the Bureau, its founders hoped not just to improve the quality of small house design but to capture a sector of the building industry not previously controlled by architects. Bureau members felt this could be accomplished by providing a more complete house plan service than that

available from builders, contractors, and lumber-yards. They believed "good taste is always conservative" and favored revival designs, avoiding the latest in "architectural fashion."[11] Colonial Revival designs ultimately proved to be the Bureau's most popular.

With the help of architect Edwin H. Brown, a member of the Minneapolis Civic and Commerce Association and the newly formed American Institute of Architects' Small House Committee, the Architects' Small House Service Bureau was endorsed by both the AIA and the Department of Commerce in 1921.[12] At the same time the Bureau was restructured into a national organization, with the original Minnesota Bureau reconstituted as the Northwestern Division, one of thirteen regional bureaus.[13] Other divisions were located in Denver, Indianapolis, New York City, Milwaukee, Seattle, Pittsburgh, Boston, Chicago, and St. Louis. None were ever formed in the southern or southwestern regions of the country.

The regional divisions were limited dividend stock corporations, as was the original Minnesota Bureau. Members joined the Bureau by paying $100 for one share of common stock in the closest regional bureau and $10 for one share in the national

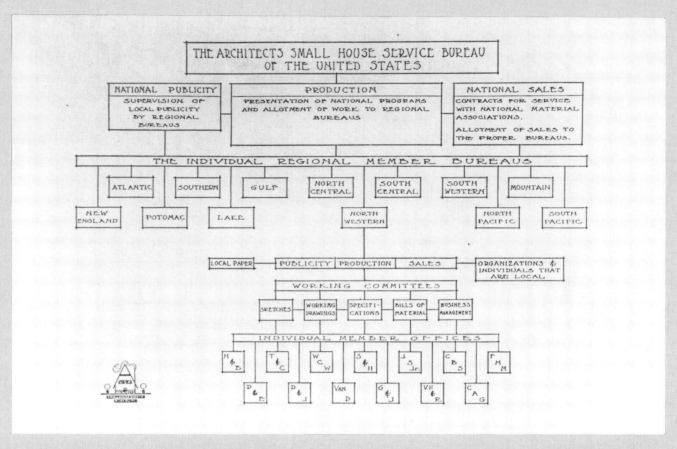

bureau.[14] They were known as "the eight-dollar-a-year-architects" because dividends were limited to eight percent per annum. Each member could sell plans for a 25 percent commission and had the chance to secure the position of supervisor on any resulting construction projects. Members could also execute design work for the Bureau and sell on consignment the books, plans, specifications, agreements, and other forms produced by the Bureau. The real value in their participation, however, was in architects "assisting in a movement for the betterment of architecture."[15]

The Bureau's national office developed ties with other organizations concerned with the quality of small houses and built an impressive network of publications and programs. The latter were intended to carry out the Bureau's educational mission as stated in its constitution: "To inform the public by means of social education about the application of the principles of good architecture to building. To advance the present widespread movement to encourage persons of limited means to build and own their own homes; to assist such persons in obtaining, at the lowest possible cost, desirable and attractive plans . . . which shall

Two years after the Minnesota Bureau was founded in 1919, it was restructured as a national organization with thirteen regional bureaus, outlined on the map at left. The chart above delineates the work to be performed at the national and regional levels.

Architects joined the ASHSB by paying $100 for one share of stock in a regional bureau and $10 for one share in the national bureau.

conform to correct artistic principles of design, and to enable such persons to secure the benefit of the advice and skill of architects . . . ."[16] The regional divisions developed designs adapted to local taste, historical precedents, and climate. They distributed Bureau books and pamphlets and carried out other educational activities, including building demonstration houses, staffing exhibit booths at conventions, and writing articles for local publications.

Each Bureau architect pledged to contribute two house sketches a month to the stock plan service and was paid an hourly rate of $1.50 rather than royalties on specific plans sold.[17] All designs had to conform to two conditions: No plan could contain more than six main rooms, and the resulting house had to contain less than 30,000 cubic feet of space.[18]

The first seventeen completed plans were published in May 1920 in *How to Plan, Finance and Build Your Home*. The following spring, 102 Bureau designs were distributed in a book of the same title for the Southern Pine Association, an organization of 6,000 retail lumber representatives with headquarters in New Orleans.[19] This volume became the first of many plan books, pamphlets, and other publications the Bureau produced for lumber associations, building supply distributors, and related associations.[20]

The Southern Pine Association book was completed as the result of a contract with the Bureau signed on July 27, 1920, which involved the complete preparation of designs, perspective drawings, working drawings, specifications, and quantity surveys for 100 houses. To create the designs the Bureau used an assembly line process, which was economical and efficient and contributed to the cooperative philosophy of the organization. A sketch committee created a classification schedule and assigned designs to Bureau members. On September 24, 1920, Robert Taylor Jones was hired as executive secretary to oversee production. Jules Crow of New York came to Minneapolis for two months to direct the creation of the perspective drawings. Working with him on the Working Drawings Committee were Roy Childs Jones, Jefferson M. Hamilton, and Rhodes Robertson. They checked the final drawings, and each member was responsible for a certain aspect of every design. Maurice I. Flagg wrote the editorial material, and his wife, Harriet, added personal touches to the text. The plans were completed on schedule and the Southern Pine Association edition of *How to Plan, Finance and*

The Bureau's regional offices promoted its designs in many ways, including the calendar above.

Opposite: All ASHSB plans were limited to six rooms and 30,000 cubic feet. Members were to submit plans for two houses each month.

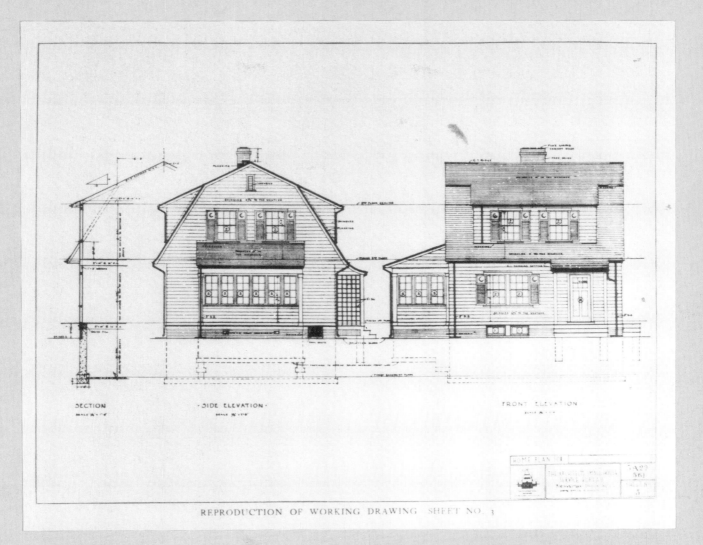

REPRODUCTION OF WORKING DRAWING · SHEET NO. 3

Build Your Home came out in the early spring of 1921.[21]

The Bureau did not intend its plan service to replace the individual architect.[22] Builders were strongly encouraged to use a Bureau architect for alterations and advice when needed, and one of the most important Bureau services was professional consultation for homeowners. From these sessions with an architect, individuals could learn more about choosing a site, financing construction, or other matters involved in building a house.[23]

To illustrate the problems inherent in making alterations without a qualified architect, the Bureau commonly compared "correct" interpretations and poorly modified versions of the same Bureau plan. These comparisons began with the article "Good Taste and Savings—Bad Taste and Waste" in the Southern Pine Association plan book. The idea reappeared as a feature in the Bureau's monthly plan bulletin, *The Small Home,* in 1926.[24] The article illustrated the horrors of the "carpetect"—a member of the building trades pretending to be an architect—sending an unequivocally clear message to home builders to either build according to the plan or hire an architect to make desired changes. Despite these caveats and the fact that only 5 percent of small houses were then designed by architects, some architects, primarily on the East Coast, saw the Bureau as a threat and it remained controversial until its demise.[25]

Sales of the Bureau's plans indicate the public's interest lay in the larger designs.[26] Although 44 percent of the plans in its first book and 36 percent of those in *Your Future Home* were three- and four-room plans, the larger, five- and six-room plans sold most often.

As for interior layouts, Bureau members found that only minimal variations in plan were possible

The Bureau found that plans for houses in the Colonial Revival style sold best. The house above was built from plan 6-A-37, which accounted for almost one-seventh of ASHSB sales in its first four years. The Dutch Colonial house on the facing page was built from another popular design (5-A-29).

because of the limited number of rooms and the small size of the houses.[27] Only a few practical layouts were developed, and the best-selling designs included the simplest floor plans. One-story plans typically consisted of a living room, dining room, and kitchen, with bedrooms and a bathroom to one side or in the rear. The largest difference in two-story designs was the presence of stairs, which were placed either at the center or the side of the house. The first floor consisted of a living room, dining room, and kitchen. The living room either ran across the front of the house or down one side; the kitchen almost always stood in the rear. The upstairs bedrooms and bathroom were located in relation to the stairs.

The Bureau found it easier to develop variety in exterior designs. In a 1929 article William Gray Purcell, director of the Northern Pacific Division, discussed how almost any room arrangement could serve any "style" with the adjustment of windows, proportions, roof lines, and construction materials.[28] The Bureau created up to five different facades for one plan and strove to "offer any elevation in any material for any given plan type."[29] The Bureau tried to adhere

to traditional revival designs such as Dutch and New England Colonial, English Tudor, Spanish, and Italian, as such "authentic styles" were found to add between 10 and 20 percent to the resale value of a house.[30]

The majority of the Architects' Small House Service Bureau plans were Colonial Revival designs. The members believed that houses in this style were "models of good taste, logic and strength" and that the popularity of the style was due to the "homelike effect, the dignity and convenience of the modern Colonial type."[31] Nonetheless, the Bureau's first edition of *How to Plan, Finance and Build Your Home* included only six Colonial designs and two English designs; most of the plans were for bungalows.

Six out of the seven top-selling plans created for the Southern Pine Association edition of *How to Plan, Finance and Build Your Home* were Colonial in design.[32] "Southern" designs made up 20 percent of the total plans in accordance with the Bureau's agreement with the Southern Pine Association, but most of these plans did not sell well and did not appear in later publications.[33] The successful plans from the

Southern Pine Association book reappeared along with several new designs in *Your Future Home,* published for Weyerhaeuser Corporation in 1923.[34]

Considerably more than half the plans in *Your Future Home* are in a Colonial Revival style. The New England Colonial (6-A-37) with side entrance (originally numbered 669) sold 141 copies and accounted for almost one-seventh of all sales during the Bureau's first four years.[35] The plan was described in the Southern Pine Association book as simple, straightforward, and dignified in proportions and lines, but practical and economical.[36] In the Bureau's 1929 book, *Small Homes of Architectural Distinction,* the same plan was characterized as "a monument to the common sense of the American home builder."[37]

The second and third most popular plans had sold eighty-nine copies each by 1924. Plan 6-A-17, a New England Colonial with central entrance and side porch, was marketed as a design able to "lessen labor and lighten housekeeping."[38] Plan 6-A-20, a Dutch Colonial, included a central stair, a front vestibule, and "ten good closets."[39] The fourth most popular plan was 5-A-29, a Dutch Colonial design described as

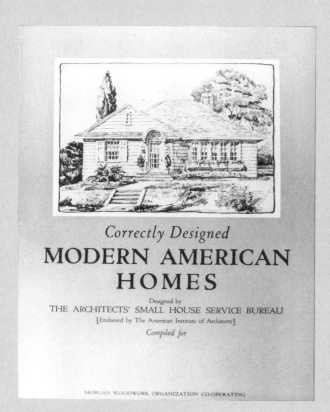

Correctly Designed

MODERN AMERICAN HOMES

Designed by
THE ARCHITECTS' SMALL HOUSE SERVICE BUREAU
[Endorsed by The American Institute of Architects]

Compiled for

MORGAN WOODWORK ORGANIZATION CO-OPERATING

Above: "Modern American" was a label the ASHSB used to encompass designs that did not appear to have roots in the Colonial, Spanish, or English traditions.

Opposite: The Bureau did not espouse the Prairie School style and published only very few designs with its horizontal lines, wide overhanging eaves, casement windows, and hipped roof.

"homelike" with an "inviting, comfortable feel."[40] Both the New England and Dutch Colonial facades were designed to use stock millwork for decorative elements and clapboard or brick for facing.

Colonial designs continued to be popular around the country throughout the life of the Bureau. Sixteen out of the seventeen six-room plans the Northwestern Division created for the 1941 plan book *Two Story Homes* were Colonial in design.

The creation of regional bureaus provided a wide selection of designs suited to the local environment and local taste. Many of the plans designed by the Mountain Division in Denver and published in a third book entitled *How to Plan, Finance and Build Your Home* had a Mediterranean flavor reflective of the Spanish influences in the Southwest. A majority were one-story dwellings of stucco and brick, with roofs of red or variegated tiles and arched windows. A plan book published by the New England Division around 1927 was entitled *New England Homes* and included Cape Cod plans with pitched roofs and "Garrison" plans with overhanging second stories. The Spanish and New England plans contrasted sharply with the Midwestern designs created by the Minnesota architects. These tended to have steeply pitched roofs with dormers in a variety of styles.

Despite the Bureau's regional focus, plan sales were spread evenly across the country. William Gray Purcell saw "Colonial, English, [and] Spanish [houses] built in New York, Florida, Los Angeles, [and] Minnesota."[41] Roy Childs Jones reported in 1924 that "sales have been distributed over the country almost equally with the exception of the strip along the Gulf Coast, the Pacific Coast and the Rocky Mountain District. Apparently there is no difference, in spite of our sentimental desire to have local differences, in the demands of the public in houses through the entire U.S. except for peculiar areas."[42]

Plan sales for designs produced by the Northwestern Division were concentrated in the Midwest, with highest sales in Minnesota, Illinois, Ohio, Pennsylvania, and New York. Certain specific plans had a much wider distribution; for example, the English Tudor 6-A-64, the Dutch Colonial 5-A-29, and the New England Colonial 6-A-37 all sold in more than twenty-five states and Canada.[43] One colonial plan, advertised in the *Saturday Evening Post*, brought inquiries from China, Japan, India, and New Zealand.[44] The Bureau regularly sent plans to the

Low-Lying Five Room Bungalow

Design No. 5-K 12

Soviet Union, China, Japan, India, Australia, and South American and European countries.[45] In 1925 plans from *Your Future Home* were published in France under the title *Cottages Rustiques, Façades et Plans.*

The Bureau used five major categories of exterior design in later years: Colonial, Spanish, English, Bungalow, and Modern American.[46] Several house plans appeared in different categories in various Bureau publications, including the "Correctly Designed" series.[47] The designs that could not be classified as Colonials, English, or Spanish were labeled Modern American. This category was described in *Small Homes of Architectural Distinction* as "rather indefinite" but appropriate as "these so-called American houses do not display the distinctive national characteristic ordinarily associated with the other styles."[48] According to the Bureau's "Modern American" books, the one truly American feature common to many of the houses was the front porch.[49]

Robert T. Jones, executive secretary of the national Bureau, proclaimed that "the Bureau does not cater to popular taste in the design of its houses," but this attitude became a major handicap in the

Bureau's ability to sell a large number of plans.[50] Even with the involvement of Prairie School architect William Gray Purcell, Prairie and other "modern" designs were noticeably absent from the Bureau's work, although several plans did incorporate Prairie School features. These plans may have been designed by former Prairie School architect John Van Bergen, who was a member of the Bureau during the mid-1930s when these designs appeared. Bureau plan 5-K-12 featured horizontal lines, wide overhanging eaves, casement windows, and a hipped roof with a wide chimney. The Bureau did not classify it as a Prairie School design, however.[51] Its opinion of the style is reflected in a 1927 "Modern American" book that states that Prairie School houses "represented a certain fad in small house architecture," and "like other fads their value is ephemeral."[52]

None of the houses in the "Modern American" publication would be classified as "modern" by stylistic standards. The Bureau did publish two "modern" designs in a book of low-cost concrete houses that appeared in the mid-1930s. Plan 5-K-35 included a flat roof with an overhanging cornice, corner and

broad groupings of windows, and plain flat surfaces typical of designs by European Modernists. It was described in *Twenty-Two Low Cost Concrete Homes* as "modern in style and up to the minute in plan and construction."[53] The second plan, 4-K-24, included a flat roof usable as "an outdoor living room or terrace" and had a concrete masonry and Portland cement stucco finish.[54] There is no record, however, of these plans selling.

Even though the almost 400 plans produced by the Architects' Small House Service Bureau were well publicized and well designed by Bureau members, the actual number of plans sold reached only a fraction of the Bureau's expectations. How many houses were actually built is difficult to ascertain, since Bureau records documenting construction of houses are sketchy and many plans sold were not used. An estimate places the number of Bureau houses built around the country at somewhat more than 5,000.[55] Blocks of Bureau houses were built in Lincoln, Nebraska, and Montclair, Colorado, and large groups are located on Kostner Avenue in Chicago and suburban Park Ridge, Illinois.[56] Smaller clusters are located

Bureau designs were often altered or imitated by owners and builders; the brick-faced house above is an interpretation of a Bureau plan.

Opposite above: The Bureau published two designs that followed principles of modern design in *Twenty-Two Low Cost Concrete Homes*. Plan 5-K-35, with a flat roof with overhanging cornice, corner and broad groupings of windows, and plain flat surfaces typical of designs by European Modernists, did not sell.

Opposite below: Blocks of Bureau houses such as this one were built in Nebraska, Colorado, and Illinois.

In 1923 the *Minneapolis Journal* and the Bureau's Northwestern Division cosponsored the construction of a demonstration house to showcase the work of the Bureau and introduce the latest in appliances and home furnishings.

on Oxford Avenue in Rockford, Illinois, and on Lafond Avenue in St. Paul, Minnesota.[57]

In addition to houses carefully built following the Bureau's plans, many houses of similar design were built, as well as Bureau plans put up by "carpetects." Owners and builders often altered plans or copied Bureau designs already constructed. Later additions and alterations have made some Bureau houses almost unrecognizable. A digression of plan 5-E-1 can be followed in at least nine houses built in Park Ridge, Illinois.[58]

Although houses built using Bureau designs may not have directly changed the face of America, the Bureau's ideology reached millions of people through its plan books and other publications. The most important source of the Bureau's influence on the housing industry was its newspaper service. Carried in more than 300 newspapers around the country, it reached approximately five million readers a week.[59] The stated purpose of the newspaper service was to sell "the idea of architecture to a class of

Ray Russell, the architect in charge of the Chicago office of the Bureau, was the consulting architect for three demonstration houses built for the fictional sons of "John Daily News." Above is Tom's house.

people who knew little or nothing about architecture and who have for the most part depended on the jerry builder, lumber dealers and other sources for architectural services."[60] Each newspaper insert, entitled "The Home Builder's Clinic," included a Bureau design accompanied by an explanation of its features, spatial arrangement, and method of construction. A technical column offered information on financing, planning, and building, and a question-and-answer column served as an open forum for readers. Beginning in 1923 several books containing "The Home Builder's Clinic" articles were published under the title *Help for the Man Who Wants to Build.*[61] By 1926 more than 115,000 copies were distributed by newspapers and a variety of other related organizations.[62]

In addition to the newspaper service, the Bureau began promoting its monthly bulletin, *The Small Home,* in March 1922. Circulation ranged from 3,000 to 10,500.[63] Each issue included a statement of the Bureau's purpose and a description of the services it provided. In addition to illustrating ten to fifteen

Models were built of Tom's, John's, and Charles's houses, built by the Bureau for the "sons" of "John Daily News," to demonstrate how they could be landscaped.

Opposite above: The Bureau built a model house for the Celotex Company to demonstrate the use of its product, an artificial lumber with a sugar cane fiber insulation material.

Opposite below: The Bureau exhibited at building shows, including that of the American Institute of Architects, to help publicize its work.

Bureau designs, *The Small Home* contained educational articles such as "How Much to Pay for Your Home" and "Why Colonial Architecture is Economical."[64] In 1927 an enlarged format was introduced, and the publication was transformed from a pattern book into a commercial home magazine.

In connection with the *Minneapolis Journal,* the Bureau's Northwestern Division sponsored a demonstration house in 1923 and three more houses the following year. Each step of the building process was documented in the *Journal* through the mythical home builder John W. Journal and his family.[65] Readers could follow the construction each week on the front page of the *Journal's* real estate section, as Mr. Journal interacted with a loan association, the Bureau, contractors, and others in the building process. Expenditures were outlined and each phase of construction documented. In addition to demonstrating the work of the Bureau, the houses included the latest in appliances and home furnishings.[66]

The Bureau established a Chicago office in 1924

with architect Ray Russell in charge. Russell became the consulting architect for three Bureau demonstration houses built for the three fictional sons of John Daily News. All of the models were Colonial Revival in design. John Jr.'s house was built of brick just south of Jackson Park, Charles's house was sided in stucco and built in Rogers Park, while Tom's house was built of wood just north of Lake Street on Lathrop Avenue in suburban River Forest.[67] All sites were located close to public transportation.

Maurice I. Flagg, the Bureau's director of service, was proficient in attracting free publicity through articles and an editorial service published in magazines and journals.[68] Approximately 75 different magazines and "house organs" made use of the Bureau's editorial service between 1920 and 1930.[69] Articles about the Architects' Small House Service Bureau were published in *Good Housekeeping, McCall's, House Beautiful, Country Life, Popular Mechanics,* and other magazines.[70]

The Bureau had display booths at building shows such as the 1921 Own Your Own Home Exposition in Chicago and conventions such as that of the American Institute of Architects.[71] It engaged in a number of projects with the Better Homes Institute, mounting national exhibits with that organization in the 1920s, and worked closely with other organizations interested in raising the standard of small house design.[72] In the early 1920s the Bureau built a model house for Celotex Company on a lot worth more than $200,000 on Michigan Avenue in the shadows of the Tribune Tower.[73]

The Architects' Small House Service Bureau never realized the level of success its members had forecast, and the Bureau's financial situation was continuously bleak. As early as 1922 plan sales were, in the Bureau's own words, "extra-ordinarily meager" and were insufficient to balance the expense of conducting services.[74] Only 231 plans were sold in 1921, a small fraction of the anticipated ten thousand sales for that year.[75] Sales followed the national housing trend, peaking in 1925 and decreasing slowly until 1929, when they slumped along with the depressed housing industry.

The AIA rescinded its endorsement in 1934 under pressure from "money-hungry" architects from the East Coast and South who saw the Bureau as an "aggressive price-cutting competitor."[76] The Bureau's strength was further sapped by the resignation of Maurice Flagg in 1927 and the death of Edwin Brown in 1930. Still, it did not officially disband until 1942.[77]

The Bureau's attempt to increase the role of professional architects in small house design was largely unsuccessful. The stock plan service made almost no mark on the housing landscape of America. Sales never reached the predicted figures, and the Bureau's major impact on the housing industry came from promoting its ideas, advice, and plan designs through publications and articles. As Bureau member Rollin C. Chapin noted in a 1932 *Pencil Points* article, "Without question the greatest service the Bureau has rendered is its educational work in the field of small home owning, planning and building. Public appreciation of good architecture not only as it pertains to homes but to building in general is undoubtedly on a higher level than it was ten years ago."[78]

Though the Architects' Small House Service Bureau disbanded in 1942, the interest of architects in the residential market for small houses and the need for higher quality in small house design remained. After World War II the Bureau's goal of raising the standard of small house design was continued by a second group of Minneapolis architects, who formed the Architects' Home Plan Institute in 1945.[79]

This reprint of the 1923 edition of the Bureau's book *Your Future Home* offers a glimpse of the American housing industry between World War I and the Depression. The elevations and floor plans of these houses, also publicized in many other ways, influenced many American houses built in the first half of the twentieth century and thus will seem familiar to many of us. The Bureau's purpose, put forward with plan books such as this one, was to be a dependable and authoritative source for well-designed houses at nominal cost. The idea also was to close the gap between architects and small house builders and homeowners who could not afford their services. It is hoped that this volume, with its articles about financing a house, selecting a design, and reading plans, will illuminate the Bureau's purposes and open a window on moderate house design of the period.

Lisa D. Schrenk

No 653

No 654

No 654 with changes

No 651

No 552

No 622

No 561

No 6510

This page from the first edition of *How to Plan, Finance, and Build Your Home* shows eight houses built from Bureau designs circa 1920.

[1]Many people have contributed their energy and expertise to my research on the Architects' Small House Service Bureau (ASHSB), including my thesis committee—Charles E. Brownell, James A. D. Cox, and Richard Guy Wilson. David Lanegran and David Gebhard provided direction and introduced me to the ASHSB through the book *Legacy of Minneapolis: Preservation Amid Change* (Minneapolis: Voyageur, 1983). Thomas Harvey's work on the Bureau served as a stepping-stone for my own. Records from the ASHSB of Minnesota and the ASHSB of the United States and its Northwestern Division are located at the Minnesota Historical Society in St. Paul (ASHSB Papers), where John Wickre and Ruth Bauer guided me through numerous dusty boxes of Bureau records. Assistance was provided by Alan Lathrop at the Northwest Architectural Archives in St. Paul and Tony Wrenn at the American Institute of Architects Archives and Library in Washington, D.C.

[2]These restrictions reduced house construction to only 4 percent of normal by November 1918. Building increased markedly after the war, but not nearly enough to meet the need. *Housing Plans for Cities* (New Orleans: Southern Pine Association, 1920), 8.

[3]Gwendolyn Wright, *Building the Dream: A Social History of Housing in America* (New York: Pantheon Books, 1981), 195; and Edwin H. Brown, *Report of the [AIA] Committee on Small Houses to the Fifty-Fifth Annual Convention*, May 1922, ASHSB Papers, Box 52.

[4]Herbert Hoover, *Memoirs: The Cabinet and the Presidency 1920-33* (New York: MacMillan, 1952), 92. Hoover led a campaign to involve the federal government in promoting better housing in the early 1920s. He was a founding member of the Better Homes in America movement and supported the Department of Labor's "Own Your Own Home" campaign. Herbert Hoover, "Foreword," *How to Own Your Own Home* ([Chicago]: Better Homes in America, [circa 1921]), 2; Wright, 195, 200, 217.

[5]The concept of mail-order plan service resulted from improvements in the postal system and the standardization of millwork. Cleveland & Backus Brothers of New York is believed to have been the first design firm to supply plans by mail, in 1856. Alan Gowans, *The Comfortable House: North American Suburban Architecture 1890-1930* (Cambridge, Mass.: The MIT Press, 1986), 42-43; James L. Garvin, "Mail-Order House Plans and American Victorian Architecture," *Winterthur Portfolio*, vol. 16, #4 (1981): 310, 312.

[6]Mail-order designers included Walter J. Keith, Jens Pedersen, George Saxton, J. W. Lindstrom, and Charles Sedgwick, all of Minneapolis; Robert W. Shoppell of New York; George Barber of Knoxville; Frank L. Smith of Boston; and David S. Hopkins, Frank P. Allen, and W. K. Johnston, all from Grand Rapids, Michigan. Garvin, 314, 329.

[7]Two of the largest mail-order services were the Radford Company and the Gordon-Van Tine Company. Organizations that produced plans included the American Brick Face Association, Chicago; National Lumber Manufacturers Association, Washington, D.C.; Southern Pine Association, New Orleans; Arkansas Soft Pine Association, Little Rock; and Weyerhaeuser Forest Products, St. Paul. Other ready-made house services included Pacific Systems of Los Angeles; Rogers and Manson, Home Builders of Chicago; Bennett Lumber Company of Tonawanda, New York; Southern Mill and Manufacturing Company of Tulsa; and Montgomery Ward. Gowans, 41, 46, 50, 55.

[8]Clifford Edward Clark, *The American Family Home, 1800-1960* (Chapel Hill: University of North Carolina Press, 1986), 73.

[9]Gowans, 65.

[10]Robert T. Jones, "The Architects' Small House Service Bureau," *Architectural Forum* (March 1926): 201. The inadequate housing conditions in Minneapolis were recounted in *The Housing Problem in Minneapolis: A Preliminary Investigation*, published in 1918 by the Minneapolis Civic and Commerce Association. Carl A. Gage was an architect with the firm Tyrie and Chapman; Beaver Wade Day was a principal in the St. Paul firm of Toltz, King and Day; Frederick Mann was instrumental in setting up the school of architecture at the University of Minnesota; and Roy Childs Jones taught in the architecture schools at the universities of Illinois and Minnesota before becoming head of Minnesota's school of architecture in 1937. ASHSB offices were located at 1200 Second Avenue South, Minneapolis.

[11]ASHSB of US, *Building Value into Your Home* (Minneapolis: ASHSB of US, [circa 1923]), 6, ASHSB Papers, Box 53.

[12]The Bureau was first introduced to the AIA at the 1919 annual convention, during the initial report of the Committee on Small Houses. The 1921 AIA resolution for endorsement read: "The American Institute of Architects, in Convention assembled hereby endorses and approves the formation and proposed operation of the Architects' Small House Service Bureau of the United States, Incorporated, and encourages it to carry on its programs with all dispatch and energy. It further directs the Board of Directors of the American Institute of Architects to follow the work of the Bureau in detail, and the management and control of the Bureau as it may deem advisable. It further suggests to its Chapters that they take an active part in the formation of Regional and Branch Bureaus and do all in their power to make the work of the Bureau a complete success." Minutes from the meeting of the AIA Committee on Small Houses, Fifty-Fourth Annual Convention of the AIA, 1921, ASHSB Papers, Box 52.

[13]On March 10, 1921, the certificate of incorporation of the Architects' Small House Service Bureau, Inc. was signed and witnessed by Brown, Mann, and Chapman. Agreement between the ASHSB of the United States and the ASHSB of Minnesota, 14 April 1921, ASHSB Papers, Box 52.

[14]Edwin H. Brown, "A Short Story of One Year's Work of the Bureau," (ASHSB of US, [circa 1921]), 13-14, ASHSB Papers.

[15]Brown, *Report of Committee on Small Houses*, May 1922.

[16]"Purpose of the ASHSB Statement" (ASHSB of US, [circa 1923]), ASHSB Papers; and William Stanley Parker, "A Statement From: The President of the Architects' Small House Service Bureau, Inc., To: Members of the American Institute of Architects," in *The Movement to Improve Small Home Architecture: A Report of the Progress of the ASHSB, Inc.* [circa 1930], 4-5, ASHSB Papers, Box 52.

[17]Minutes of ASHSB of Minnesota board of directors meeting, 24 September 1920, ASHSB Papers, Box 56.

[18]Minutes of ASHSB of Minnesota board meeting, 1 February 1923.

[19]During the spring of 1920 the ASHSB received a proposal from the Southern Pine Association to develop a series of plans for local builders. On June 19, 1920, King H. Pullen, acting trade extension manager of the Southern Pine Association, wrote to Ernest Flagg: "I shall be glad to co-operate with you in extending your Bureau's field of usefulness. It is my idea that this end can be accomplished most effectively through the medium of the retail lumber dealer, who comes in closer contact with the small home builder than perhaps any other single agency. We have a list of some 6,000 dealers in all parts of the country who regularly subscribe to our advertising and sales help service. This service included a stock plan service which is very good in its way, but which has defects that have long been apparent to me. I would therefore welcome the opportunity of assisting you in merchandising to our dealer friends an architecturally correct plan service such as your organization has created. To this end I suggest an arrangement be entered into between the Architects' Small House Service Bureau, Inc. and the Southern Pine Association, whereby a special Southern Pine Association edition of your 'number two' booklet be issued when the subject matter for such booklet is ready, this edition to be practically identical with your regular edition except that the advertisements would be eliminated and the front cover design would contain our name along with your own. I would also desire that there be included a correct presentation on the subject of 'the use of Southern Pine in home building.' This, perhaps, in the back of the book. The text matter for such article to be prepared by a member of your staff and to contain only such statements as your Bureau could subscribe to with entire propriety."

On June 24, 1920, at the Bureau's executive committee meeting, Maurice I. Flagg presented the SPA proposal and two others involving dealer distribution through lumberyards and independent organizations. The following July, the Bureau's board of directors considered a proposal for the two organizations to develop a merchandising campaign and distribute an enlarged publication, plans, and accompanying services for SPA retail lumber dealers. Letter from Maurice I. Flagg to Downs & Eads, 9 August 1920; letter from King H. Pullen to Maurice I. Flagg, 19 June 1920; and minutes from ASHSB of Minnesota executive committee meeting, 24 June 1920, and board of directors meeting, 26 July 1920; ASHSB Papers.

[20]The previous Southern Pine Association plans were not free; they cost $1.50 each. Other lumber company plan books the ASHSB produced included *Help for the Man Who Wants to Build a Small Home,* for Thompson Lumber Company of Minneapolis (1924); *Beauty in Brick,* for the Finzer Brothers Clay Company in Sugarcreek, Ohio [circa 1925]; *A Portfolio of Distinguished Homes,* for Dierks Lumber and Coal Company, Kansas City, Missouri (circa 1930); and *A Dozen Suggestions for the Home Builder,* for the Standard Lumber Company of Chicago (1928).

[21]Edwin H. Brown, "The Architects' Small House Service Bureau of Minnesota, Inc.," *Journal of the American Institute of Architects* (April 1921): 136-37; minutes of the president's report from the ASHSB of Minnesota annual meeting, 27 January 1921, ASHSB Papers, Box 47.

[22] Robert T. Jones, "The Architects' Small House Service Bureau," *Architectural Forum* (March 1926): 202.

[23] News release from the ASHSB of US, "Northwest Architects Join to Help Builders Lower Costs," June 1921, ASHSB Papers, Box 52.

[24] The initial column in *The Small Home* was written by William Gray Purcell and titled "What's Wrong With this House—This House Gives You the Answer" (August 1926): 17. The Minneapolis Public Library has a complete run of *The Small Home*.

[25] Letter from William G. Dorr, president of the Minnesota Society of the AIA, to Harry Lucht, secretary of the Architecture League of Northern New Jersey, 31 October 1929, ASHSB Papers, Box 51.

[26] A chart illustrating ASHSB houses built, by number of rooms, was published in 1927. It showed that six-room houses accounted for 52.8 percent, five-room houses 29.2 percent, four-room houses 14.6 percent, and three-room houses 3.4 percent of total plan sales. "Reaching the Small Home Market" (ASHSB of US, 1927), 4, ASHSB Papers, Box 52.

[27] Memo from Roy C. Jones to Robert T. Jones, 2 April 1923, ASHSB Papers, Box 39.

[28] William Gray Purcell, "Early America," *The Small Home* (May 1929): 8.

[29] Thomas Harvey, "Mail-Order Architecture of the Twenties," *Landscape* vol. 25, #3 (1981): 5.

[30] Harvey, 3.

[31] "Why Colonial Style is Popular" in *When You Build—Build Right: How the Smallest Home Can Have the Architects' Services* (ASHSB of US, [circa 1925]), 20, ASHSB Papers, Box 38.

[32] *How to Plan, Finance and Build Your Home of Three, Four, Five or Six Rooms*, vol. 1, #1 (ASHSB of Minnesota, 1921) [no other issues were ever published]; and *How to Plan, Finance and Build Your Home* (ASHSB of Minnesota for the Southern Pine Association, 1921).

[33] Minutes of the ASHSB of US executive committee meeting, 12 February 1924, 4, 5, ASHSB Papers.

[34] Roy C. Jones, report of the Sketch Committee, 1921, ASHSB Papers, Box 39. The contract between the Northwestern Division and the Weyerhaeuser Forest Products Corporation was spelled out in a letter from Robert T. Jones to Arthur C. Holden, director of service of the Atlantic Division, dated March 26, 1926, but labeled "NOT SENT." It stated that "the Northwestern Division agreed to perfect certain of the designs which had been prepared by the Minnesota corporation and to rerender others, and also to rerender certain designs of the Mountain Division and to maintain its standard service in connection with these designs. The Weyerhaeuser Corporation agreed to advance the funds necessary for actual work involved in producing these drawings and to print a catalogue at the expense of the Weyerhaeuser Corporation showing the designs in question, and to give publicity to the service. The cost of producing the catalogue was a matter of concern only to the Weyerhaeuser corporation. In producing the designs, an expense of about $10,000 was incurred, which under the terms of the contract was to be repaid out of sales of the plans. Nearly half of this sum has now been repaid. The contract also provides that the Weyerhaeuser Corporation is to have about 20% commission on the net proceeds that accrue to the Northwestern Division from sales of these particular designs. As a final item in this agreement, there was the provision that in the case the whole sum advanced by the Weyerhaeuser Corporation should not have been paid off in a period of five years next succeeding the publishing of the catalogue the indebtedness would be waived. The plans, of course, have always been the property of the Northwestern Division."

[35] Letter from George A. Chapman, secretary of the ASHSB of the US Lake Division, 16 August 1924, Box 30; minutes of the ASHSB of US executive committee meeting, 12 February 1924, 6, ASHSB Papers, Box 51. ASHSB plans were originally numbered using a three-digit system in which the first digit indicated the number of rooms the plan contained. When the Bureau became a national organization, the system was changed to a number-letter-number system, in which the first number indicated the number of rooms, the second letter which regional division the plan came from, and the last the number of the specific plan.

[36] *How to Plan, Finance and Build Your Home*, 1921.

[37] ASHSB of US, *Small Homes of Architectural Distinction* (New York: Harper, 1929), 130.

[38] Minutes of the ASHSB of US executive committee meeting, 12 February 1924, 6, ASHSB Papers, Box 51; and *Small Homes of Architectural Distinction*, 126.

[39] ASHSB of US, *When You Build—Build Right: How the Smallest Home Can Have the Architects' Services*, 6.

[40] *How to Plan, Finance and Build Your Home*, 9.

[41] Harvey, 6.

[42] Minutes of the ASHSB of US executive committee meeting, 12 February 1924, 11, ASHSB Papers, Box 51.

[43] Information on plan sales was compiled from ASHSB plan sale records at the Minnesota Historical Society.

[44] Plan 6-A-17 was published on page 64 of the June 18, 1921, issue of *The Saturday Evening Post* and plan 6-A-20 was published on page 76 of the March 11, 1922, issue. Both were in advertisements for the book *How to Plan, Finance and Build Your Home*. Report of the director of services, ASHSB of US Northwestern Division, 1921, 3, ASHSB Papers, Box 47.

[45] Report of director of services, Northwestern Division, 1921, 3; editorial policy, circulation statement, and services to advertisers of *The Small Home* [circa 1926], ASHSB Papers, Box 53; and report of the AIA Committee on Small Houses, 1923, 4, ASHSB Papers, Box 49.

[46] The Modern American label was given to designs that could not be classified as Colonial, English, or Spanish.

[47] Published for the Morgan Woodworking Organization for distribution among their dealers. Many more than 50,000 were distributed in the first year. Letter from Robert T. Jones to officers and directors of the Architects' Small House Service Bureau at their annual meeting, April 14, 15, and 16, at San Antonio, Texas [circa 1931], 7, ASHSB Papers.

[48] *Small Homes of Architectural Distinction*, 43.

[49] "One of the most striking characteristics of the Modern American home was the front porch," a "truly American feature." "Introduction" in *Modern American: A Selected Group of Homes of Architectural Distinction*, Home Builders' Library, Publication #4, (Minneapolis: ASHSB of US, 1927): 2.

[50] Harvey, 5.

[51] *Correctly Designed Modern American: A Selected Group of Homes of Architectural Distinction* (Minneapolis: ASHSB of US, 1930): 5.

[52] *Modern American: Selected Group of Homes*, 2.

[53] *Twenty-Two Low Cost Concrete Homes* (Minneapolis: ASHSB of US, 1935), 23.

[54] *Twenty-two Low Cost Concrete Homes*, 5.

[55] ASHSB sent out surveys to those who bought Bureau plans to try and find out if houses were ever built, but in many cases the survey forms were never completed or returned. Some of these records are on file at the Minnesota Historical Society; and Harvey, 5.

[56] The Kostner Avenue houses are located on the 5800 and 5900 blocks in the neighborhood of Sauganash in the Woods, where the development partnership of Koester & Zander reported they had built between thirty-five and forty houses. Park Ridge includes one of the largest numbers of ASHSB houses identified at this time. More than thirty houses using Bureau plans or altered Bureau designs are located between Touey and Devon avenues. "Streets of Bureau Houses," *The Small Home* (December 1924): 12-13.

[57] The Rockford houses are located between 2225 and 2233 Oxford Avenue; the St. Paul houses at 1178, 1186, 1194, and 1200 Lafond Avenue.

[58] Houses using or resembling ASHSB plan 5-E-1 in Park Ridge, Illinois, include 1128 Vine Avenue, 709 Cumberland Avenue, 841 Fairview Avenue, 904 Fairview Avenue, 903 Prospect Avenue, 901 Courtland Avenue, 920 Cumberland Avenue, 1104 Vine Avenue, and 605 Chester Avenue.

[59] ASHSB of US report on newspapers [circa 1931]; and letter from Robert T. Jones to ASHSB officers [circa 1931], 5, ASHSB Papers.

[60] Edwin H. Brown, statement and recommendations covering past and future advertising, promotion, and merchandising policies of the ASHSB of the US, Inc., 9 May 1923, ASHSB Papers, Box 39.

[61] Newspapers that sold editions of *Help for the Man Who Wants to Build* included the *Minneapolis Journal*, the *Chicago Daily News*, the *Milwaukee Journal*, the *Boston Herald*, the *Duluth News Press*, the *Buffalo Express*, the *Toledo Blade*, the *Omaha World Herald*, the *Evansville Courier*, the *Mankato Free Press*, the *Waterloo Courier*, and the *Saint Paul Pioneer Press*. Organizations that sold the books include the Dierks Lumber and Coal Company of Kansas City, the Arkansas Soft Pine Bureau of Little Rock, and *Popular Mechanics* magazine. Report of service bureau promotional activities, ASHSB of US, Northwestern Division, 1923, ASHSB Papers.

[62] Robert. T. Jones, "The Architects' Small House Service Bureau," *Architectural Forum* (March 1926): 203.

[63] Letter from Robert T. Jones to the directors of the ASHSB of the US, 6 July 1928, ASHSB Papers, Box 51.

[64] "How Much to Pay for Your Home," *The Small Home* (August 1926): 7; and "Why Colonial Architecture is Economical," *The Small Home* (June

1925): 15.

[65]John W. Journal, "How I Financed and Built My Home," *The Small Home*, vol. 1, #3 [circa 1923]: 13-21.

[66]The 1923 house was built at 2919 Johnson Street NE, Minneapolis, from ASHSB plan 654A (later renumbered 6-A-20) at a cost of $5,400. It was completed in sixty working days. The 1924 Demonstration Houses were a brick house at 4353 France Avenue South from plan 5-B-7 at a cost of $6,584.81; a stucco house at 4449 17th Avenue South at a cost of $4,821.98; and a wood house at 1920 44th Avenue North, built at a cost of $4,644.34, from plan 4-A-29. John W. Journal, *The Houses that John Built* (Minneapolis: Minneapolis Journal, 1924).

[67]The Chicago Daily News houses were located at 6847 Cregier Avenue (John Jr., probably plan 6-A-37), 2206 Lunt Avenue (Charles, plan 6-A-69), and 250 Lathrop Avenue, River Forest (Tom, plan 5-A-52). *A Handbook for Home Builders* (Chicago: Chicago Daily News Model Demonstration Homes, 1924), section 2.

[68]Maurice I. Flagg was the former director of the Minnesota State Art Commission. He inaugurated a number of model farm, village, and urban house competitions for the government of Minnesota. According to Purcell, "Flagg had a positive genius for the peculiar sort of publicity which was necessary to reach the house-plan bombarded public." Letter from William Gray Purcell to Edwin H. Brown, 14 September 1926, ASHSB Papers; and "Northwest Architects Join to Help Home Builders Lower Building Costs," news release, June 1921, Purcell Papers, Northwest Architectural Archives, University of Minnesota, St. Paul.

[69]"An Educational Force of Tremendous National Power" in *The Movement to Improve Small House Architecture: A Report of the Progress of the ASHSB, Inc.* (ASHSB of US, [circa 1930]): 6, ASHSB Papers, Box 53.

[70]ASHSB records show that these publications also printed Bureau plans: *American Builder, American Lumberman, American Magazine, Builders' Guide, Builders' Journal, Building Age, Building Materials, Chicago Journal of Commerce, Christian Science Monitor, Collier's Weekly, The Contractor* (Canadian), *Country Gentleman, The Coupler* (General Electric), *Furniture Age, Hearthstone* (H. O. Reno Co.), Hearst's International, *House and Garden, The House and Its Management, House Betterment, How to Own Your Own Home, Journal of Home Economics, Keith's Magazine, Ladies Home Journal,* Long-Bell Lumber Pamphlet, Wm. J. McConnell Company, *Modern Priscilla, Modern Woman, National Builder, National Real Estate Journal, Permanent Builder, Pictorial Review, Saturday Evening Post,* Universal Portland Cement, *Wellsworth Life, Woman's Home Companion, Woman's Weekly,* and *Woman's World.*

[71]Shows in 1922 included the Building Show at Des Moines, Iowa; the Own Your Own Home shows at St. Louis and Omaha; the Real Estate and Building shows at Buffalo and Cleveland; the Minnesota State Fair; the convention of the American Civic Association at Chicago; and the convention of the National Federation of Construction Industries at Chicago. Edwin H. Brown, minutes of the AIA Committee on Small Houses meeting at the fifty-fifth convention of the AIA, May 1922, ASHSB Papers, Box 52.

[72]The Better Homes in America began in 1922, under the auspices of Mrs. William Brown Meloney, editor of *The Delineator,* as a public service institute to provide people with unbiased aid in matters relating to home building, furnishings, and subjects related to social and community welfare. Herbert Hoover served as president of the organization. By 1930 there were 7,279 local Better Homes committees across the country. During Better Homes week, each committee sponsored contests, demonstrations, and lectures on home improvement and home building techniques. Many of the committees sponsored a demonstration house, which was opened during the week for tours and special events. The ASHSB became involved in the Better Homes in America Movement through Hoover and the Department of Commerce. The plan book *Better Homes in America* was published by the Bureau for Better Homes in 1924 to illustrate and detail the work of the regional divisions. In addition, Bureau plans were used for model houses and to illustrate the yearly publications, which explained to municipalities how to organize their own Better Homes campaigns. Five ASHSB houses were built for the 1925 campaign in Atlanta, Georgia. Other Bureau work for the Better Home movement included providing design 5-A-50 for the Permanent Home Information Center in Minneapolis and a brick training center, built from design 6-A-17, for the Girl Scouts' Sesqui-Centennial Exhibition in Philadelphia. James Ford, "Better Homes in America," *The Scholastic* (March 1928): 29; *How to Organize the 1926 Campaign* (Better Homes in America, [circa 1926]), 13, 44, 49; *How to Organize the 1928 Campaign* (Better Homes in America, [circa 1928]), 26; and Wright, 197-98.

[73]The plan—4-A-48, a Spanish Colonial design—was built at 641 North Michigan Avenue. According to Martin Charles Huggett, service counsel of the Celotex Company, "The little house is dedicated to the strength, efficiency, beauty and general usefulness of Celotex Insulation Lumber." *The Small Home* (March 1925): 14. *Your Home,* a book of twenty-five plans prepared for the Celotex Company, is the only known example of plans referred to with names rather than numbers. Plan names were historical and included the Washington (6-A-67), the Columbus (5-A-72), the Adams (4-A-36), and Ponce de Leon (6-A-92). *Your Home* (Chicago: The Celotex Company, 1924).

[74]Report of the technical director, ASHSB of US, Northwestern Division, 1921, ASHSB Papers, Box 47.

[75]The 231 plan sales resulted from 500 inquiries; there were 2,568 plan book sales in 1921. Report of the director of services, ASHSB of US, Northwestern Division, 1921; and report of the technical director, ASHSB of US, Northwestern Division, 1921, ASHSB Papers.

[75A]Northwestern Division sales figures for 1925 were $750; sales for all divisions totaled $1,340. Report of technical director, ASHSB of US, Northwestern Division, 1926, 3, 10, ASHSB Papers.

[76]The fight was documented in issue after issue of *American Architect* and *Pencil Points.* Albert L. Brockway, "Should the AIA Continue to Sponsor the Architects' Small House Service Bureau: 'Results Justify Affiliation of Bureau with AIA,'" *American Architect* (February 1932): 17; and minutes of the board of directors meeting, American Institute of Architects, 30 March 1934, AIA Archives and Library.

[77]At the final meeting of the board of directors and stockholders of the Northwestern Division on April 10, 1942 (the first meeting held since October 8, 1936), Roy C. Jones made a motion, which passed unanimously, to initiate the dissolution of the regional bureau. Members C. B. Stravs and Rollin C. Chapin were allowed to take some of the drawings; the remainder were to "be turned over to some agency for their salvage value." Robert T. Jones was authorized to sell old paper blueprints on hand and dispose of financial records as an attorney recommended. Roy C. Jones moved that the perspective drawings be sent to "the University," and Robert T. Jones was to "dispose of the historical archives wherever he can." Finally, a motion was made by Robert T. Jones to "divide unencumbered assets among surviving members." Minutes of the board of directors and stockholders meeting, ASHSB of US, Northwestern Division, 10 April 1942, ASHSB Papers, Box 56.

[78]Rollin C. Chapman, "Should AIA Endorse Architects? Yes!" *American Architect* (April 1932): 22. This belief was in agreement with a 1932 *Pencil Points* article noting a "marked improvement in the architectural design and construction of good architecture since 1920; and coincident with this development there has been an equal improvement in the architectural design and construction quality of the stock plans for small houses produced by nearly all agencies." "The Affiliation of the AIA with the Architects' Small House Service Bureau, Inc.," *Pencil Points* (March 1932): 197.

[79]The Architects' Home Plan Institute was begun in 1945 by approximately twenty-five American Institute of Architects' members from Minneapolis and St. Paul. This group included at least one former member of the ASHSB—Rollin C. Chapin. Endorsed by the Minnesota Chapter of the AIA, the organization was intended "to give the small house owner the benefits of the best in architectural advice." Members paid twenty-five dollars and created three plans for the Institute during the first six months of membership. Plans were distributed solely through architect members of the AHPI but were publicized in local newspapers and leaflets. The Institute's first publication was *Northwest Homes.* Published in October 1945, it included forty-four plans and was available at bookstands and certain banks. The AHPI sold 150 plans in the first seven months they were available. "Membership List," *Northwest Homes: Folio Number Two* (Minneapolis: The Architects' Home Plan Institute, 1946); and Dale Robert McEnary, "The Architects' Home Plan Institute of Minneapolis," 5 March 1946, a manuscript in the local history collection of the Minneapolis Public Library.

YOUR
FUTURE HOME

*A Selected Collection of Plans for Small Houses
from three to six rooms, for which
complete working drawings may
be secured at nominal cost*

HOUSE PLANS AND SERVICE
By the Northwestern and Mountain Divisions of
THE ARCHITECTS' SMALL HOUSE SERVICE BUREAU
OF THE UNITED STATES, Inc.
Controlled by The American Institute of Architects

EDITED AND PUBLISHED BY
WEYERHAEUSER FOREST PRODUCTS
Saint Paul, Minnesota

Contents

	Page
INTRODUCTION - - - - - - - - - -	5
THE TRADE MARK OF THE ARCHITECTS' SMALL HOUSE SERVICE BUREAU AND WHAT IT STANDS FOR - - - -	9
ENDORSEMENTS OF THE ARCHITECTS' SMALL HOUSE SERVICE BUREAU BY THE AMERICAN INSTITUTE OF ARCHITECTS AND THE DEPARTMENT OF COMMERCE - - - - - -	10
SOME FUNDAMENTAL HINTS ON FINANCING THE BUILDING OF A HOME	11
HOW TO SELECT A PLAN TO SUIT YOUR NEEDS - - - -	12
HOW TO READ AND UNDERSTAND PLANS - - - - -	14

Portfolio of House Plans

	Page
INTRODUCTION - - - - - - - -	15
SIX-ROOM HOUSES - - - - - - - - - -	16
Twenty-two Designs with Key Floor Plans and Descriptions	
FIVE-ROOM HOUSES - - - - - - - -	60
Twenty-Two Designs with Key Floor Plans and Descriptions	
FOUR-ROOM HOUSES - - - - - - - -	104
Seventeen Designs with Key Floor Plans and Descriptions	
THREE-ROOM HOUSES - - - - - - - -	138
Eight Designs with Key Floor Plans and Descriptions	

Contents—*Continued*

WHAT THE ARCHITECTS' SMALL HOUSE SERVICE BUREAU HAS
to OFFER - - - - - - - - - 154

BUILDING DOCUMENTS SUPPLIED BY THE ARCHITECTS' SMALL HOUSE
SERVICE BUREAU - - - - - - - - 156

REPRODUCTIONS OF A COMPLETE SET OF WORKING DRAWINGS AND
DETAILS - - - - - - - - - 158

NATIONAL HEADQUARTERS OF THE ARCHITECTS' SMALL HOUSE SERVICE BUREAU
OF THE UNITED STATES, INC., 1200 SECOND AVENUE SOUTH,
MINNEAPOLIS, MINNESOTA.

Introduction

THE Architects' Small House Service Bureau is a coöperative organization composed of architects who are men of reputation and successful experience, associated through regional or territorial Service Bureaus, and finally through a National body known as The Architects' Small House Service Bureau of the United States, Inc.

The fundamental idea behind the Bureau movement is the desire to improve the architecture of the small house, to eliminate waste in the building thereof, and to insure good, safe, and at the same time economical building.

The Bureau is practically a non-profit making organization. The members are professional men who have no "axe to grind." They have been referred to as the "Eight-Dollar-A-Year" Architects. Each member in the Bureau has invested one hundred dollars in one share of stock and no member can hold more than one share of the common stock. The articles of incorporation limit the dividends from earnings to 8% a year, and in the event of the earnings exceeding this amount such surplus is to be devoted to the betterment of the service.

Because the Bureau is nation-wide in its membership, it becomes possible for it to offer, from personal knowledge, first hand advice to the home-builder, covering contingencies that arise from climatic and other local conditions.

The designs reproduced in this book are for six, five, four and three-room houses. The Bureaus' service stops with the six-room house. They do no special designing. Beyond this limited service the Bureaus recommend that home-builders employ an individual practicing architect.

Persons who imagine that money is to be saved by dispensing with the services of an architect usually place themselves in the hands of some firm which undertakes to combine the functions of architect and builder. Unfortunately, however, a builder is rarely a good designer, nor should he be, for these are two distinct and widely separated functions, yet the time consumed by whoever makes the design must be, and in all fairness should be, paid for. It is not surprising that a home-builder should fail to grasp this point, though a little reflection might convince him that the work of preparing any character of plans must be paid for in some way.

Offers of cheap plans and plans "free of charge" are calculated to attract the class of mind that wants "something for nothing." It is strange, however, that persons bent on economy should not perceive that the expense of furnishing plans, through a free plan service, to a large number of prospective builders, who in so many cases do not use them, must be borne by the few who do use them. To those who consider whether there is any real benefit in architectural service it is not difficult to make plain its many advantages, but to those who will not consider the matter only a costly experience can enlighten them. The interests of an owner and an architect must be identical, whereas the relation of an owner and a contractor are those of buyer and seller.

An honest contractor welcomes a full set of plans and specifications, for he knows that they save him time and money. He knows exactly what he is expected to deliver and he is therefor able to figure closely on an intelligent basis. In all fairness the money thus saved should be passed on to the home-builder. Money paid out for mistakes and deceits, which professionally prepared plans and advice could have saved, is wasted. It can never be regained. Buying sound building advice is buying insurance against inefficiency and disappointment. It is hazardous not to have it.

For the first time in the history of American home-building, the gap which has existed between the small home-builder and the architect has been spanned. For the first time there is now a dependable and authoritative source from which the small home-builder can get well-designed houses and good planning at a nominal cost. The Architects' Small House Service Bureau now makes it possible for anyone desiring to build a small dwelling, up to six rooms in size, to secure professional help at modest cost. Home-builders may now secure complete working plans, specifications, bill of materials, and contract agreement forms, prepared by experienced architects, each checked and finally approved by associate architects of the Bureau. These men have devoted years to the particular problem of small houses. The cost of this service for any of the houses shown in this book is within the reach of all.

These designs are not merely pretty pictures of an artistic imagination. They are real pictures of your possible future home as it is bound to look if you follow the plans which the Architects' Bureau has studied and prepared. Each house has been worked out with the painstaking care that an architect gives to an individual client. The drawings are just as honestly tested for accuracy as though an individual architect's reputation depended upon the designing of that particular house.

Since you do not come into personal contact with your architect when you buy the Bureau service, and since no two problems are absolutely alike, The Architects' Small House Service Bureau is so organized that it can answer perplexing questions if they arise. In many cases one of the houses shown might be quite perfect if the porch could be moved to the other side, or if the stove were in another position in the kitchen, or if the fireplace were in a different location. It is realized that "facing" a house is most important and for this reason the Bureau supplies at your request, and without charge, extra working drawings printed in reverse for the facing that your lot dictates. There is no additional charge for this particular service. If other minor changes in the plans are desired, the Bureau will be glad to make them at the cost only of the actual time necessary to revise the drawings.

The Architects' Small House Service Bureau also gives counsel and help in all matters relating to small home-building. This advice is unbiased and prompted by a desire to give the man who is building the truths and basic facts about materials, equipment, construction, and costs, in order to protect his interests and save him money.

We have all seen the commonplace and ugly houses which have been built so many times in our cities and villages—houses that are badly planned and with poor accommodation, in which the placement of rooms is wrong and the proportion of rooms to hallways and passageways is out of balance—houses in which the depreciation is high, where the owner pays annually for repairs a sum almost equal to rent—houses that are so ugly both outside and inside that, if offered for sale, no one wants to buy them.

Such houses are usually built from plans furnished by strictly commercial house plan concerns or by inexperienced draftsmen, neither of whom have had experience in the actual building of houses nor adequate training in architectural design. Seldom can such failures be traced to practicing architects.

From actual experience it can be demonstrated that a well and simply designed, commodiously planned small house can be built at a price which is often less than the packing-box type of house loaded with gingerbread ornament. It is no more costly to work from a good pattern than a poor one.

The Architects' Small House Service Bureau idea originated in and is approved by The American Institute of Architects, which is the national association of the leading architects of this country, and in order that the development of the idea may retain the character of a professional service and be prevented from expanding into a purely commercial undertaking for unlimited profit, the organization of the Bureau involves a certain control of its policies by the Institute. The Board of Directors of The American Institute of Architects looks upon an architect's work in the various Regional Small House Service Bureaus as primarily a contribution to the improvement of the small house architecture of this country, where it involves houses of not more than six primary rooms. The Bureau's work in no way displaces the architect, for his is a very real function and his service to home-builders is a real economic necessity.

The national scope and the importance of the work The Architects' Small House Service Bureau of the United States is doing is perhaps best illustrated by the fact that it not only has the approval of and is controlled by The American Institute of Architects, but that it also has the endorsement of Herbert Hoover, Secretary of the Department of Commerce, United States Government.

Copyright 1920

What This Sign Stands For

THIS SIGN is the trade-mark of The Architects' Small House Service Bureau of the United States, Inc. Regional member bureaus are licensed to use the trade-mark plus the territorial designation or name assigned each Bureau by The Architects' Small House Service Bureau of the United States, Inc., depending on the location of the individual bureaus.

This trade-mark stands for co-operative effort and service by groups of architects who in addition to their regular practice are able to supply professional service and counsel, well studied, carefully prepared plans, specifications, and quantity surveys—at low cost—for the erection of homes up to and including six primary rooms.

For specially designed or larger homes an individual practicing architect should be employed at an adequate fee.

This trade-mark signifies professional architectural service at low cost because The Architects' Small House Service Bureau of the United States, Inc., and its regional member bureaus are primarily non-profit making enterprises. Each Bureau is a limited dividend corporation with small capital.

Home builders who use the service this trade-mark stands for are insured the best possible ready-to-use home plans, designed to eliminate extra materials and labor without loss of maximum home comforts, conveniences and beauty.

THE ARCHITECTS' SMALL HOUSE SERVICE BUREAU OF THE UNITED STATES, INC.

National Headquarters, 1200 Second Avenue South, Minneapolis, Minnesota

Thirteen Regional Service Bureaus will make up The Architects' Small House Service Bureau of the United States, Inc. These bureaus will be so located that home builders in any part of the country can get prompt service, each bureau being thoroughly familiar with local building conditions and the architectural types best suited to its locality.

REGIONAL SERVICE BUREAUS IN OPERATION MAY 1, 1923

THE NORTHWESTERN DIVISION, Inc.
Main Office: 1200 Second Avenue South, Minneapolis, Minn.

THE MOUNTAIN DIVISION, Inc.
Main Office: 415 Chamber of Commerce Building, Denver, Colorado

THE NORTH CENTRAL DIVISION, Inc.
Main Office: Room 813, 141 Wisconsin Street, Milwaukee, Wisconsin

THE ATLANTIC DIVISION, Inc.
Main Office: Room 610, 19 West 44th Street, New York, N. Y.

THE LAKE DIVISION, Inc.
Main Office: 413 Penway Building, Indianapolis, Ind.

THE POTOMAC DIVISION, Inc.
Main Office: 302 Ferguson Building, Pittsburgh, Pa.

THE NORTH PACIFIC DIVISION, Inc.
Headquarters: 814 Couch Bldg., Portland, Oregon

9

WILLIAM B. FAVILLE, President, San Francisco
ERNEST J. RUSSELL, 1st Vice President, St. Louis
ROBERT D. KOHN, 2nd Vice President, New York

WILLIAM STANLEY PARKER, Secretary, Boston
D. EVERETT WAID, Treasurer, New York
EDWARD C. KEMPER, Executive Secretary, Washington, D.C.

1857   1922

THE AMERICAN INSTITUTE OF ARCHITECTS
THE OCTAGON HOUSE, WASHINGTON, D. C.

San Francisco, Calif.
August 4th, 1922.

Mr. Edwin Brown,
1200 Second Avenue, South,
Minneapolis, Minn.

My dear Brown:

The wider field of activity
and the increased usefulness of the
Architects Small House Service Bureau
by the creation of new Regional Bureaus,
during the last year is most gratifying.

This activity was warmly
indorsed by the Convention of the
Institute and the Bureau's activity,
I am sure, will become more and more
appreciated by persons who previously
have felt that Architectural service
for the Small House was unavailable.

Wishing you unqualified success
in this field of professional usefulness,
I am

Very truly yours,

William B. Faville

PRESIDENT.

WBF:W

---

*Under date of October 11, 1921, Mr. Herbert Hoover wrote to Mr. Henry
H. Kendall, then President of The American Institute of Architects:*

I HAVE looked into the work of The Architects' Small House Service Bureau of The United States with its divisions and branches and have examined its organization and incorporation papers. The complete plans, specifications, documents and bills of materials with the designs —worked out for local conditions and to use stock materials and eliminate waste—materially simplify home building problems. The form of control by The American Institute of Architects should guarantee a high standard of service. It gives me pleasure to endorse this work and to assure you that the Department of Commerce will do all it can to co-operate with the Institute and the Bureau.

Herbert Hoover

Some Fundamental Hints
on Financing the Building of a Home

While this is strictly a house plan service book, financing is for many such a determining factor in the building of a home, that it seemed advisable to include a few fundamental hints on this subject.

PERSONS of moderate means generally find it necessary to borrow a part of the money needed if they are to build a home; in fact, most of the houses built in this country have, to a large extent, been financed with borrowed money. Ways are provided for financing the building of a home which make it possible, even for persons with a very modest income, to build a house with less ready money than most people realize.

With the thought of building, these questions usually arise: "Have I sufficient money to build?" "Can I finance the building of a home?" In assisting you to answer these questions, the following is meant to be helpful.

The cost of the lot should represent not to exceed 20% or ⅕ of the total contemplated investment; in other words, if the total investment is to be $2,500 the lot should cost approximately $500 and the house $2,000; likewise with an investment of $5,000, the lot should cost somewhere near $1,000 and the house $4,000; and again, if the total investment is to be $10,000, the lot should cost not to exceed $2,000, and the house $8,000. If the lot has been fully paid for, or if there has been not less than ⅕ of the total investment saved up to start with, this is sufficient to ask for a mortgage loan on which to build, and any amount available over 20% makes it just that much easier.

Naturally the greater the amount of money available above 20% the better the security for the money borrowed and consequently the more advantageous the terms upon which you can place a mortgage loan.

Mortgage loans are nothing more not less than promissory notes. A mortgage loan is simply a recorded statement that, because of money advanced, the title to land and building is offered as an assurance that the borrower will pay the full value of the loan with interest.

The usual sources from which loans as above outlined can be obtained are Savings Banks; Building and Loan Associations; Title Insurance and Trust Companies; Life Insurance Companies; Real Estate Firms; Mortgage Brokers; Private Individuals.

Before making a loan, bankers and other financial agencies will investigate the title to and will study carefully the location of your building site, whether or not it is in an improved district, and the probability of a year by year increase in its land value; they will thoroughly go over the plans and specifications of the house you propose to build to determine that it will be well and economically built; and they will want to know that the borrower has a reputation for honesty and for meeting his obligations promptly.

In different localities different accredited ways have grown up for making mortgage loans, and to endeavor to cover these would only tend to confuse. In conclusion therefore, be it said, if your lot is paid for, and better still if you have any funds left over after your lot has been paid for, you are in a position to approach without embarrassment any organization making mortgage loans and to ask for a loan that will make possible the building of your home.

In addition to mortgage loans there is one other and much used manner of financing the building of a home. This is the so-called "Contract for Deed" method. Under this method, building can be begun with very little or no ready money. The builder pays for his house in monthly installments, very much as if he were paying rent, but the title to the property does not rest in the builder until all the payments have been made. Since this method of financing is more hazardous to the lender than is the mortgage loan method, larger commissions are usually charged, and the interest rates are higher. This method of financing therefore, with the possibility of excessive commissions and higher interest rates, can be and has been abused, but if rightly handled is in every way legitimate. The usual channels through which a "Contract for Deed" can be made are house financing companies, speculative builders and private individuals.

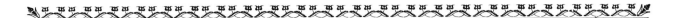

How to Select a Plan to Suit Your Needs

THERE are sixty-nine different designs illustrated in this book from which to choose your future home. The plan that will best meet your requirements and the exterior that is most pleasing to you is no doubt somewhere included in this collection. Where there are so many plans to choose from it may be that you will have difficulty in making your selection. The Architects' Small House Service Bureau wants to help you with this problem so that you will not make the mistake of selecting the wrong plan and so as to make the selection of the right plan as easy as possible for you. If you will follow these suggestions in the rotation in which they are offered, you will be surprised to find how quickly the right design for your particular needs can be found.

First decide whether you want a three, four, five or six-room house. Next make certain whether you want a one-story or a two-story house. Do not bother at this time as to whether the exterior be of wood, stucco, or brick—as that problem, if it arises, can usually be overcome. You will find in this book grouped together, six-room houses, five-room houses, four-room houses and three-room houses, each design for identification being numbered. The first figure in these identifying numbers indicates the number of "Principal Rooms" in the house. By "Principal Rooms" is meant living room, dining room, kitchen and bedrooms, and not hall, enclosed sun porches, bath rooms, or closets. Thus 6A20, is a six-room house; 5B11 is a five-room house; 4A15, is a four-room house; and 3B9 is a three-room house. The letters "A" and "B" indicate the division of The Architects' Small House Service Bureau which made the designs, "A" indicating "Northwestern Division" of Minneapolis, and "B" indicating "Mountain Division" of Denver.

When you have determined the number of rooms you want, you then eliminate a large number of designs in which you otherwise might have become interested. For example, suppose you have decided on a six-room house. You therefore have all the six-room designs from which to choose. The exteriors of some of these are of wood, some of brick and

some of stucco. For the time being do not think of these exterior materials. In fact it would be much better if you do not consider the exterior at all until after you have selected the plan.

Next eliminate those plans which you do not care for. Then eliminate the houses that cannot be accommodated to your lot. In this connection perhaps the setting of your house is such that a living room across the front with stairway at the side will be much more satisfying than a plan wherein the living room runs from front to back with stairway in the center of the house. With this decided it is possible to drop out a further number of plans. Next the outlook from your different windows is important. Not every plan will give you the best view from your living room, it being all important that your living room have the best possible outlook. By this time you have now left perhaps eight or ten designs which provide in general for the things that you most wish to have. From these plans you should then make such further eliminations as will reduce the more satisfactory plans to the smallest number.

Now look at the outside of these houses, and definitely select the combination of exterior and plan that you like best.

In making this final decision it will help you to know that The Architects' Small House Service Bureau can make minor changes for you in these plans if you wish to have this done. They can add or omit porches or change open porches to sun porches. They can change double hung windows to the casement type of window, or vice versa. They can add or omit fireplaces. For exterior use stucco can be substituted for weather boarding in many of the designs without serious harm to appearance. Brick, stucco and wood can often be interchanged. Minor changes can always be made, and the Bureau makes them for you at slight additional expense, depending upon how much time it takes to make the revisions. They will try to tell you in advance what the maximum charge will be for any such work. Please remember also that many of the houses are so designed that they can be enlarged. You may, for instance, find among the four-room group plans like 4A16, in which provision is made for an extra room under the roof, thus making it a five-room house. This makes it possible for you to finish off this extra room when you build or at some later time.

It may be that you will find a plan which in all respects exactly meets your requirements, but which is too large for your lot. In such cases possibly you can adjust this house to your lot by putting the porches at the rear instead of at the side, without seriously injuring the design, or by slightly decreasing the "over all" dimensions of the house, or by turning the end of the house to the front. These changes can almost always be made without difficulty. In the same way most of the designs can be extended if you wish to have the rooms larger. It is part of the Bureau service to tell you about this. Please do not hesitate to ask for an opinion. You will be told frankly what they think can be done wisely and to your advantage.

In selecting the house you wish to build, there are thus four definite steps to consider. *First,* Determine how many rooms you want. *Second,* Group together and study only those designs that have the desired number of rooms. *Third,* Eliminate from this group those plans that you do not wish to consider. *Fourth,* Select from the finally retained plans the one which has the exterior you most prefer.

Read the Plans First and Choose the Exterior Afterward. In this if you will even go so far as to first cover with paper the drawing that shows the outside of the house, so as not to allow the exterior to confuse you, you will find it very much easier to study the plan and you will have a far better assurance of getting the plan arrangement best suited to your needs. Remember that the plan is far more important to your comfort than the exterior.

With a definite amount in mind for the building of your home, the cost of any selected house plan becomes the final determining factor. To help you in determining this cost, The Architects' Small House Service Bureau has closely followed the construction costs of a large number of houses built from these plans—the houses from which this information was gathered having been built in widely separated localities, under varying conditions, in different climates, and using different specifications. If desired they will be glad indeed to tell you with reasonable accuracy what the cost of your house should be.

In conclusion it should be pointed out, that the final cost is largely determined by the specifications, the decision as regards the selection of materials resting with the owner, after consultation with some reliable local contractor and advice from The Architects' Small House Service Bureau. If the owner specifies the highest grade of materials and finishes, the cost of necessity will be higher. If he adds expensive equipment, it adds to the ultimate cost. By using moderate or low priced equipment the final cost of the building will in turn be materially reduced. It should always be remembered, however, that the cheapest is not always in the end the most economical, nor are the highest priced materials always necessary. Every care should be used in determining in each case the most economical material to use. Again be it said, the final decision as regards the quality of materials and therefore the cost of building rests with the owner.

How to Read and Understand Plans

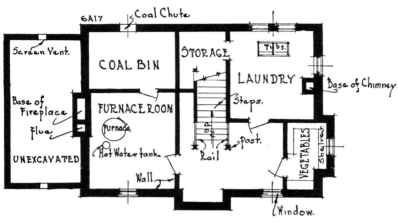

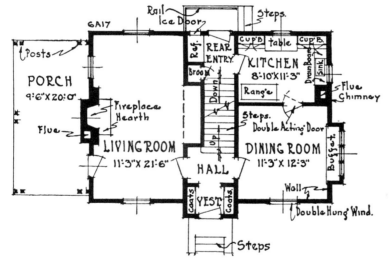

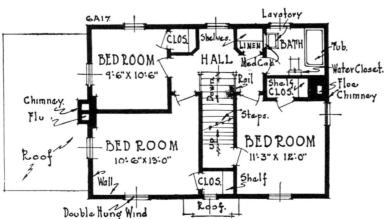

PERHAPS it is difficult for you to read plans; many people find it so. If you will refer to the three illustrations on this page you will find typical floor plans with the different parts clearly named:

Wide black lines indicate the walls.

Chimneys are indicated by a thickening of the wall with one or more light spaces to show the flues.

Fireplaces are indicated by a thickening of the wall with a recess for the fireplace opening. The light lines in front of fireplace indicate the hearth.

Windows are indicated by breaks in outside walls with connecting light lines across these breaks.

Doors are indicated by a light line set at an angle with the door opening, and a curved line which shows direction in which the door is to swing.

Stairs are indicated by light parallel lines.

An arrow and word tell you whether the stairs go "Up" or "Down."

Porch columns are indicated by solid squares or circles.

Plumbing fixtures are separately indicated.

Other features such as closets, porches, porch roofs, location of furnace, etc., are plainly marked on the drawings.

Practice reading over these plans. You will soon find it easy to tell where the cupboards are, where the ice box is located, where the range and sink are placed in the kitchen, and so on. When you have done this with one of the plans, all the others will be easy to read. You will find all the rooms plainly marked and the dimensions of each given.

Portfolio of House Plans

ON the following pages—16 to 153—are shown sixty-nine house plans—twenty-two six-room houses, pages 16 to 59; twenty-two five-room houses, pages 60 to 103; seventeen four-room houses, pages 104 to 137; and eight three-room houses, pages 138 to 153.

Complete working plans, specifications, quantity survey and forms of agreement for all of the houses are ready for immediate distribution. Where a house is designed to face North or West, as explained in the description, the Bureau will supply an extra set of working drawings printed in reverse for the house to face South or East.

Each house is presented in perspective and accompanied by key floor plans and a complete description. By studying these carefully you may know what Your Future Home will look like when built, and exactly what it will contain.

The cubic contents of each house is given at the bottom of the middle column in the descriptive matter to enable you to get an idea of the cost of the house built in your locality. Architects, reliable contractors or building material dealers can give you the approximate building cost per cubic foot. Get this cost per cubic foot from them, multiply it by the figure given and you will get the approximate cost of the house built in your locality. The actual cost will, of course, depend upon your final specifications, but this approximate cost will at least give you a starting point for your calculations.

HOUSE PLAN NO. 6A1

A DELIGHTFULLY SATISFYING HOME, ACHIEVING THE TRUE COLONIAL ATMOSPHERE OF GRACE AND REPOSE

THE SIMPLICITY OF THE ARRANGEMENT OF ROOMS ASSURES COMFORT AND FREEDOM FROM HOUSEHOLD CARES BUT DOES NOT ADD TO THE COST OF CONSTRUCTION

FIRST FLOOR

CEILING HEIGHT 8'-6"

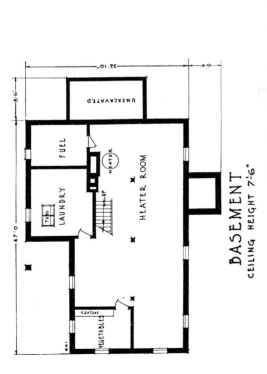

BASEMENT

CEILING HEIGHT 7'-6"

Note—For guidance in reading floor plans, see explanation on page 14

EXTERIOR

STYLE: New England Colonial. Bungalow type.

SIZE OF LOT REQUIRED: 65 feet in width if placed on lot as illustrated; from 37 to 42 feet in width if house is turned so that porch faces the street, which will bring the entrance on the side; plan especially suited to corner lot.

CONSTRUCTION: Wood frame on masonry foundations.

FINISH: Wide wood siding or shingles for walls, shingled roof.

PORCHES: Large living porch opening off the living room; entrance terrace; kitchen porch at the rear.

CHIMNEY: One inside brick chimney, containing heater, fireplace and kitchen range flues.

DECORATIVE FEATURES: The use, throughout, of forms which have been demonstrated as successful for execution in wood; the texture of the plan surfaces serves to enhance the proportions of the doors, windows and cornice; the slender columns and delicate open balustrade of the porch have the lightness and grace that distinguish Colonial design.

COLOR SCHEME SUGGESTED: Siding painted white; blinds bottle green; shingles stained in variegated colors of green, red and brown.

ALTERNATE EXTERIOR: This same basic plan with a different exterior, may be found on Page 26, House Plan No. 6A6.

INTERIOR

NUMBER OF ROOMS: 6 Main rooms, Bath-room, and 8 Closets.

SIZE OF ROOMS:

Living Room	13' 6" x 20' 0"
Dining Room	13' 0" x 11' 0"
Kitchen	10' 0" x 13' 6"
Bed Room	13' 6" x 10' 6"
Bed Room	11' 6" x 10' 6"
Bed Room	10' 0" x 11' 6"
Bath Room	5' 6" x 7' 6"

BASEMENT: Under the entire house, containing Laundry, Heater-room, Vegetable-storage and Fuel-bins.

PLAN TYPE: Living room and dining room running from front to back or across the front of the house if placed with porch toward the street.

DESIGNED TO FACE: So that principal rooms can be toward the South. Plans may be reversed.

FIREPLACE: One large open fireplace in end wall of living room, with Colonial mantel and adjoining built-in seat and bookcase.

VENTILATION: 17 windows with double hung sash; one pair of French doors opening onto porch; 2 outside doors; semi-circular louvre window for free circulation of air under roof.

WALL SPACES: Ample for large pieces of furniture.

CUBIC CONTENTS: Approximately 31,000 cubic feet.

SPECIAL FEATURES

ENTRANCE VESTIBULE: Takes the place of a hall, breaking the draft, and providing a handy hat and coat closet.

LIVING ROOM: The proportions are excellent; it is large enough for entertaining but not so big that a few people will feel lost in it; the sunny dining room may be seen through the cased opening at the rear and the hospitable porch opens directly from this room.

KITCHEN: Equipped with all modern conveniences for doing work with fewest steps, and least labor; windows on two sides, one group directly over the sink. Refrigerator iced from outside.

REAR ENTRY HALL: Opening off back porch and providing direct passage to basement stairs, to the kitchen, and to the inner hall; the bath room and bed rooms are only a step from the kitchen through this hall. It contains a fine broom closet.

BED ROOMS: Entirely shut off from the living rooms by an inner hall which contains a linen closet and an extra coat closet; all the rooms have ample light and ventilation.

PLUMBING: Includes bath tub, lavatory, water closet, laundry tubs, kitchen sink, hot and cold water supply.

ELECTRIC OUTLETS: Properly placed, available for iron, washing machine, vacuum cleaner, toaster, floor and table lamps, heaters, etc., if any or all of them are desired.

17

HOUSE PLAN NO. 6B2

Architects' Small House Service Bureau

THE SMALL MODERN ENGLISH HOUSE IS MUCH ADMIRED FOR ITS PICTURESQUENESS AND FOR ITS HOMELIKE ATMOSPHERE

THE PLANS PROVIDE FOR HOUSEKEEPING FACILITIES AND CONVENIENCES FOR INDOOR AND OUTDOOR FAMILY LIFE

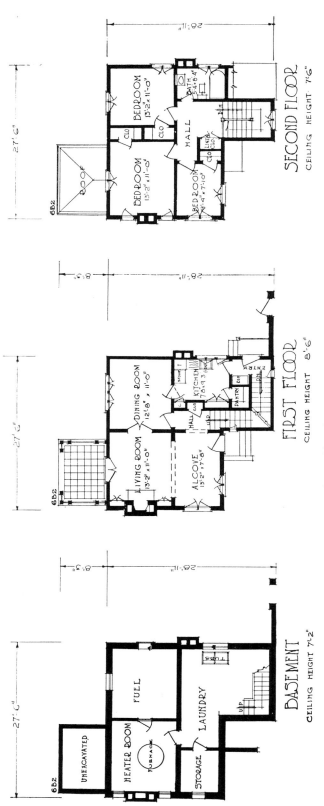

BASEMENT

CEILING HEIGHT 7'-2"

UNEXCAVATED

HEATER ROOM — FURNACE

FUEL

STORAGE

LAUNDRY

6B2

FIRST FLOOR

CEILING HEIGHT 8'-6"

DINING ROOM 12'8" x 11'-0"

KITCHEN 7'8" x 9'3"

LIVING ROOM 13'2" x 11'-0"

HALL CLO — PANTRY — ENTRY

ALCOVE 13'2" x 7'-8"

6B2

SECOND FLOOR

CEILING HEIGHT 7'-6"

BEDROOM 13'2" x 11'-0"

BATH 5'4" x 8'4"

CLO — CLO

HALL

CLO LINEN CLO

BEDROOM 13'2" x 11'-0"

BEDROOM 9'4" x 7'-10"

ROOF

6B2

Note—For guidance in reading floor plans, see explanation on page 14

EXTERIOR

STYLE: Modern English Domestic. Two-story type.

SIZE OF LOT REQUIRED: From 45 to 40 feet in width.

CONSTRUCTION: Wood frame on masonry foundations.

FINISH: Floated stucco above brick water table; roof shingled.

PORCHES: Hooded main entrance porch, with brick floor; covered living porch 12' 0" x 8' 0" opening off living room on the garden end.

CHIMNEYS: Two exterior chimneys, each with two flues.

DECORATIVE FEATURES: The picturesque roof slopes; the plain wall spaces pleasantly broken by windows, and the hooded entrance insure an exterior that will make an excellent appearance from any point of view. The garden wall and gate add interest to the general contour of the house.

COLOR SCHEME SUGGESTED: Walls cream colored, floated finish stucco; brickwork variegated rough textured brick; variegated stain for the roof shingles. Exterior woodwork stained a weathered oak color.

ALTERNATE EXTERIORS: None.

INTERIOR

NUMBER OF ROOMS: 6 Main rooms, Alcove, Bathroom and 6 Closets.

SIZE OF ROOMS:

First Floor

Living Room	13' 2" x 11' 0"
Alcove	13' 2" x 7' 8"
Dining Room	12' 8" x 11' 0"
Kitchen	7' 8" x 9' 3"

Second Floor

Bed Room	13' 2" x 11' 0"
Bed Room	13' 2" x 11' 0"
Bed Room	9' 4" x 7' 10"
Bath Room	5' 4" x 8' 4"

BASEMENT: Under entire house, containing Laundry, Heater-room, Storage-room, and Fuel-bins.

PLAN TYPE: Living room running from front to rear; stairs in center of house.

DESIGNED TO FACE: North or East. For other facings, plans should be reversed.

FIREPLACE: One large open fireplace in the living room with well designed wood mantel, and book cases on each side.

VENTILATION: 28 casement windows. One pair of French doors; 2 outside doors; louvres in gable ends to permit free circulation of air under roof.

WALL SPACES: Ample for large pieces of furniture.

CUBIC CONTENTS: Approximately 18,200 cubic feet.

SPECIAL FEATURES

LIVING ROOM: The alcove is really part of one big living room, but as occasion may demand it can be converted into a most useful additional room.

DINING ROOM: Opens off the living room by French doors; faces the garden, visible through the bank of casement windows.

KITCHEN: In addition to being perfectly equipped and well lighted, it also contains a storage pantry; it is reached from the outside through an entry, enclosed in the main body of the house; the basement stairs descend from this entry, which also provides space for ice box with cupboards over it.

BED ROOMS: The two principal bed rooms overlook the garden; generous closets for all three rooms, and each has windows on two sides.

LINEN CLOSET AND BATH ROOM open off the upstairs hall.

PLUMBING: Includes bath tub, lavatory, water closet, laundry tubs, kitchen sink and hot and cold water supply.

ELECTRIC OUTLETS: In the proper places, available for iron, washing machine, vacuum cleaner, toaster, floor and table lamps, and heater, etc., if any or all of them are desired.

6B4

A MODERN AMERICAN HOUSE IN WHICH PRETENSION AND ARCHITECTURAL STYLE ARE SECONDARY TO HUMAN CHARM
BEAUTY OF DESIGN OBTAINED BY HARMONY OF GRACEFUL LINES, BALANCED MASS AND SIMPLE TREATMENT

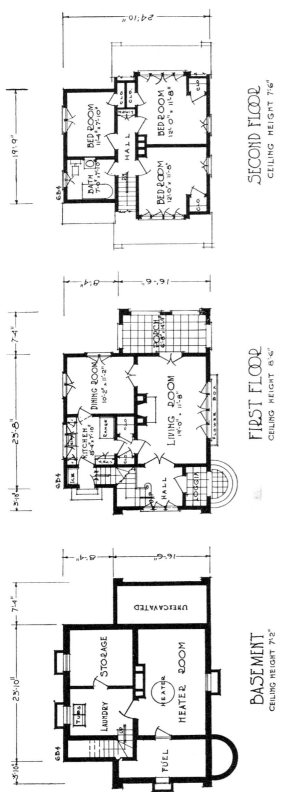

BASEMENT
CEILING HEIGHT 7'-2"

FIRST FLOOR
CEILING HEIGHT 8'-6"

SECOND FLOOR
CEILING HEIGHT 7'-6"

Note—For guidance in reading floor plans, see explanation on page 14

EXTERIOR

STYLE: American with Italian Influence. Story-and-a-half type.

SIZE OF LOT REQUIRED: From 42 to 45 feet in width.

CONSTRUCTION: Wood frame on masonry foundations.

FINISH: Trowel-marked stucco; shingled roof.

PORCHES: Arched entrance loggia and arched living porch 6' 8" x 14' 9".

CHIMNEY: Central brick chimney, covered with stucco. Three flues.

DECORATIVE FEATURES: The graceful lines of the roof, the arched buttress on each side, the plain wall surfaces and the excellent window spacing make this a beautiful and distinctive house. The appropriate flower box below the living room windows gives a touch of color.

COLOR SCHEME SUGGESTED: Light cream colored wall surfaces. Roof a brownish-green with shutters to harmonize with roof. Wood doors and frames painted white.

ALTERNATE EXTERIORS: This same basic plan with different exteriors may be found on Pages 54 and 58, House Plan Nos. 6A37 and 6A43.

INTERIOR

NUMBER OF ROOMS: 6 Main rooms, Bath-room and 6 Closets.

SIZE OF ROOMS:

First Floor

Living Room	19' 0" x 11' 8"
Dining Room	10' 2" x 11' 2"
Kitchen	8' 4" x 7' 10"

Second Floor

Bed Room	12' 0" x 11' 8"
Bed Room	12' 0" x 11' 8"
Bed Room	11' 4" x 7' 10"
Bath Room	7' 0" x 7' 10"

BASEMENT: Under entire house, containing Laundry, Heater-room, Storage-room and Fuel-bins.

PLAN TYPE: Living room running across front of house with stair-hall at one side.

DESIGNED TO FACE: North or West. For other facings, plans should be reversed.

FIREPLACE: One large open fireplace in center of inside wall of living room.

VENTILATION: 30 single casement windows in groups of 2, 3 and 4 windows each. 2 outside doors and pair of French windows opening onto porch. Louvres in gable end for free circulation of air.

WALL SPACES: Ample for large pieces of furniture.

CUBIC CONTENTS: Approximately 16,800 cubic feet.

SPECIAL FEATURES

LIVING ROOM: Well lighted and spacious with balanced openings on each side of fireplace, one leading to the dining room, the other to a real hall. The four windows in front, and the French doors to the porch make an attractive vista whichever way one looks.

DINING ROOM: Lighted by windows on two sides, one pair of windows overlooking the garden.

KITCHEN: Most complete with its working space along the outside wall under three windows.

REAR ENTRY: To kitchen and to basement stairs, direct from outside. Ice box is here with cupboards above.

BED ROOMS: Generous size and well arranged and ventilated. Four closets for three bed rooms.

LINEN CLOSET: Occupies the space at the end of second story hall.

PLUMBING: Includes bath tub, lavatory and water closet, laundry tubs, kitchen sink, and hot and cold water.

ELECTRIC OUTLETS: In the proper places, available for iron, washing machine, vacuum cleaner, toaster, floor and table lamps, heaters, etc., if any or all of them are desired.

THE REMOTE LOVELINESS OF THE OLD HOMES BELOW THE MASON AND DIXON LINE IS RECALLED IN THIS RAMBLING BUNGALOW
HOSPITALITY IS THE KEYNOTE OF THE HOUSE, AND IS WELL SOUNDED BY THE TWO HUGE PORCHES AND GENEROUS LIVING QUARTERS

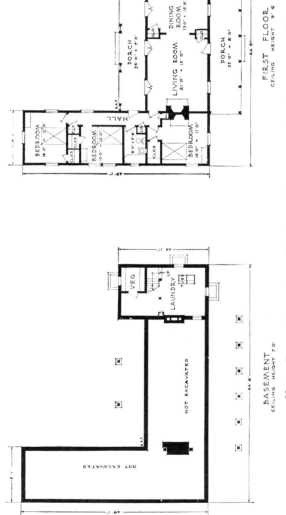

BASEMENT
CEILING HEIGHT 7'0"

FIRST FLOOR
CEILING HEIGHT 9'6"

Note—For guidance in reading floor plans, see explanation on page 14

EXTERIOR

STYLE: Southern Colonial Adaptation. Bungalow type.

SIZE OF LOT REQUIRED: House designed for a large piece of land.

CONSTRUCTION: Wood frame on masonry foundations.

FINISH: Wide wood siding for walls; shingled roof.

PORCHES: Cooling shade assured at all times, by the two long, spacious porches; one in the front 35' long and the one at the rear of living room 34' long; there is also a kitchen porch 9' 0" x 7' 0".

CHIMNEYS: Two inside brick chimneys for the flues of the three fireplaces and the kitchen range.

DECORATIVE FEATURES: The long front is attractively divided by elevating the ridge of the central portion and bringing the roof down over the porch, producing a central mass with wings on each side; the cornice line of all parts is kept at the same level, tying the design together; splendid arrangement of windows and door openings; the house rambles with real ease and informality and clings closely to the ground.

COLOR SCHEME SUGGESTED: Siding, cornice and columns painted white; blinds blue-green; roof variegated greens and browns.

ALETRNATE EXTERIORS: None.

INTERIOR

NUMBER OF ROOMS: 6 Main rooms, Bath-room, Toilet-room and 8 Closets.

SIZE OF ROOMS:
Living Room	21' 0" x 15' 0"
Dining Room	13' 0" x 15' 0"
Kitchen	14' 0" x 11' 0"
Bed Room	14' 0" x 11' 0"
Bed Room	10' 0" x 12' 0"
Bed Room	14' 0" x 11' 0"
Bath Room	8' 0" x 5' 6"

BASEMENT: Under kitchen only, containing Laundry and Vegetable-storage space.

PLAN TYPE: L-shaped plan, with bed rooms running from front to rear.

DESIGNED TO FACE: This house may face in any direction; plans may be reversed, however, if desired.

FIREPLACES: Three open fireplaces, to provide adequate heat, as there is no furnace. Each has a Colonial wood mantel.

VENTILATION: 16 windows with double hung sash; 3 pairs of French doors, 4 outside doors; louvres in gable ends to admit free circulation of air.

WALL SPACES: Ample for large pieces of furniture.

CUBIC CONTENTS: Approximately 34,000 cubic feet.

SPECIAL FEATURES

THIS PLAN is especially designed for regions of moderate winters or for a summer home, anywhere. The ceilings are 9½ feet high and every room has abundant fresh air.

LIVING AND DINING ROOMS: Are really one huge room, and can be further enlarged to take in the rear porch, by opening the three pairs of French doors; a closet in the living room at the right of the front door is for hats and coats; a closet balancing this in the dining room is for china.

KITCHEN: Modern, well-planned and equipped; the refrigerator is conveniently placed, and may be iced from the outside; the kitchen porch is large enough to be used as an outdoor room for the preparation of meals.

LAVATORY: Opening off the kitchen entry gives an opportunity to freshen up before sitting down to meals, or, it may be that a servant is employed, and it would then be doubly useful.

PLUMBING: Includes bath tub, 2 lavatories, 2 water closets, laundry tubs, kitchen sink, hot and cold water supply.

ELECTRIC OUTLETS: Properly placed, available for iron, washing machine, vacuum cleaner, toaster, floor and table lamps, heaters, etc., if any or all of them are desired.

House Plan No. 6B5

6B5

THE POPULARITY OF THE DUTCH GAMBREL ROOF HAS STOOD THE TEST FOR MANY GENERATIONS

ALTHOUGH SMALL, THIS HOUSE, WITH CONNECTING GARAGE, HAS EXCELLENT STYLE AND WILL HOLD ITS OWN AMONG LARGER HOUSES

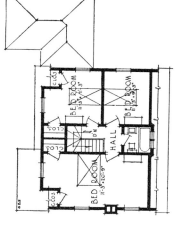

SECOND FLOOR PLAN
7'6" CEILING

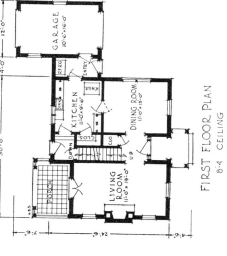

FIRST FLOOR PLAN
8'4" CEILING

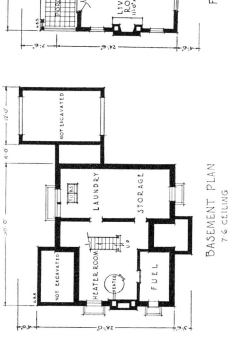

BASEMENT PLAN
7'6" CEILING

Note—For guidance in reading floor plans, see explanation on page 14

EXTERIOR

STYLE: Dutch Colonial Adaptation. Story-and-a-half type.

SIZE OF LOT REQUIRED: From 55 to 60 feet in width; will go on 40-foot lot if garage is omitted.

CONSTRUCTION: First story walls of brick on masonry foundations. Wood frame from second story.

FINISH: Wire cut face brick for first story. Wide wood siding for gable ends and dormer window.

PORCHES: Front entrance porch with recessed entry, affording partial protection from the elements. Living porch 8' 0" x 12' 6" covered by projection of main roof.

CHIMNEY: One outside brick chimney with fireplace and heater flues.

DECORATIVE FEATURES: Unusually good proportion, well formed roof and octagon shaped dormer. The curved roof of the entrance porch recedes into the cornice line and makes a graceful treatment. The delicate boxed columns and latticed panels on each side of the porch are most attractive. The beam and trellis effect on the garage tends to mold this feature into the main body of the house.

COLOR SCHEME SUGGESTED: Dark red face brick laid in white mortar joints. Main roof stained a bright green. The woodwork painted white and the outside blinds a turquoise blue.

ALTERNATE EXTERIORS: This same basic plan with different exteriors may be found on Pages 34, 42, 44, 46 and 48, House Plans No. 6B11, 6A18, 6A19, 6A20 and 6A22.

INTERIOR

NUMBER OF ROOMS: 6 Main rooms, Bath-room and 6 Closets.

SIZE OF ROOMS:

First Floor		
Living Room	11' 0" x 19' 0"
Dining Room	11' 0" x 13' 0"
Kitchen	11' 0" x 9' 6"
Second Floor		
Bed Room	11' 3" x 20' 9"
Bed Room	11' 3" x 11' 3"
Bed Room	11' 3" x 9' 3"
Bath Room	5' 6" x 5' 6"

BASEMENT: Under entire main portion of house, containing Laundry, Heater-room, Storage and Fuel-bins.

PLAN TYPE: Living room running from front to rear. Stairs in the center of house.

DESIGNED TO FACE: South or West. For other facings, plans should be reversed.

FIREPLACE: One large open fireplace in center of outside wall of living room.

VENTILATION: 16 windows with double hung sash; 3 outside doors. Louvres in gable ends to admit air under roof.

WALL SPACES: Due consideration given to the possibilities for placing large pieces of furniture.

CUBIC CONTENTS: Approximately 20,225 cubic feet.

SPECIAL FEATURES

HALL: Of sufficient width to permit of a stairway and a hall coat closet.

LIVING ROOM: Excellent proportions, light and airy with well placed windows on three sides. Fireplace centrally located, making a pleasing feature on the outside as well as the inside.

DINING ROOM: Balances the living room on the opposite side of the hall, with light on two sides.

KITCHEN: Spacious, well lighted with a modern equipment of fixtures, arranged to save extra steps in the day's work.

SIDE ENTRY: Providing access to the kitchen and forms a passage to the garage without going outdoors. Place provided for ice box.

REAR ENTRY: Provided so that basement may be reached directly from outdoors.

BED ROOMS: One of exceptionally large size. Two with windows on two sides. Ample closet space.

PLUMBING: Includes bath tub, lavatory and water closet, laundry tubs, kitchen sink, and hot and cold water supply.

ELECTRIC OUTLETS: In the proper places, available for iron, washing machine, vacuum cleaner, toaster, floor and table lamps, heaters, etc., if any or all of them are desired.

HOUSE PLAN NO. 6A6

6A6

THE NOTE OF HOMELINESS RATHER THAN OF STATELINESS IS STRUCK BY THIS BUNGALOW OF MILD ENGLISH FLAVOR
AMPLENESS COMBINED WITH CHARM, CONVENIENCE WITH GOOD TASTE, MEET ONE EVERYWHERE IN THE STUDY OF THIS HOME

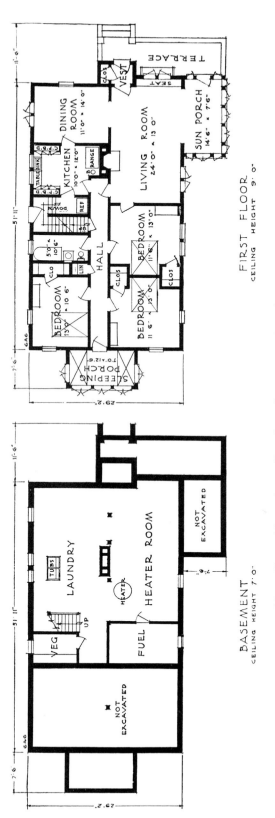

BASEMENT
CEILING HEIGHT 7'-0"

FIRST FLOOR
CEILING HEIGHT 9'-0"

Note—For guidance in reading floor plans, see explanation on page 14

EXTERIOR

STYLE: English Cottage. Bungalow type.

SIZE OF LOT REQUIRED: From 42 to 47 feet in width. Narrower lot would do if sun room is omitted. Plan especially suited to a corner lot.

CONSTRUCTION: Wood frame on masonry foundations.

FINISH: Stucco and siding combined. Could be built of brick with porches in half timber.

PORCHES: Sun porch, 14' 6" x 7' 6" and sleeping porch 7' 0" x 12' 6". Entrance terrace.

CHIMNEY: One chimney containing the heater, fireplace and kitchen range flues.

DECORATIVE FEATURES: The general excellence of the composition and the fine use of contrasting materials. The pleasing roof lines. The enclosed sun porch. The settee on the terrace.

COLOR SCHEME SUGGESTED: Cream colored stucco, brown stained timbers. Roof stained variegated greens.

ALTERNATE EXTERIOR: This same basic plan with different exterior can be found on page 16, House Plan No. 6A1.

INTERIOR

NUMBER OF ROOMS: 6 Main rooms, Sun porch, Sleeping porch, Bath-room, and 5 Closets.

SIZE OF ROOMS:

Living Room	24' 0" x 13' 0"
Dining Room	11' 0" x 14' 0"
Kitchen	10' 0" x 12' 0"
Bed Room	11' 6" x 13' 0"
Bed Room	11' 6" x 13' 0"
Bed Room	13' 0" x 10' 6"
Bath Room	5' 0" x 10' 6"

BASEMENT: Under two-thirds of house, containing Laundry, Heater-room, Vegetable-storage and Fuel-bins.

PLAN TYPE: Living room and dining room running from front to back or across the front of the house as shown in the illustration above.

DESIGNED TO FACE: South or East. For other facings, plans should be reversed.

FIREPLACE: Open fireplace in living room.

VENTILATION: 10 double hung windows, 30 casement windows, arranged to assure cross ventilation; 2 outside doors.

WALL SPACES: Ample for large pieces of furniture.

CUBIC CONTENTS: Approximately 36,500 cubic feet.

SPECIAL FEATURES

ENTRANCE VESTIBULE: Takes the place of a hall, breaking the drafts and providing a handy hat and coat closet.

SUN ROOM: Is so placed with cased opening connecting with living room that the two rooms count as one great room.

COMPACT KITCHEN: With cupboards and dressers: and direct connection with the dining room, side entry and inner hall.

ICE BOX: In the side entry within a few steps of the outside door and directly accessible to kitchen.

WINDOW SEAT: Built-in under a window in the living room.

LINEN CLOSET: Next to bath room and convenient to all parts of the house.

ATTIC: Generous in size, with light and ventilation from dormer windows.

TERRACE: With patterned brick flooring and cement coping and steps.

PLUMBING: Includes bath tub, water closet, lavatory, kitchen sink, laundry tubs, and hot and cold water supply.

ELECTRIC OUTLETS: In the proper places, available for iron, washing machine, vacuum cleaner, toaster, floor and table lamps, heaters, etc., if any or all of them are desired.

6B6

IN SUBURBS, RURAL COMMUNITIES OR FARMING COUNTRY THIS AMERICAN BUNGALOW WOULD BE AN ACQUISITION

THE DESIGN IS A FREE TRANSLATION, IN WORDS OF FEW SYLLABLES, OF EARLY AMERICAN HOUSES, BUT POSSESSES THE ESSENTIALS OF BUNGALOW PLANNING

FIRST FLOOR
CEILING HEIGHT 8'-6"

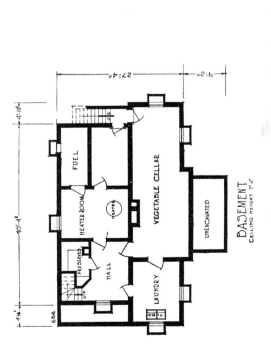

BASEMENT
CEILING HEIGHT 7'2"

Note—For guidance in reading floor plans, see explanation on page 14

EXTERIOR

STYLE: Early American. Bungalow type.

SIZE OF LOT REQUIRED: About 60 feet in width if an inside lot; can be placed on a corner lot 45 feet in width on one street.

CONSTRUCTION: Wood frame on masonry foundations.

FINISH: Wide wood siding for walls; movable slat blinds; shingled roof.

PORCHES: Living porch across the central mass of the house; side porch opening off dining room, ideal for meals out-of-doors.

CHIMNEY: Central brick chimney, containing heater and fireplace flues. Separate flue for kitchen range.

DECORATIVE FEATURES: Like the farm houses built by the early settlers on the Atlantic coast, this house depends for its beauty upon two things only: the proportion of very simple masses grouped together and the excellence of sparingly employed detail.

COLOR SCHEME SUGGESTED: Outside walls, doors and frames painted white; green shutters; brown or green stain on shingles; chimney brick red or common brick whitewashed.

ALTERNATE EXTERIORS: None.

INTERIOR

NUMBER OF ROOMS: 6 full sized rooms all on one floor, Bath-room, 5 Closets.

SIZE OF ROOMS:

Living Room	20' 0" x 13' 0"
Dining Room	14' 0" x 11' 0"
Kitchen	12' 0" x 11' 2"
Bed Room	14' 0" x 11' 0"
Bed Room	9' 11" x 11' 0"
Bed Room	9' 11" x 10' 0"
Bath Room	5' 10" x 7' 2"

BASEMENT: Under entire house, containing Laundry, Heater-room, Vegetable-storage, Preserve-closet and Fuel-bins.

PLAN TYPE: Symmetrical, with living room the central feature.

DESIGNED TO FACE: South or North. For other facings, plans should be reversed.

FIREPLACE: One large open fireplace with attractive mantel on axis with the front door.

VENTILATION: 13 windows with double hung sash; 3 outside doors; louvres in gable ends for free circulation of air under roof; cooler in hot weather.

WALL SPACES: Ample for large pieces of furniture.

CUBIC CONTENTS: Approximately 23,400 cubic feet.

SPECIAL FEATURES

LIVING ROOM: Spacious in size with direct access to all rooms of the house.

KITCHEN: Very large for a house of this size; for farm or suburban use it will be found adequate for all possible necessities. A wash sink has been placed on porch outside kitchen for farm help.

REAR ENTRY: Serves the kitchen and the basement with direct communication out-of-doors, and provides a place for the ice box.

BED ROOM HALL: Opens off living room, and is so arranged that all three bed rooms and bath room are easily reached, giving as much privacy as second floor bed rooms.

LINEN PRESS AND ADDITIONAL HANGING CLOSET: Open off the hall.

OUTSIDE BASEMENT STEPS: Provided so that basement may be accessible for the storage of garden truck brought from the fields.

PLUMBING: Includes bath tub, lavatory, water closet, laundry tubs, kitchen sink, outside wash sink, and hot and cold water supply.

ELECTRIC OUTLETS: In the proper places, available for iron, washing machine, vacuum cleaner, toaster, floor and table lamps, heaters, etc., if any or all of them are desired.

HOUSE PLAN NO. 6B8

Mountain Division

COMPOSED OF OLD FRENCH CHATEAU MOTIVES MORE FREELY USED THAN BY THEIR ORIGINATORS

THE PLANS SATISFY THE AVERAGE FAMILY'S NEEDS AND DO SO WITHOUT EXACTING EXCESSIVE WORK OR EXPENSIVE CONSTRUCTION

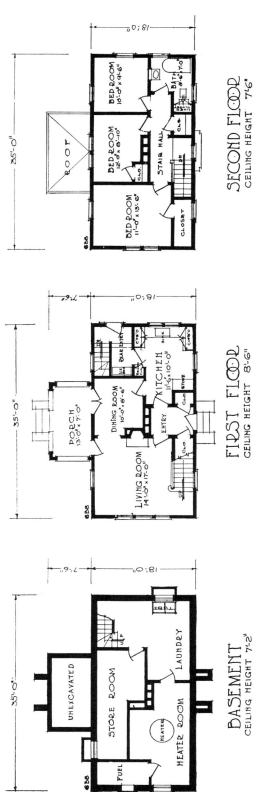

SECOND FLOOR
CEILING HEIGHT 7'-6"

BED ROOM 10'-0" x 9'-6"

BATH 8'-6" x 7'-0"

BED ROOM 12'-0" x 8'-10"

ROOF

STAIR HALL

CLO.

CLO.

CLO.

BED ROOM 11'-0" x 13'-6"

CLOSET

35'-0"

18'-0"

FIRST FLOOR
CEILING HEIGHT 8'-6"

PORCH 13'-0" x 7'-0"

DINING ROOM 10'-0" x 13'-6"

KITCHEN 11'-6" x 10'-0"

LIVING ROOM 14'-0" x 17'-0"

ENTRY

SINK

REAR ENTRY

CUP'D

CUP'D

STOVE

35'-0"

18'-0"

7'-6"

BASEMENT
CEILING HEIGHT 7'-2"

UNEXCAVATED

STORE ROOM

LAUNDRY

HEATER ROOM

FUEL

HEATER

UP

35'-0"

18'-0"

7'-6"

Note—For guidance in reading floor plans, see explanation on page 14

EXTERIOR

STYLE: Modified French Chateau. Story-and-a-half style.

SIZE OF LOT REQUIRED: From 42 to 45 feet in width.

CONSTRUCTION: Wood frame on masonry foundations, brick base course.

FINISH: Wide wood siding, roof slate, or shingled.

PORCHES: Front entrance stoop with brick floor. Living porch facing the garden, 13' 0" x 7' 0" arranged to be screened for summer or enclosed with glass for winter use.

CHIMNEY: Central brick chimney containing the fireplace and heater flues.

DECORATIVE FEATURES: Symmetrically balanced design following the lines and traditions of the French roofs and cut-in dormer windows. The doorway is refined in detail, and is the outstanding feature of the street front. The downspouts serve both utility and design by adding another detail, well considered.

COLOR SCHEME SUGGESTED: Drop siding painted white, shingles stained in variegated colors of greens, reds and browns; outside blinds bottle green.

ALTERNATE EXTERIORS: None.

INTERIOR

NUMBER OF ROOMS: 6 Main rooms, Bath-room and 6 Closets.

SIZE OF ROOMS:

First Floor

Living Room	14' 0" x 17' 0"
Dining Room	10' 0" x 8' 6"
Kitchen	11' 6" x 10' 0"

Second Floor

Bed Room	11' 0" x 13' 6"
Bed Room	12' 0" x 8' 10"
Bed Room	10' 0" x 9' 6"
Bath Room	8' 6" x 7' 0"

BASEMENT: Under entire house, containing Laundry, Heater-room, Store-room and Fuel-bins.

PLAN TYPE: Living room running from front to back. Central hall, stairs ascend from living room.

DESIGNED TO FACE: North, East or South. For West facing, plans should be reversed. May be placed close to street, as the principal front faces the garden.

FIREPLACES: One large open fireplace in the living room, with attractive wood mantel.

VENTILATION: 20 windows with double hung sash; 4 outside doors.

WALL SPACES: Ample for large pieces of furniture.

CUBIC CONTENTS: Approximately 16,600 cubic feet.

SPECIAL FEATURES

LIVING ROOM: Exposure on three sides with entrance to garden through the garden porch. The fireplace is nicely placed opposite the triple window.

DINING ROOM: Admirably located in relation to living room, kitchen and garden porch.

KITCHEN: Placed in front of the house with direct access to the rear entry, the dining room and front entrance. Unusually large with complete equipment. Windows on two sides insure adequate circulation of air.

COAT CLOSETS: On each side of front entry; an especially good feature where there are children in the house.

REAR ENTRY: To kitchen and to stairs to basement. Excellent place for ice box.

BATH ROOM: Located directly above kitchen, insuring minimum plumbing costs. Linen closet in one corner.

PLUMBING: Includes bath tub, lavatory and water closet; laundry tubs and kitchen sink, hot and cold water supply.

ELECTRIC OUTLETS: In the proper places available for iron, washing machine, vacuum cleaner, toaster, floor and table lamps, heaters, etc., if any or all of them are desired.

Architects' Small House Service Bureau

Northwestern Division

HOUSE PLAN NO. 6A11

SUGGESTIVE OF THE TRIM, PRIM HOUSES OF AN ENGLISH COUNTRYSIDE
EXTERIOR PROMISE OF TRIMNESS IS JUSTIFIED BY THE COMPACT, ECONOMICAL AND LIVABLE INTERIOR

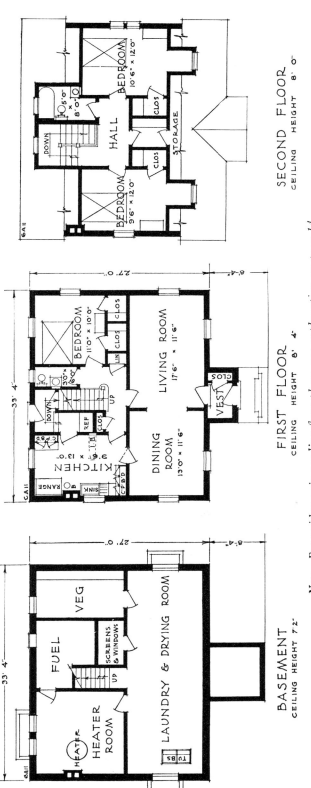

SECOND FLOOR
CEILING HEIGHT 8' 0"

BEDROOM 10'6" × 12'0"
BEDROOM 9'6" × 12'0"
HALL
5'0" × 8'0"
DOWN
CLOS
CLOS
CLOS
STORAGE

FIRST FLOOR
CEILING HEIGHT 8' 4"

27' 0"
33' 4"
BEDROOM 11'0" × 10'0"
CLOS
LIN CLOS
CLOS
LIVING ROOM 17'6" × 11'6"
DINING ROOM 13'0" × 11'6"
KITCHEN 9'6" × 13'0"
RANGE
SINK
REF
UP
DOWN
CP'B'D
VEST
CLOS

Note—For guidance in reading floor plans, see explanation on page 14

BASEMENT
CEILING HEIGHT 7' 2"

27' 0"
33' 4"
FUEL
VEG
HEATER ROOM
SCREENS & WINDOWS
UP
LAUNDRY & DRYING ROOM
TUBS

EXTERIOR

STYLE: English Cottage Adaptation. Story-and-a-half type.

SIZE OF LOT REQUIRED: From 40 to 45 feet in width.

CONSTRUCTION: Frame construction with brick veneer; on masonry foundations.

FINISH: Brick walls and entrance; shingled roof and dormers; wood trim.

PORCHES: A brick-paved entrance stoop.

CHIMNEY: One exterior brick chimney, containing heater and kitchen range flues.

DECORATIVE FEATURES: The restrained, but attractive entrance, with its pointed roof and softening rounded doorway, set off by patterned brickwork, is the outstanding feature. The wrought iron side lights, the partially glazed door and transom are in keeping; the first floor windows and the dormers are nicely placed, and of good proportion. The fact that the dormers are shingled ties them to the roof; the roof lines are exceptionally good, both in front and on the ends.

COLOR SCHEME SUGGESTED: Variegated wire-cut brick walls; roof and dormer roofs stained slate color; dormers painted white; exterior trim, mahogany brown; shutters, apple green; door, white.

ALTERNATE EXTERIORS: This same basic plan with different exteriors, may be found on Pages 36, 128 and 132. House Plan Nos. 6A12, 4A15 and 4A16.

INTERIOR

NUMBER OF ROOMS: 6 Main rooms, Bath-room, Lavatory and 8 Closets.

SIZE OF ROOMS:

First Floor

Living Room	17' 6" x 11' 6"
Dining Room	13' 0" x 11' 6"
Kitchen	9' 6" x 13' 0"
Bed Room	11' 0" x 10' 0"
Lavatory	3' 0" x 6' 0"

Second Floor

Bed Room	10' 6" x 12' 0"
Bed Room	9' 6" x 12' 0"
Bath Room	5' 0" x 8' 0"

BASEMENT: Under entire house, containing Laundry and Drying-room, Heater-room, Fuel-bins, Vegetable-room and Storage-room.

PLAN TYPE: Living room and dining room extending across the front.

DESIGNED TO FACE: North or West.

For other facings, plans should be reversed.

FIREPLACES: None.

VENTILATION: 16 windows with double hung sash; 2 outside doors.

WALL SPACE: Ample for large pieces of furniture.

CUBIC CONTENTS: Approximately 23,000 cubic feet.

SPECIAL FEATURES

VESTIBULE AND CLOSET: Serve the purpose of an entrance hall.

LIVING AND DINING ROOMS: Really one large room, separated by wide opening. The living room has a door into the rear hall, the dining room, one into the kitchen, insuring easy circulation; each has two exposures, their openness practically giving each room, or both rooms, three exposures.

KITCHEN: Is equipped with all conveniences, including built-in ironing board; beautifully lighted and ventilated.

REAR ENTRY: Contains ice box; gives direct access to kitchen and to basement.

DOWNSTAIRS BED ROOM AND LAVATORY: Most convenient arrangement; bed room most attractive, having two large closets, their doors opening so that each may have a mirror, and the space between be glazed, making a triple mirror, something every woman will enjoy.

UPSTAIRS BED ROOMS: Comfortably large, with excellent closets and two exposures.

PLUMBING: Includes bath tub, 2 lavatories, 2 water closets, laundry tubs, kitchen sink, hot and cold water supply.

ELECTRIC OUTLETS: Properly placed, available for iron, washing machine, vacuum cleaner, toaster, floor and table lamps, heater, etc., if any or all of them are desired.

33

House Plan No. 6B11

6B11

A PLEASING MODERN ADAPTATION OF THE SMALL COLONIAL GAMBREL ROOF HOUSE

THE DAY HAS PASSED WHEN BOX-LIKE HOUSES WILL SATISFY. TODAY A HOME MUST BE PLEASANT TO LOOK AT AS WELL AS CONVENIENT TO LIVE IN

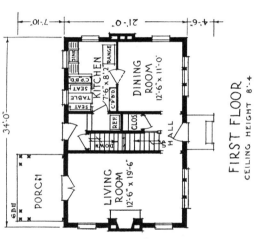

SECOND FLOOR
CEILING HEIGHT 7'-4"

BEDROOM 9'-9" x 8'-0"
BEDROOM 9'-9" x 9'-6"
BEDROOM 12'-6" x 17'-6"
CLOS
CL
CL
CL
LIN
DOWN
6'-6" x 5'-6"

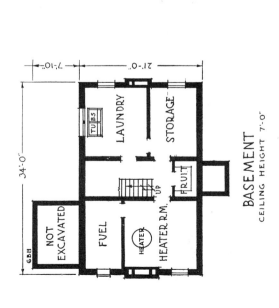

FIRST FLOOR
CEILING HEIGHT 8'-4"

PORCH
LIVING ROOM 12'-6" x 19'-6"
DINING ROOM 12'-6" x 11'-0"
KITCHEN 7'-6" x 8'-2"
HALL
RANGE
CP'B'D
SEAT
TABLE
SEAT
REF
CLOS
DN
UP
DINN

BASEMENT
CEILING HEIGHT 7'-0"

NOT EXCAVATED
FUEL
HEATER
HEATER RM.
LAUNDRY
STORAGE
FRUIT
UP
TU BS

Note—For guidance in reading floor plans, see explanation on page 14

EXTERIOR

Style: Dutch Colonial Adaptation. Story-and-a-half type.

Size of Lot Required: From 41 to 45 feet in width.

Construction: Exterior walls of brick on masonry foundations. May be of stucco if desired.

Finish: Wire cut brick for walls; matched wood siding or stucco for dormer window; moulded wood frontispiece; roof, slate or shingled.

Porches: Principal porch 12' 0" x 8' 0", faces the garden, and opens out of the living room. Brick entrance stoop.

Chimneys: Two attractive exterior chimneys each with two flues.

Decorative Features: Brick gables "topped out" with well designed chimneys. The expansive dormer across the front moulds naturally into the main roof. The flower boxes and shutters and the stunning doorway add greatly to the appearance.

Color Scheme Suggested: Reddish-brown brick with brownish-green stained shingles. White woodwork and green blinds.

Alternate Exteriors: This same basic plan, with different exteriors, can be found on Pages 24, 40, 42, 44, 46 and 48. House Plan Nos. 6B5, 6A17, 6A18, 6A19, 6A20 and 6A22.

INTERIOR

Number of Rooms: 6 Main rooms, Bath-room and 7 Closets.

Size of Rooms:

First Floor

Living Room .... 12' 6" x 19' 6"
Dining Room .... 12' 6" x 11' 0"
Kitchen .... 7' 6" x 8' 2"

Second Floor

Bed Room .... 12' 6" x 17' 6"
Bed Room .... 9' 9" x 9' 6"
Bed Room .... 9' 9" x 8' 0"
Bath Room .... 6' 6" x 5' 6"

Basement: Under entire house, containing Laundry, Heater-room, Storage-space and Fuel-bins.

Plan Type: Living room running from front to back: stairs in the center of the house.

Designed to Face: East or South. For other facings, plans should be reversed.

Fireplace: One large open fireplace in living room, nicely balancing the outside wall; fine mantel.

Ventilation: 22 windows with double hung sash; full length casement window opening onto porch; 2 outside doors.

Wall Spaces: Ample for large pieces of furniture.

Cubic Contents: Approximately 19,500 cubic feet.

SPECIAL FEATURES

Central Entrance Hall: Containing the stairs and a large coat closet; it serves to isolate the dining room.

Living Room: Good proportion with windows well spaced on three sides; opens onto the living porch.

Dining Alcove: In addition to the dining room there is provision for a table and for seats in the kitchen.

Kitchen: Contains the most modern equipment and is lighted on two sides.

Rear Entry: Makes it possible to reach both the kitchen and basement from outside without entering any other portion of the house; also provides space for ice box.

Bed Rooms: One large and two smaller rooms, each provided with closets.

Linen Closet: In upstairs hall, well located in relation to bed rooms and bath room.

Plumbing: Includes bath tub, lavatory, water closet, laundry tubs, kitchen sink and hot and cold water supply.

Electric Outlets: In the proper places, available for iron, washing machine, vacuum cleaner, toaster, floor and table lamps, heaters, etc., if any or all of them are desired.

House Plan No. 6A12

6A12

HARKING BACK TO THE DELIGHTFUL HOUSES OF EARLY PENNSYLVANIA ORIGIN

A HOME THAT WILL ENDEAR ITSELF TO ITS OWNER BECAUSE OF ITS ECONOMICAL AND LIVABLE INTERIOR AND MODEST, HOMEY EXTERIOR

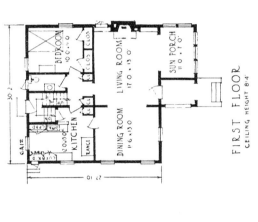

SECOND FLOOR
CEILING HEIGHT 8'0"

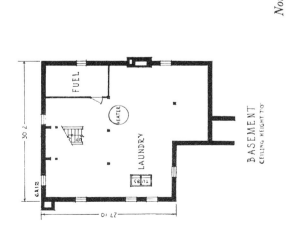

FIRST FLOOR
CEILING HEIGHT 8'4"

Note—For guidance in reading floor plans, see explanation on page 14

BASEMENT
CEILING HEIGHT 7'0"

EXTERIOR

STYLE: Pennsylvania Colonial influence. Story-and-a-half type.

SIZE OF LOT REQUIRED: From 40 to 45 feet in width.

CONSTRUCTION: Wood frame on masonry foundation, brick base course.

FINISH: Wood siding, shingled roof.

PORCHES: Sun porch, 11' 0" x 7' 0" and entrance stoop combined and projected from the main walls of the house.

CHIMNEY: One outside brick chimney, containing the heater and fireplace flues.

DECORATIVE FEATURES: There are houses that need no "decorations," and this is such an one. It is distinctive because it is well designed; the incorporation of the sun porch, not only with the main roof, but within the walls of the house, makes what is sometimes obviously a "tacked on" feature, an integral part of this design. The miniature Germantown hood, running along the side of the house, completes the feeling of cohesion and adds a pleasing softness and shadow.

COLOR SCHEME SUGGESTED: Cream colored siding, white trim and variegated green roof shingles.

ALTERNATE EXTERIORS: This same basic plan, with different exteriors, may be found on Pages 32, 128, and 132, House Plan Nos. 6A11, 4A15, and 4A16.

INTERIOR

NUMBER OF ROOMS: 6 Main rooms, Bath-room, Lavatory and 8 Closets.

SIZE OF ROOMS:

First Floor

Living Room	17' 0" x 13' 0"
Dining Room	11' 6" x 13' 0"
Kitchen	12' 0" x 13' 0"
Bed Room	10' 0" x 11' 0"
Lavatory	3' 0" x 6' 0"

Second Floor

Bed Room	14' 0" x 14' 6"
Bed Room	15' 0" x 10' 0"
Bath Room	8' 0" x 5' 6"

BASEMENT: Under entire house, containing Laundry, Heater-room and Fuel-bins.

PLAN TYPE: Living room and dining room extending across the front of house.

DESIGNED TO FACE: North or West. For other facings, plans should be reversed.

FIREPLACE: Large open fireplace in the living room.

VENTILATION: 17 windows with double hung sash; 7 casement windows; 2 outside doors.

WALL SPACES: Ample for large pieces of furniture.

CUBIC CONTENTS: Approximately 20,500 cubic feet.

SPECIAL FEATURES

LIVING ROOM, SUN PORCH AND DINING ROOM are really one sunny open space; each is separated from the other just enough to define it, without taking away from the appearance of spaciousness. The living room has a door into the bed room hall, and the dining room one into the kitchen; on each side of the living room mantel is a built-in bookcase.

KITCHEN: Small and compact, but in no sense cramped; it has ample cupboard space, light and air from two sides and the refrigerator, with outside icing door, is in the corner of the kitchen.

REAR ENTRY: Provides direct passage to kitchen and to basement from outdoors. The lower hall and stairs are also convenient to it.

DOWNSTAIRS BED ROOM AND LAVATORY: An arrangement that has much to commend it; it is saving of steps, it has all the privacy of an upstairs bedroom and every possible convenience, closet space, lavatory, cross ventilation.

PLUMBING: Includes bath tub, 2 lavatories, 2 water closets, laundry tubs, kitchen sink, hot and cold water supply.

ELECTRIC OUTLETS: Properly placed, available for iron, washing machine, vacuum cleaner, toaster, floor and table lamps, heaters, etc., if any or all of them are desired.

Northwestern Division

Architects' Small House Service Bureau

THE EFFECTIVENESS OF THE OLD DUTCH COLONIAL HOUSES IS SUSTAINED BY THIS QUAINT AND STURDY HOUSE
NUMEROUS CONVENIENCES AND FINE ARRANGEMENT OF ROOMS MAKE THIS A GENUINELY COMFORTABLE HOME FOR ANY SECTION OF THE COUNTRY

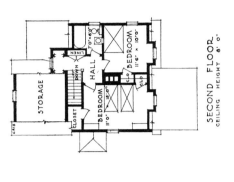

SECOND FLOOR
CEILING HEIGHT 8' 0"

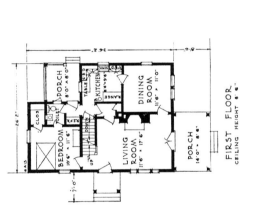

FIRST FLOOR
CEILING HEIGHT 8' 6"

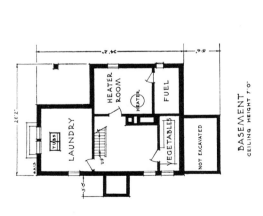

BASEMENT
CEILING HEIGHT 7' 0"

Note—For guidance in reading floor plans, see explanation on page 14

EXTERIOR

STYLE: Modified Dutch Colonial. Story-and-a-half type.

SIZE OF LOT REQUIRED: From 32 to 37 feet in width if porch is faced toward the street; from 48 to 53 in width if the stoop is faced to the street. Plan is especially desirable for a corner lot.

CONSTRUCTION: Wood frame on masonry foundation.

FINISH: Wide wood siding for walls; shingled roof.

PORCHES: Covered living porch 14' 0" x 8' 6"; covered entrance stoop; large kitchen porch 8' 0" x 8' 0".

CHIMNEY: One inside brick chimney containing the heater, fireplace and kitchen range flues.

DECORATIVE FEATURES: There is a snug effect produced by the two gambrel roofs. The one over the first floor bed room ties in beautifully with the full two story gambrel. The house would look equally attractive if the rear wing were omitted. The dormer windows are in excellent scale and do not look as if they were stuck on.

COLOR SCHEME SUGGESTED: White walls and trim; apple green shutters; variegated green and brown stain for roof.

ALTERNATE EXTERIORS: This same basic plan with different exteriors may be found on pages 52, 90, and 92, House Plan Nos. 6A31, 5A31 and 5A33.

INTERIOR

NUMBER OF ROOMS: 6 Main rooms, Bath-room, Toilet and 7 Closets.

SIZE OF ROOMS:

First Floor

Living Room	11' 6" x 17' 6"
Dining Room	11' 6" x 11' 0"
Kitchen	8' 6" x 9' 6"
Bed Room	10' 6" x 11' 6"

Second Floor

Bed Room	11' 0" x 15' 0"
Bed Room	11' 6" x 10' 0"
Bath Room	7' 0" x 6' 0"

BASEMENT: Under the entire house, containing Laundry, Heater-room, Vegetable-storage and Fuel-bins.

PLAN TYPE: Living room running from front to back with stairway at one end of living room.

DESIGNED TO FACE: East or South. For other facings, plans should be reversed.

FIREPLACES: Large open brick fireplaces in the living room with attractive Colonial mantelpiece.

VENTILATION: 17 windows with double hung sash, 1 casement window; pair of French doors opening onto living porch; 2 outside doors.

WALL SPACES: Ample for large pieces of furniture.

CUBIC CONTENTS: Approximately 20,700 cubic feet.

SPECIAL FEATURES

THIS HOUSE may readily be built as a five-room house by omitting the rear wing.

FIRST FLOOR BED ROOM: With large closet, cross ventilation and a toilet adjoining. If not needed as a sleeping room it can be used as a den or study.

LIVING ROOM: A big cheery room with windows on two sides and beautiful staircase across one end.

KITCHEN: Planned according to the most approved ideas of kitchen efficiency. Windows on two sides.

REAR ENTRY AND HALL: Allows direct passage from yard both to kitchen and to basement stairs and provides excellent place for refrigerator. Broom closet opens off hall.

BED ROOMS: Each has a large closet and each has cross ventilation.

LARGE TRUNK OR STORAGE ROOM: Above the first floor bed room; is accessible from the upstairs hall.

LINEN CLOSET: Built-in at the head of stairs, convenient to rooms on both floors.

PLUMBING: Includes bath tub, two water closets, two lavatories, kitchen sink, laundry tubs and hot and cold water supply.

ELECTRIC OUTLETS: Properly placed, available for iron, washing machine, vacuum cleaner, toaster, floor and table lamps, heaters, etc., if any or all of them are desired.

39

House Plan No. 6A17

THE DESIGN HOLDS CLOSELY TO THE LETTER AS WELL AS TO THE SPIRIT OF THE DIGNIFIED NEW ENGLAND COLONIAL HOUSES

EMBODYING ALL THE VIRTUES OF REAL COLONIAL HOMES—RIGID ECONOMY, GOOD TASTE, GOOD PROPORTION, ALL SET OFF BY THE RIGHT USE OF MATERIALS

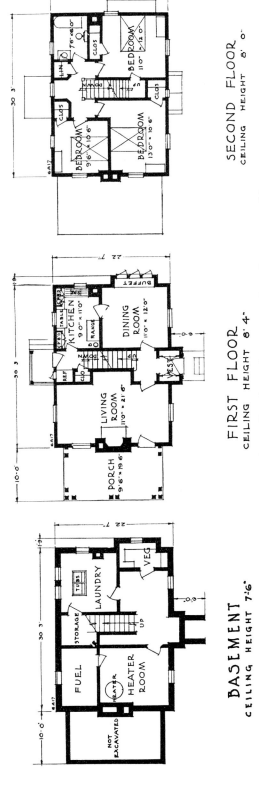

SECOND FLOOR
CEILING HEIGHT 8' 0"

FIRST FLOOR
CEILING HEIGHT 8' 4"

Note—For guidance in reading floor plans, see explanation on page 14

BASEMENT
CEILING HEIGHT 7' 6"

EXTERIOR

STYLE: New England Colonial. Full two-story type.

SIZE OF LOT REQUIRED: From 45 to 50 feet in width if porch is placed as shown. From 35 to 40 feet in width if porch is omitted or placed at rear.

CONSTRUCTION: Wood frame on masonry foundation, brick base course.

FINISH: Wide wood siding, roof shingled.

PORCHES: One large open porch, 9'-6"x19'-6"

CHIMNEYS: Two outside brick chimneys, one containing the heater and fireplace flues, the other the kitchen range flue.

DECORATIVE FEATURES: Texture and scale given to the wall spaces by the skillful use of wide siding; the symmetrical placing of window openings and the decorative treatment of the projecting vestibule do not represent accidents, but skill on the part of the designer; the conservative use of ornament also helps it to achieve the atmosphere associated with the old houses.

COLOR SCHEME SUGGESTED: Siding white; shutters and front door green. Roof variegated green.

ALTERNATE EXTERIORS: This same basic plan with different exteriors can be found on Pages 24, 34, 42, 44, 46 and 48, House Plan Nos. 6B5, 6B11, 6A18, 6A19, 6A20, and 6A22.

INTERIOR

NUMBER OF ROOMS: 6 Main rooms, Bath-room and 7 Closets.

SIZE OF ROOMS:

First Floor

Living Room	11' 0" x 21' 6"
Dining Room	11' 0" x 12' 0"
Kitchen	9' 0" x 11' 0"

Second Floor

Bed Room	13' 0" x 10' 6"
Bed Room	11' 0" x 12' 0"
Bed Room	9' 6" x 10' 6"
Bath Room	7' 6" x 6' 0"

BASEMENT: Under entire house, containing Laundry, Heater-room, Fuel-bins and Vegetable-storage.

PLAN TYPE: Living room running from front to back. Stairway in the center of the house.

DESIGNED TO FACE: East or South. For other facings, plans should be reversed.

FIREPLACE: One large brick fireplace, with Colonial wood trim, in the living room.

VENTILATION: 15 windows with double hung sash. 3 casement windows; 3 outside doors; louvres in gable ends to insure ventilation of attic.

WALL SPACES: Ample for large pieces of furniture.

CUBIC CONTENTS: Approximately 22,500 cubic feet.

SPECIAL FEATURES

LIVING ROOM: Has windows at each end, as well as window and glazed door opening on the porch, so it is well lighted. An alcove 8 feet long with lights on each side is a splendid place for davenport or piano.

DINING ROOM: Has a bay with built-in buffet with casement windows above it.

KITCHEN: Is well lighted and carefully planned to lessen labor. Ice box is in rear entry, ice delivered direct from outside. A broom closet is provided.

ENTRANCE VESTIBULE: With coat closets on each side of door.

BED ROOMS: All corner rooms each with a closet and windows on two sides for cross ventilation.

LINEN CLOSET: In upper hall.

ATTIC STORAGE SPACE: Reached by stairs leading from closet in front bedroom.

PLUMBING: Includes bath tub, water closet, lavatory, kitchen sink, laundry tubs and hot and cold water supply.

ELECTRIC OUTLETS: In the proper places, available for iron, washing machine, vacuum cleaner, toaster, floor and table lamps, heaters, etc., if any or all are desired.

HOUSE PLAN NO. 6A18

6A18

THE DUTCH COLONIAL STYLE HAS A VIRILITY AND STURDINESS WHICH MAKES IT MOST SUITABLE FOR MODERN HOUSES

THE SNUG, AND INTIMATE QUALITY OF THE STYLE AND THE ELIMINATION OF WASTE IN SPACE AND BUILDING COST MAKE AN IMMEDIATE APPEAL TO EVERYONE

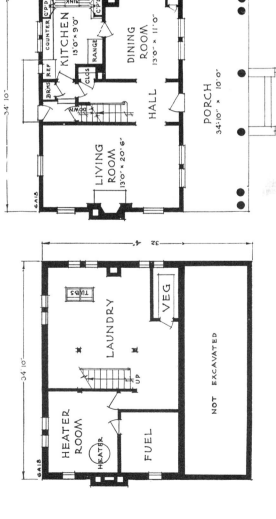

SECOND FLOOR
CEILING HEIGHT 8' 0"

SLEEPING PORCH 13'0" x 8'0"

BEDROOM 13'0" x 9'0"

BEDROOM 13'0" x 12'0"

BEDROOM 13'0" x 15'6"

HALL

CLOS LIN CLOS

34'10"

FIRST FLOOR
CEILING HEIGHT 8' 6"

21'6"

14'6"

KITCHEN 13'0" x 9'0"

DINING ROOM 13'0" x 11'0"

LIVING ROOM 13'0" x 20'6"

HALL

PORCH 34'10" x 10'0"

CPD SINK CPD COUNTER REF RMS RANGE CLOS

34'10"

BASEMENT
CEILING HEIGHT 7' 6"

32'

HEATER ROOM

LAUNDRY

VEG

FUEL

NOT EXCAVATED

34'10"

Note—For guidance in reading floor plans, see explanation on page 14

EXTERIOR

STYLE: Dutch Colonial. Combination of story-and-a-half and two-story type.

SIZE OF LOT REQUIRED: From 40 to 45 feet in width.

CONSTRUCTION: Wood frame on masonry foundation. Roof shingled.

FINISH: Design shows wide wood siding; may be built of shingles. Roof shingled.

PORCHES: Large brick paved front porch, 34' 10" x 10' 0"; sleeping porch in rear of second story 13' 0" x 8' 0".

CHIMNEYS: Two brick chimneys, one at each end of the house.

DECORATIVE FEATURES: The long, low home-like effect produced by bringing the gambrel roof down over the porch; the large dormer window across the front; the sturdy round columns of the front porch.

COLOR SCHEME SUGGESTED: White walls; variegated green roof; dark green shutters.

ALTERNATE EXTERIORS: This same basic plan with different exteriors can be found on Pages 24, 34, 40, 44, 46 and 48, House Plan Nos. 6B5, 6B11, 6A17, 6A19, 6A20 and 6A22.

INTERIOR

NUMBER OF ROOMS: 6 Main rooms, Sleeping Porch, Bath-room and 9 Closets.

SIZE OF ROOMS:

	First Floor
Living Room	13' 0" x 20' 6"
Dining Room	13' 0" x 11' 0"
Kitchen	13' 0" x 9' 0"
	Second Floor
Bed Room	13' 0" x 15' 6"
Bed Room	13' 0" x 12' 0"
Bed Room	13' 0" x 9' 0"
Sleeping Porch	13' 0" x 8' 0"
Bath Room	6' 6" x 9' 0"

BASEMENT: Under main portion of house, containing Laundry, Heater-room, Vegetable-storage, and Fuel-bins.

PLAN TYPE: Central stairs and hallway; living room running from front to back of the house.

DESIGNED TO FACE: South or East. For other facings, plans should be reversed.

FIREPLACE: One large open fireplace in living room.

VENTILATION: 23 double hung windows, 3 casement sash windows, arranged for cross ventilation.

WALL SPACES: Ample for large pieces of furniture.

CUBIC CONTENTS: Approximately 25,500 cubic feet.

SPECIAL FEATURES

LIVING ROOM: Has windows on three sides and wide cased openings into hall.

DINING ROOM: Is well lighted and so planned that a recessed bay is formed for placing sideboard under high casement windows. There is a built-in china closet in one corner of the room.

KITCHEN: Is compactly and efficiently planned, with light and ventilation on two sides, ample dresser and work counters. Ice delivered direct to ice box without entering house.

CLOTHES CHUTE: From second floor to laundry.

COAT CLOSET: In extreme rear of rear hall.

BROOM CLOSET: Opening on rear hall.

LINEN CLOSET: Off the second floor hall.

BED ROOMS: Have windows on two sides and each has a closet.

PLUMBING: Includes bath tub, water closet, lavatory, kitchen sink, laundry tubs and hot and cold water supply.

ELECTRIC OUTLETS: Properly placed, available for iron, washing machine, vacuum cleaner, toaster, floor and table lamps, heaters, etc., if any or all are desired.

Architects' Small House Service Bureau

Northwestern Division

THERE IS A TRULY AMERICAN FEELING ABOUT THIS STRAIGHTFORWARD, CONSERVATIVE SIX-ROOM HOUSE
NICELY BALANCED EXTERIOR AND INTERIOR WHERE EVERY ELEMENT HAS BEEN CAREFULLY STUDIED TO HARMONIZE THE NEEDS OF THE HOUSEKEEPER
WITH LOW BUILDING COSTS

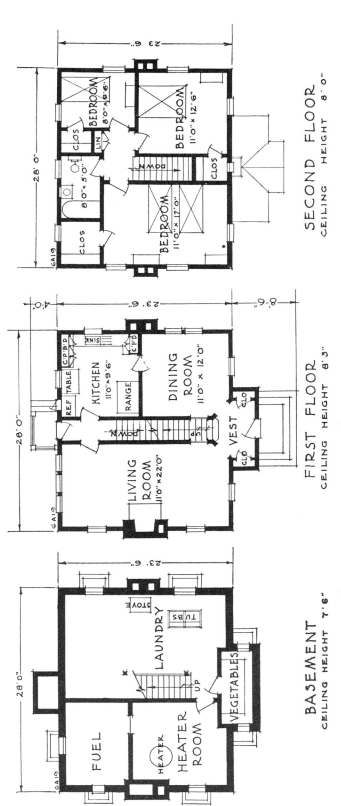

SECOND FLOOR
CEILING HEIGHT 8'0"

BEDROOM 8'0" x 9'6"

BEDROOM 11'0" x 12'6"

BEDROOM 11'0" x 17'0"

CLOS

LIN

CLOS

CLOS

DOWN

8'0" x 5'0"

28' 0"

23' 6"

FIRST FLOOR
CEILING HEIGHT 8'3"

KITCHEN 11'0" x 9'6"

SINK

CP'B'D

CP'B'D

TABLE

REF

RANGE

DINING ROOM 11'0" x 12'0"

LIVING ROOM 11'0" x 22'0"

DOWN

UP

VEST

CLO

CLO

28' 0"

23' 6"

4' 0"

8' 6"

BASEMENT
CEILING HEIGHT 7'6"

LAUNDRY

TUBS

STOVE

FUEL

HEATER ROOM

HEATER

VEGETABLES

UP

28' 0"

23' 6"

Note—For guidance in reading floor plans, see explanation on page 14

EXTERIOR

STYLE: Colonial Adaptation. Full two-story type.

SIZE OF LOT REQUIRED: From 35 to 40 feet in width.

CONSTRUCTION: Wood frame on masonry foundations, with brick base carried up two feet.

FINISH: First story, wide wood siding; second story, stucco or matched boards; brick veneer could be used for first story if desired; roof shingled.

PORCHES: Entrance vestibule; and rear stoop.

CHIMNEYS: Two outside brick chimneys, on opposite sides of the house; finished in stucco, topped with brick.

DECORATIVE FEATURES: A straightforward, balanced and dignified design, displaying a pleasing and harmonious variety in wall treatment, obtained by the clever use of different materials. The simple hipped roof adds to the charm of the composition.

COLOR SCHEME SUGGESTED: Siding painted white, stucco cream color; blinds dark green; roof shingles stained variegated greens and browns.

ALTERNATE EXTERIORS: This same basic plan, with different exteriors, may be found on Pages 40, 42, 46 and 48, House Plan Nos. 6A17, 6A18, 6A20, and 6A22.

INTERIOR

NUMBER OF ROOMS: 6 Main rooms, Bath-room and 6 Closets.

SIZE OF ROOMS:

First Floor

Living Room	11' 0" x 22' 0"
Dining Room	11' 0" x 12' 0"
Kitchen	11' 0" x 9' 6"

Second Floor

Bed Room	11' 0" x 17' 0"
Bed Room	11' 0" x 12' 6"
Bed Room	8' 0" x 9' 6"
Bath Room	8' 0" x 5' 0"

BASEMENT: Under entire house, containing Laundry, Heater-room, Vegetable-storage and Fuel-bins.

PLAN TYPE: Living room running from front to back; stairway in the center of the house.

DESIGNED TO FACE: East or South. For other facings, plans should be reversed.

FIREPLACE: Large open fireplace in the living room.

VENTILATION: 21 windows with double hung sash; 2 outside doors.

WALL SPACES: Ample for large pieces of furniture.

CUBIC CONTENTS: Approximately 19,000 cubic feet.

SPECIAL FEATURES

ENTRANCE VESTIBULE: Projects slightly from the body of the house and forms a hall; two coat closets are obtained, one on each side of the entrance.

LIVING ROOM: A cheerful room, the whole year around; it extends the full depth of the house and has windows on three sides; splendid fireplace in outside wall.

KITCHEN: Windows on two sides, many cupboards; and is laid out according to modern ideas of efficiency; outside icing door for the refrigerator.

BED ROOMS: Two good sized bed rooms and one smaller one which may serve as a child's room, or as a sewing room. There is a glorious owner's room running the full depth of the house, with windows on three sides, affording almost as much air as the average sleeping porch; each room has a large closet.

LINEN CLOSET: Special closet with shelves in the upstairs hall; and a built-in medicine cabinet in the bath room.

PLUMBING: Includes bath tub, lavatory, water cabinet, laundry tubs, kitchen sink, hot and cold water supply.

ELECTRIC OUTLETS: Properly placed, available for iron, washing machine, vacuum cleaner, toaster, floor and table lamps, heater, etc., if any or all of them are desired.

HOUSE PLAN NO. 6A20

Architects' Small House Service Bureau

THE LOW, GENTLE LINES AND OVERHANGING EAVES OF THE STYLE CREATED BY THE DUTCH COLONISTS

A COMPACT PLAN, INGENIOUS IN THE LOGICAL PLACING AND SIZE OF ROOMS IN RELATION TO EACH OTHER

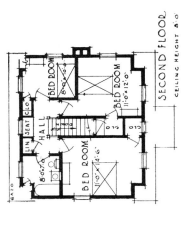

SECOND FLOOR
CEILING HEIGHT 8'-0

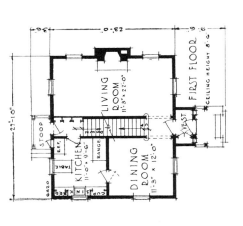

FIRST FLOOR
CEILING HEIGHT 8'-6

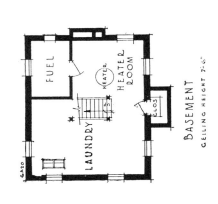

BASEMENT
CEILING HEIGHT 7'-6"

Note—For guidance in reading floor plans, see explanation on page 14

EXTERIOR

STYLE: Dutch Colonial Adaptation. Story-and-a-half type.

SIZE OF LOT REQUIRED: From 33 to 38 feet in width.

CONSTRUCTION: Wood frame on masonry foundation.

FINISH: Wide wood siding for walls. Roof shingled.

PORCHES: Front entrance stoop with brick floor, sheltered by projection of roof over vestibule. A living porch can be added either at the side or at the rear.

CHIMNEY: Outside brick chimney containing heater and fireplace flues.

DECORATIVE FEATURES: Broad three window dormer introduced for the double purpose of lighting the second story rooms and of adding interest to the exterior.

COLOR SCHEME SUGGESTED: Siding painted white; roof variegated green; blinds bottle green; door white or bottle green.

ALTERNATE EXTERIORS: This same basic plan with different exteriors can be found on Pages 24, 34, 40, 42, 44 and 48, House Plan Nos. 6B5, 6B11, 6A17, 6A18, 6A19 and 6A22.

INTERIOR

NUMBER OF ROOMS: 6 Main rooms, Bath-room and 9 Closets.

SIZE OF ROOMS:

First Floor

Living Room	11' 3" x 22' 0"
Dining Room	11' 3" x 12' 0"
Kitchen	11' 0" x 9' 6"

Second Floor

Bed Room	11' 0" x 14' 6"
Bed Room	11' 0" x 12' 0"
Bed Room	8' 0" x 10' 0"
Bath Room	8' 0" x 7' 0"

BASEMENT: Under entire house, containing Laundry, Heater-room, Closet and Fuel-bins.

PLAN TYPE: Living room running from front to back; stairs in center of the house.

DESIGNED TO FACE: West or North. For other facings, plans should be reversed.

FIREPLACE: One large open fireplace in living room, with mantel.

VENTILATION: 17 windows with double hung sash; 2 outside doors. Windows in gable ends to admit air to attic.

WALLSPACES: Ample for large pieces of furniture.

CUBIC CONTENTS: Approximately 19,100 cubic feet.

SPECIAL FEATURES

VESTIBULE: This convenience solves the hat and coat problem. The excellent six panelled front door is flanked by glass panes which let in plenty of light.

LIVING ROOM: A large airy room with windows on three sides; arched openings throw it into the hall and dining room.

KITCHEN: Planned to include all the necessary features of cupboards, worktable, etc., all close to windows. Ice-box is easily accessible for both housewife and iceman. It has a door for outside icing.

BASEMENT STAIRS: Descend from rear hall under main stairs. Easily reached from kitchen and rear stoop.

BED ROOMS: All three rooms have cross ventilation and each a good closet.

LINEN CLOSET: In the upstairs hall with plenty of shelf room.

BUILT-IN SEAT: In upper hall with hinged cover, giving additional storage space.

ATTIC STORAGE SPACE: Reached by stairs which ascend from a closet in the front bed room.

PLUMBING: Includes bath tub, lavatory, water closet, kitchen sink, laundry tubs and hot and cold water supply.

ELECTRIC OUTLETS: In the proper places, available for iron, washing machine, vacuum cleaner, toaster, floor and table lamps, heaters, etc., if any or all of them are desired.

47

HOUSE PLAN NO. 6A22

AN UNUSUALLY FINE EXAMPLE OF A WELL DESIGNED, COMFORTABLE, TRULY AMERICAN HOUSE

A PLEASING VARIATION OF THE POPULAR AND PRACTICAL RECTANGULAR HOUSE WITH SIMPLE HIPPED ROOF, WHICH CAN BE BUILT AT REASONABLE COST

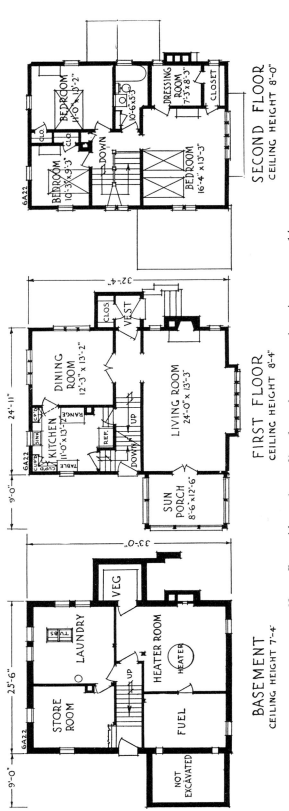

SECOND FLOOR

CEILING HEIGHT 8'-0"

BEDROOM 11'-0" x 13'-2"

DRESSING ROOM 7'-3" x 8'-3"

CLOSET

6A22

BEDROOM 10'-3" x 9'-3"

DOWN

10'-6" x 5'-3"

CLO.

CLO.

BEDROOM 16'-4" x 13'-3"

FIRST FLOOR

CEILING HEIGHT 8'-4"

32'-4"

24'-11"

9'-0"

CLOS.

VEST.

DINING ROOM 12'-3" x 13'-2"

CUP'D

CUP'D

RANGE

KITCHEN 11'-0" x 13'-2"

SINK

TABLE

REF.

CUP'D

CUP'D

6A22

UP

DOWN

LIVING ROOM 24'-0" x 13'-3"

SUN PORCH 8'-6" x 12'-6"

BASEMENT

CEILING HEIGHT 7'-4"

33'-0"

25'-6"

9'-0"

VEG

STORE ROOM

LAUNDRY

UP

HEATER ROOM

HEATER

6A22

FUEL

NOT EXCAVATED

Note—For guidance in reading floor plans, see explanation on page 14

EXTERIOR

STYLE: Western. Full two-story type.

SIZE OF LOT REQUIRED: From 45 to 50 feet in width, if sun porch is placed as shown. If porch is put at rear of dining room a 40-foot lot will do.

CONSTRUCTION: Wood frame on masonry foundation, brick base course to first story window sills.

PORCHES: Fine sun porch 8' 6"x12' 6", opening off living room. Entrance stoop at side with brick steps and parapet.

CHIMNEY: One outside brick chimney containing the heater and fireplace flues. One inside brick chimney containing kitchen flue, may be omitted.

DECORATIVE FEATURES: The use of different materials to make a happy contrast in wall textures. Attractive projecting bay with grouped windows and ornamental cornice. The hipped roof over the main portion of the house has a pleasant slope and looks well with the steep pitch of the roof over the entrance vestibule.

COLOR SCHEME SUGGESTED: Light cream colored stucco and reddish brown brick for walls. Variegated stain for roof shingles.

ALTERNATE EXTERIORS: This same basic plan with different exteriors may be found on Pages 24, 34, 40, 42, 44 and 46, House Plan Nos. 6B5, 6B11, 6A17, 6A18, 6A19, and 6A20.

INTERIOR

NUMBER OF ROOMS: 6 Main rooms, Bath-room, Dressing-room and 5 Closets.

SIZE OF ROOMS:

First Floor

Living Room	24' 0" x 13' 3"
Dining Room	12' 3" x 13' 2"
Kitchen	11' 0" x 13' 2"

Second Floor

Bed Room	16' 4" x 13' 3"
Bed Room	11' 0" x 13' 2"
Bed Room	10' 3" x 9' 3"
Dressing Room	7' 3" x 8' 3"
Bath Room	10' 6" x 5' 3"

BASEMENT: Under entire house, containing Laundry, Heater-room, Vegetable-room, Store-room and Fuel-bins.

PLAN TYPE: Living room running across the front. Stairway in the center of the house with entrance at the side.

DESIGNED TO FACE: South or East. For other facings, plans should be reversed.

FIREPLACE: Handsome brick fireplace dominates one end of living room. Excellent mantelpiece.

VENTILATION: 23 windows with double hung sash; 7 windows in sun porches; 7 casement windows; 2 outside doors.

WALL SPACES: Ample for large pieces of furniture.

CUBIC CONTENTS: Approximately 25,200 cubic feet.

SPECIAL FEATURES

FIRST FLOOR: Roomy coat closet in the vestibule; the dual purpose stairway serving both the front of the house and the kitchen; the finely proportioned hall between; and the dining room with cased opening into living room; and double French doors opening into dining room.

SECOND FLOOR: One large bedroom extending across the front of the house. It has so many windows that is has all the advantages of a sleeping porch. Opening from this room is a smaller room with outside window. This might be used as a child's bedroom or dressing room. The other bedrooms have windows on two sides and good clothes closets. There is a linen closet in the upper hall and an additional closet in the bath room.

KITCHEN: A spacious room but designed and equipped to lighten labor and minimize steps. Cross ventilation with windows on two sides.

PLUMBING: Includes bath tub, lavatory, water closet, laundry tubs, kitchen sink, hot and cold water supply.

ELECTRIC OUTLETS: Properly placed, available for iron, washing machine, vacuum cleaner, toaster, floor and table lamps, heaters, etc., if any or all of them are desired.

49

House Plan No. 6A28

THIS TYPE OF HOUSE IS KNOWN AS "THE AIRPLANE" BUNGALOW, A GREAT FAVORITE IN CALIFORIA

IT AFFORDS EXCEPTIONALLY LIGHT, AIRY ROOMS THAT ARE IN EFFECT SLEEPING PORCHES, BECAUSE THEY HAVE SO MANY WINDOWS

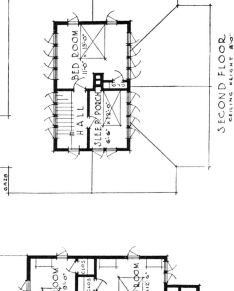

SECOND FLOOR
CEILING HEIGHT 8'-0"

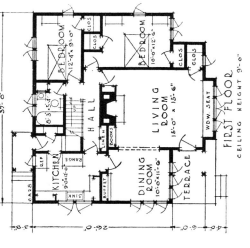

FIRST FLOOR
CEILING HEIGHT 9'-0"

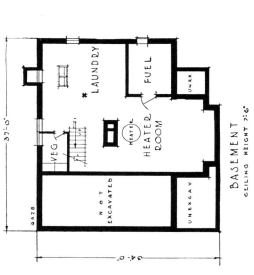

BASEMENT
CEILING HEIGHT 7'-6"

Note—For guidance in reading floor plans, see explanation on page 14

EXTERIOR

STYLE: Airplane bungalow. Story-and-a-half type.

SIZE OF LOT REQUIRED: From 42 to 47 feet in width.

CONSTRUCTION: Wood frame on masonry foundations, brick base course.

FINISH: Very wide wood siding for walls; brick base course; composition or canvas for roof; shingles may be used for roof if desired.

PORCHES: The dining room has six casement windows, so arranged that one corner of it becomes a sun porch; brick terrace partly sheltered by main roof.

CHIMNEY: One inside brick chimney, which contains heater and living room fireplace flues.

DECORATIVE FEATURES: Designed along "airplane" lines. The roof has a very low pitch, and wide spread; and is covered with canvas with raised ridges; a portion of the building extends above the main roof to form a small second story, with the roofs as wings and the large cupola as the driver's cabin, it is easy to see how the bungalow gets its name.

ALTERNATE EXTERIOR: This same basic plan, with a different exterior, may be found on Page 66, House Plan No. 5A4.

INTERIOR

NUMBER OF ROOMS: 6 Main rooms, Sleeping Porch, Bath-room and 8 Closets.

SIZE OF ROOMS:

First Floor

Living Room	15' 0" x 15' 6"
Dining Room	10' 0" x 11' 6"
Kitchen	9' 0" x 12' 0"
Bed Room	10' 0" x 12' 6"
Bed Room	12' 4" x 9' 0"
Bath Room	8' 3" x 5' 4"

Second Floor

Bed Room	11' 0" x 13' 0"
Sleeping Porch	6' 6" x 12' 0"

BASEMENT: Partially excavated, but of ample size to contain Laundry, Heater-room, Vegetable-storage and Fuel-bins.

PLAN TYPE: Typical "Airplane" bungalow type.

DESIGNED TO FACE: North or East. For other facings, plans should be reversed.

FIREPLACE: One large open brick fireplace on inside wall of living room.

VENTILATION: 42 casement windows, arranged in banks of four, three, two and one. 2 outside doors.

WALL SPACES: Ample for large pieces of furniture.

CUBIC CONTENTS: Approximately 23,900 cubic feet.

SPECIAL FEATURES

FIRST FLOOR ARRANGEMENTS: All parts connect with each other through the hall back of the living room; this makes it convenient for a woman without a servant; all rooms are only a few steps from the kitchen. The stairs to the "Airplane" rooms lead from this central hall and the bathroom is placed at the foot of the stairs, so that it is convenient for bed rooms on both floors. Linen closet is handy to all rooms. If the partition is omitted between the front bedroom and the living room, or opened up, a library would be obtained which could be used as an auxiliary bedroom if a patent bed were concealed in one of the closets during the day.

BUILT-IN FEATURES: A buffet in the dining room; book-cases and window-seat in the living room; medicine closet in bathroom; dressers and cupboards in the kitchen; a broom closet in the rear entry.

REAR ENTRY: Allows direct passage from yard to both kitchen and to basement stairs.

PLUMBING: Includes bath tub, lavatory, water closet, laundry tubs, kitchen sink, hot and cold water supply.

ELECTRIC OUTLETS: Properly placed, available for iron, washing machine, vacuum cleaner, toaster, floor and table lamps, heaters, etc., if any or all of them are desired.

HOUSE PLAN NO. 6A31

Architects' Small House Service Bureau

6A31

A TWO-STORIED RECTANGULAR HOUSE, SAVED FROM BOX LIKE APPEARANCE BY THE USE OF DELICATE COLONIAL FORMS

DEMAND FOR ECONOMY CONTROLLED THE PLAN ARRANGEMENT AND BUILDING COST, YET CARE WAS TAKEN NOT TO SACRIFICE AN AGREEABLE EXTERIOR

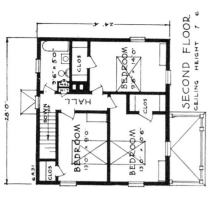

Note—For guidance in reading floor plans, see explanation on page 14

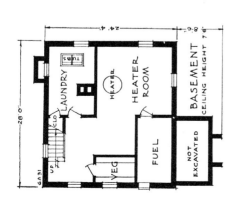

EXTERIOR

STYLE: New England Colonial. Full two-story type.

SIZE OF LOT REQUIRED: From 35 to 40 feet in width.

CONSTRUCTION: Wood frame on masonry foundations, brick base course.

FINISH: Wide wood siding for walls; corner boards; plain trim for windows. Shingled roof.

PORCHES: Front covered porch and a rear covered stoop.

CHIMNEY: One interior brick chimney containing the heater and kitchen range flues.

DECORATIVE FEATURES: Well balanced window spacing with splendid wall surfaces. The caps on the corner boards add distinction. The proportions of the porch columns and lace-like railing give the whole house a real Colonial flavor.

COLOR SCHEME SUGGESTED: Colonial yellow for siding. White cornice, corner boards and trim; green shutters and variegated stained roof.

ALTERNATE EXTERIORS: This same basic plan with different exteriors may be found on pages 38, 90, and 92, House Plan Nos. 6A15, 5A31 and 5A33.

INTERIOR

NUMBER OF ROOMS: 6 Main rooms, Bath-room and 6 Closets.

SIZE OF ROOMS:

First Floor

Living Room	13' 0" x 19' 6"
Dining Room	13' 0" x 11' 0"
Kitchen	7' 6" x 11' 6"

Second Floor

Bed Room	13' 0" x 10' 6"
Bed Room	13' 0" x 9' 0"
Bed Room	9' 6" x 14' 0"
Bath Room	9' 6" x 5' 0"

BASEMENT: Under the entire house, containing the Laundry, Heater-room, Vegetable-storage and Fuel-bins.

PLAN TYPE: Living room running from front to rear with stairs at one end.

DESIGNED TO FACE: South or West. For other facings, plans should be reversed.

FIREPLACE: None.

VENTILATION: 18 windows with double hung sash; 2 outside doors.

WALL SPACES: Ample for large pieces of furniture.

CUBIC CONTENTS: Approximately 20,300 cubic feet.

SPECIAL FEATURES

LIVING ROOM: Spacious in size and excellent in proportion, with outlook in two directions. The door leading into rear entry means a great convenience since it gives the kitchen direct access to stairs leading to second floor.

KITCHEN: Well arranged and liberally supplied with cupboard room; it has a handy broom-closet. The outside icing door provided for the ice box is a labor saving device.

AMPLE CLOSETS: In addition to the large bed room closets there is a coat closet accessible from the living room; a linen closet in the upper hall, a large towel and supply closet and a medicine cabinet in the bath room.

REAR ENTRY: Permits passage from yard to both the kitchen and to the basement stairs; a door into the living room means a saving of steps for everybody.

PLUMBING: Includes bath tub, lavatory, water closet, laundry tubs, kitchen sink, hot and cold water supply.

ELECTRIC OUTLETS: Properly placed, available for iron, washing machine, vacuum cleaner, toaster, floor and table lamps, heaters, etc., if any or all of them are desired.

HOUSE PLAN NO. 6A37

Architects' Small House Service Bureau

THE MELLOW DIGNITY OF THIS HOUSE REMINDS ONE OF A HOMESTEAD IN NEW ENGLAND. IT HAS A TANG OF THE EAST COAST

MAKES AN IMMEDIATE APPEAL BECAUSE IT IS RELATED CREDITABLY TO THE HOUSES OF PAST DAYS

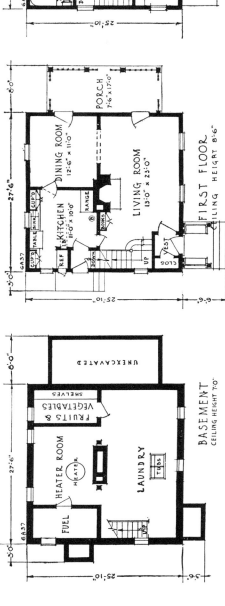

BASEMENT CEILING HEIGHT 7'0"

UNEXCAVATED

HEATER ROOM — HEATER

FUEL

LAUNDRY — TUBS

FRUITS & VEGETABLES — SHELVES

FIRST FLOOR CEILING HEIGHT 8'6"

DINING ROOM 12'6" x 11'0"

PORCH 7'6" x 17'0"

KITCHEN 11'0" x 10'0" — SINK, TABLE, CUP'D, REF, RANGE

LIVING ROOM 13'0" x 23'0"

CLOS, VEST, UP, DOWN, ROOMS

SECOND FLOOR CEILING HEIGHT 8'0"

BEDROOM 15'6" x 11'0" — WARDROBE

BEDROOM 15'0" x 11'6"

BED ROOM 10'6" x 8'0"

HALL, CLOS, LINEN, 7'6" x 7'0", DOWN

Note—For guidance in reading floor plans, see explanation on page 14

EXTERIOR

STYLE: New England Colonial. Full two-story type.

SIZE OF LOT REQUIRED: From 41 to 46 feet in width if built as shown above; if side porch is omitted, or placed at the rear, from 33 to 38 feet in width will be needed.

CONSTRUCTION: Wood frame on masonry foundations; brick base course.

FINISH: Wood siding for walls; shingled roof.

PORCHES: Covered entrance porch and side living porch, 7' 6" x 17' 0" with columns supporting a flat roof.

CHIMNEY: One central brick chimney, located to serve furnace, fireplace and kitchen range.

DECORATIVE FEATURES: The quaint entrance porch with its seats is practical and an inviting bit of decoration; the lattices on the porch are admirable in themselves, or may be used to support vines.

COLOR SCHEME SUGGESTED: Walls painted white; roof greenish-brown; blinds bottle green; exterior trim white.

ALTERNATE EXTERIORS: This same basic plan, with different exteriors, may be found on Pages 20 and 58, House Plan Nos. 6B4 and 6A43.

INTERIOR

NUMBER OF ROOMS: 6 Main rooms, Bath-room and 5 Closets.

SIZE OF ROOMS:

First Floor		
Living Room	13' 0" x 23' 0"
Dining Room	12' 6" x 11' 0"
Kitchen	11' 0" x 10' 0"
Second Floor		
Bed Room	15' 0" x 11' 6"
Bed Room	15' 6" x 11' 0"
Bed Room	10' 6" x 8' 0"
Bath Room	7' 6" x 7' 0"

BASEMENT: Under the entire house, containing Laundry, Heater-room, Vegetable-storage and Fuel-bins.

PLAN TYPE: Living room running across the front, with stairs at one side.

DESIGNED TO FACE: West or North. For other facings, plans should be reversed.

FIREPLACE: One brick fireplace on inside wall of living room, with Colonial wood mantel.

VENTILATION: 15 windows with double hung sash; 2 French doors, and 2 outside doors; small windows in attic to admit free circulation of air under roof.

WALL SPACES: Ample for large pieces of furniture.

CUBIC CONTENTS: Approximately 22,000 cubic feet.

SPECIAL FEATURES

LIVING ROOM: Is lighted from four sides, the window on the stair landing doing double duty. The living porch is reached through French doors from the dining room as well as from living room; has built-in bookcase.

DINING ROOM: Has a wide cased opening into the living room, giving an air of roominess to the whole first floor.

KITCHEN: Has direct access to stairs and front door; it is ideal in plan and arrangement; the sink and worktable are placed close to windows; ice box in convenient niche, with door for outside icing; built-in cupboards and ironing board.

THE VESTIBULE: Has a good-sized hat and coat closet.

TWO OF THE BED ROOMS are unusually large, and the third is of good size and proportion.

TWO BUILT-IN WARDROBES: One in each of the two larger bed rooms make for comfort and are excellently placed for pier glasses.

LINEN CLOSET and two other closets on the second floor are large and convenient.

PLUMBING: Includes bath tub, lavatory, water closet, laundry tubs, kitchen sink, hot and cold water supply.

ELECTRIC OUTLETS: In proper places, available for iron, washing machine, vacuum cleaner, toaster, floor and table lamps, heater, etc., if any or all of them are desired.

House Plan No. 6A39

Architects' Small House Service Bureau

6A39

BORROWED FROM ENGLAND BUT SUFFICIENTLY ACCLIMATED TO BE VERY AMERICAN

A DIGNIFIED, RESTFUL HOUSE OF SURPRISING CONVENIENCE AND NO EXTRAVAGANCE

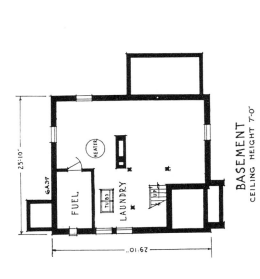

BASEMENT
CEILING HEIGHT 7'-0"

FUEL

LAUNDRY

HEATER

25'-10"

29'-10"

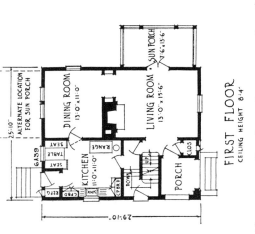

FIRST FLOOR
CEILING HEIGHT 8'-4"

ALTERNATE LOCATION FOR SUN PORCH

DINING ROOM 13'-0"x11'-0"

KITCHEN 11'-0"x10'-0"

RANGE

SUN PORCH 7'-6"x13'-6"

LIVING ROOM 13'-0"x15'-6"

PORCH

25'-10"

29'-10"

SECOND FLOOR
CEILING HEIGHT 8'-2"

BEDROOM 13'-0"x11'-0"

BEDROOM 13'-0"x14'-6"

BEDROOM 10'-6"x8'-0"

HALL

LINEN

STORAGE

25'-10"

29'-10"

Note—For guidance in reading floor plans, see explanation on page 14

EXTERIOR

STYLE: English domestic adaptation. Two-story type.

SIZE OF LOT REQUIRED: From 39 to 44 feet in width, unless sun porch is placed in alternate location, as indicated on plan, then 31 to 36 feet in width would be sufficient.

CONSTRUCTION: Wood frame on masonry foundation, brick base course.

FINISH: Trowelled stucco walls, shingled roof.

PORCHES: Covered entrance porch; sun porch 7' 6" x 13' 6".

CHIMNEY: One central brick chimney, containing heater, living room fireplace and kitchen range flues, terminating in terra cotta chimney pots.

DECORATIVE FEATURES: The long sweep of the main roof to cover the entrance porch is both quaint and effective. The stucco corners and simple but sturdy wood pilasters and the window-shaped opening all tend to attract and hold interest. The windows are carefully studied in their relation to the wall surface and to each other. The side entry and sun porch are tied into the main house in a most satisfactory manner.

COLOR SCHEME SUGGESTED: Cream colored stucco walls; white trim; variegated green and brown stain for shingles.

ALTERNATE EXTERIORS: None.

INTERIOR

NUMBER OF ROOMS: 6 Main rooms, Dining Alcove, Bath-room and 5 Closets.

SIZE OF ROOMS:

First Floor

Living Room	13' 0" x 15' 6"
Dining Room	13' 0" x 11' 0"
Kitchen	11' 0" x 11' 0"

Second Floor

Bed Room	13' 0" x 14' 6"
Bed Room	13' 0" x 11' 0"
Bed Room	11' 0" x 8' 0"
Bath Room	7' 0" x 6' 0"

BASEMENT: Under entire house, containing Laundry, Heater-room, and Fuel-bins.

PLAN TYPE: Living room and dining room running from front to back of the house.

DESIGNED TO FACE: North, West or South. For East facing, plans should be reversed.

FIREPLACE: One large open fireplace in the living room, with wood mantel.

VENTILATION: 16 windows with double hung sash; 1 pair French doors to sun porch; 3 outside doors; louvres in gable end to admit air circulation under roof.

WALL SPACE: Ample for large pieces of furniture.

CUBIC CONTENTS: Approximately 24,200 cubic feet.

SPECIAL FEATURES

LIVING ROOM: Is reached through entrance porch and small hall, containing hat and coat closet; it has direct access to the sun porch. The size, shape, lighting and ventilation make this a very livable room.

DINING ROOM: Has two exposures, and opens directly into the living room.

KITCHEN: Is so equipped and planned that there is room for a dining alcove with built-in table and seats, a time and labor-saving device when only one or two are home for meals.

REAR ENTRY AND HALL: Containing an ice box iced from outside. Basement stairs descend from here.

STAIRS: Ascend to second floor from main hall; they have a landing half-way up, lighted by a window.

BED ROOMS: There are three bed rooms of comfortable size, each with two exposures and closet.

BATH ROOM AND LINEN CLOSET: Open from upstairs hall, and are easily reached from all bed rooms.

STORAGE SPACE: Opening from the upstairs hall is a large storage space, under the eaves.

PLUMBING: Includes bath tub, lavatory, water closet, laundry tubs and kitchen sink.

ELECTRIC OUTLETS: Properly placed, available for iron, washing machine, vacuum cleaner, toaster, floor and table lamps, heaters, etc., if any or all of them are desired.

57

HOUSE PLAN NO. 6A43

EASTERN PENNSYLVANIA BUILDERS OF OLD FURNISHED THE IDEA FOR THIS HOUSE OF TODAY

A VERY SMALL OUTLAY OVER BARE NECESSITIES, BUT A HOUSE OF CHARACTER AND DIGNITY

BASEMENT
CEILING HEIGHT 7'-0"

COAL | LAUNDRY

HEATER ROOM

NOT EXCAVATED

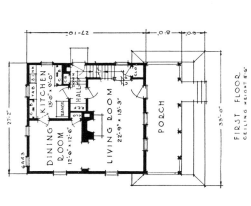

FIRST FLOOR
CEILING HEIGHT 9'-0"

KITCHEN
13'-0" x 9'-0"

DINING ROOM
12'-6" x 12'-6"

HALL

LIVING ROOM
22'-9" x 13'-3"

PORCH

SECOND FLOOR
CEILING HEIGHT 8'-0"

BED ROOM
9'-0" x 12'-3"

HALL

BED ROOM
13'-0" x 16'-0"

BED ROOM
13'-0" x 16'-0"

Note—For guidance in reading floor plans, see explanation on page 14.

EXTERIOR

STYLE: Pennsylvania Colonial. Combination story-and-a-half and full two-story type.

SIZE OF LOT REQUIRED: From 32 to 38 feet in width.

CONSTRUCTION: Wood frame on masonry foundations.

FINISH: Design shows wood siding; may be shingles if desired. Roof shingled.

PORCHES: Large living porch, under main roof, running the full width of the house; it protects the entrance and makes a vestibule unnecessary.

CHIMNEY: One brick chimney, containing heater and fireplace flues.

DECORATIVE FEATURES: The large dormer window breaking the huge stretch of roof. The projection of the roof over the porch ties the house to the terrace on which it stands. The lattice work on either end of the porch is attractive in itself and suggests the planting of vines.

COLOR SCHEME SUGGESTED: Siding painted white; roof variegated green; and blue-green blinds and door.

ALTERNATE EXTERIORS: This same basic plan with different exteriors can be found on Pages 20 and 54, House Plan Nos. 6B4 and 6A37.

INTERIOR

NUMBER OF ROOMS: 6 Main rooms, with Bath-room and 8 closets.

SIZE OF ROOMS:

First Floor

Living Room	22' 9" x 13' 3"
Dining Room	12' 6" x 12' 6"
Kitchen	13' 0" x 9' 0"

Second Floor

Bed Room	13' 0" x 16' 0"
Bed Room	16' 0" x 12' 3"
Bed Room	9' 0" x 11' 6"
Bath Room	9' 6" x 6' 0"

BASEMENT: Under main portion of house, containing Laundry, Heater-room and Fuel-bins.

PLAN TYPE: Living room running across the front of house with stairway at one end.

DESIGNED TO FACE: East or South. For other facings, plans should be reversed.

FIREPLACE: One brick fireplace in the living room, with wood mantel.

VENTILATION: 20 windows with double hung sash, located for cross-ventilation; 2 outside doors.

WALL SPACES: Ample for large pieces of furniture.

CUBIC CONTENTS: Approximately 26,000 cubic feet.

SPECIAL FEATURES

LIVING ROOM: A truly impressive room, occupying more than half of the first floor.

DINING ROOM: A square room with china closet in one corner. Wide cased openings throw this room into the living room, adding the impression of bigness to each.

KITCHEN: Carefully planned to simplify house work. It has straight line access to the front door and stairs. The ice-box is in the side hall, reached from the side door.

BED ROOMS: Each has windows on two sides, and each has a large closet; there is an extra closet in two of the rooms.

ATTIC SPACE: The design provides a large space in the third floor for storage and an extra room, reached by stairs in one of the bedrooms.

LINEN CLOSET: In a central location in upper hall. Coat closet opening off stair landing near front door.

PLUMBING: Includes bath tub, water closet, lavatory, kitchen sink, laundry tubs and hot and cold water supply.

ELECTRIC OUTLETS: In the proper places, available for iron, washing machine, vacuum cleaner, toaster, floor and table lamps, heater, etc., if any or all of them are desired.

HOUSE PLAN NO. 5A1

Architects' Small House Service Bureau

Northwestern Division

5A1

INVITING ADMIRATION FROM THE PASSERBY BECAUSE OF ITS PLEASING COMBINATION OF ROOF LINES AND WALL TREATMENT

PLANNED TO MEET THE MOST EXACTING MODERN REQUIREMENTS AND TO PROVIDE COMFORT AND CONVENIENCES FOR SMALL OUTLAY

SECOND FLOOR
CEILING HEIGHT 8'-2"

BEDROOM 10'-6" x 11'-2"

BATH 5'x7'-0"

BED ROOM 16'-6" x 11'-0"

ROOF

FIRST FLOOR
CEILING HEIGHT 8'-4"

KITCHEN 8'-6" x 11'-0"

DINING ROOM 11'-0" x 11'-0"

STOOP

HALL

VEST

LIVING ROOM 20'-3" x 11'-2"

PORCH 7'-6" x 18'-3"

BASEMENT
CEILING HEIGHT 6'-9"

TUBS

LAUNDRY

FUEL

HEATER

NOT EXCAVATED

Note—For guidance in reading floor plans, see explanation on page 14

EXTERIOR

STYLE: Western. Story-and-a-half type.

SIZE OF LOT REQUIRED: From 35 to 40 feet in width.

CONSTRUCTION: Wood frame on masonry foundations, cement base course.

FINISH: Wood shingles, wood siding or stucco for walls; shingled roof.

PORCHES: Entrance and living porch, 7' 6" x 18' 3", ended just beyond the entrance doorway so that no sunlight is cut off from the dining room. A side stoop is provided.

CHIMNEY: One inside brick chimney, containing the heater and fireplace flues.

DECORATIVE FEATURES: The ingenious way in which the roof of the main house extends over the porch adds interest; the long sweep of the roof is broken by a recessed dormer; the introduction of a gable, with the same pitch as the main roof, to emphasize the entrance and the grouping and placing of the windows make this a snug and attractive house; a flower box under the second story windows and a trellis around the first story window invites vines, which add a touch of vivid color.

COLOR SCHEME SUGGESTED: Wall shingles stained dark gray; trim cream color; roof stained dark brown.

ALTERNATE EXTERIORS: This same basic plan, with different exteriors, may be found on Pages 64, 76, 80, 82 and 84, House Plan Nos. 5B3, 5B10, 5B13, 5A21 and 5A24.

INTERIOR

NUMBER OF ROOMS: 5 Main rooms, Bath-room and 6 Closets.

SIZE OF ROOMS:

First Floor

Living Room	20' 3" x 11' 2"
Dining Room	11' 0" x 11' 0"
Kitchen	8' 6" x 11' 0"

Second Floor

Bed Room	16' 6" x 11' 0"
Bed Room	10' 6" x 11' 2"
Bath Room	5' 6" x 7' 0"

BASEMENT: Under main portion of the house, containing Laundry, Heater-room and Fuel-bins.

PLAN TYPE: Living room running across the front of the house; stairway in the center of the house.

DESIGNED TO FACE: South or West. For other facings, plans should be reversed.

FIREPLACE: One large open fireplace in center of inside wall of living room.

VENTILATION: 13 windows with double hung sash, 6 casement windows in dormers; 2 outside doors; louvres in gable ends to admit free circulation of air under roof.

WALL SPACES: Ample for large pieces of furniture.

CUBIC CONTENTS: Approximately 16,500 cubic feet.

SPECIAL FEATURES

LIVING ROOM: Everything that its name implies; it is large, sunny and has two necessities of a year round house: the porch for summer use and the fireplace for winter; it has the unusual advantage of being accessible three ways; from the entrance, from the rear porch, and from the living porch, a surprisingly useful feature.

KITCHEN: Invites the housekeeper's approval; it is saving of steps, light and contains all the fixtures she needs, within easy reach. The stoop is not only useful for passage to kitchen and to basement, but it will be found a great comfort as a summer kitchen. The ice box is in the kitchen proper, but iced from the outside.

BED ROOMS: Both rooms have windows on two sides, and each has its own closet; the bath room is easily reached from both; it contains a built-in medicine cabinet.

SPECIAL CLOSETS: On the first floor a coat closet in the vestibule, a broom closet and a general catch-all closet in the living room, have been provided; on the second floor there is a shelved linen closet.

PLUMBING: The bath room is over the kitchen, an economical plumbing arrangement; the plumbing fixtures include bath tub, lavatory, water closet, laundry tubs, kitchen sink, hot and cold water supply.

ELECTRIC OUTLETS: Properly placed, available for iron, washing machine, vacuum cleaner, toaster, floor and table lamps, heater, etc., if any or all of them are desired.

61

HOUSE PLAN NO. 5A2

5A2

AN EXAMPLE OF THE BUNGALOW WHICH ESTABLISHED THE VOGUE OF THE TYPE AND WHICH IS A HERITAGE OF CALIFORNIA

THERE IS SPLENDID VALUE IN THIS ONE STORIED, LOW ROOFED, WIDE EAVED INTIMATE HOUSE

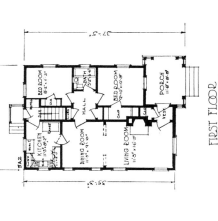

FIRST FLOOR
CEILING HEIGHT 7'-6"

Note—For guidance in reading floor plans, see explanation on page 14

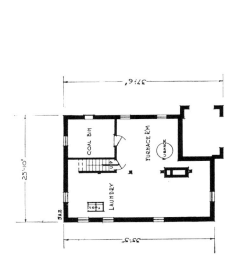

BASEMENT
CEILING HEIGHT 7'-6"

EXTERIOR

STYLE: Modern Bungalow. All rooms on one floor.

SIZE OF LOT REQUIRED: From 35 to 40 feet in width.

CONSTRUCTION: Wood frame on masonry foundations, cement base course.

FINISH: Wood siding for walls; shingled roof.

PORCHES: Living porch, 11' 8" x 8' 8" taken out of the front corner of the house, with a slight projection on front and side. Rear stoop.

CHIMNEY: One inside brick chimney, toward the front, containing heater and fireplace flues.

DECORATIVE FEATURES: The hipped roof has a pleasing pitch and is framed so that the ventilating louvres are in an attractive little gable at the ridge. The slender boxed columns and pilasters of the porch, filled in between with lattice, cut off no light; the lattice may or may not be used to train vines on.

COLOR SCHEME SUGGESTED: White siding, white trim, green shutters, variegated green roof shingles.

ALTERNATE EXTERIOR: This same basic plan with different exterior may be found on page 68, House Plan No. 5A6.

INTERIOR

NUMBER OF ROOMS: 5 Main rooms, Bath-room and 4 Closets.

SIZE OF ROOMS:
Living Room	11' 5" x 16' 2"
Dining Room	11' 5" x 9' 8"
Kitchen	11' 5" x 8' 2"
Bed Room	9' 10" x 10' 3"
Bed Room	8' 2" x 11' 2"
Bath Room	5' 2" x 6' 6"

BASEMENT: Under entire house, containing Laundry, Furnace-room, Storage and Fuel-bins.

PLAN TYPE: The living room and porch running across the front of the house.

DESIGNED TO FACE: South or East. For other facings, plans should be reversed.

FIREPLACE: One large open fireplace in center of inside wall of the living room. Wood mantel with wide shelf.

VENTILATION: 12 windows with double hung sash; 2 outside doors; louvres at the ends to permit free circulation of air under roof.

WALL SPACES: Ample for large pieces of furniture.

CUBIC CONTENTS: Approximately 18,000 cubic feet.

SPECIAL FEATURES

LIVING ROOM: In few houses of this size does one find so generous a room, or one of so attractive a shape. It is separated from the dining room by a wide cased opening, making the two rooms practically one, or if desired, the opening could be reduced in size giving privacy to the dining room. Excellent coat closet in vestibule, between this room and front porch.

KITCHEN: Ample in size, and installed with complete equipment for doing the work with the fewest steps and least labor. A window on one side is over the sink, and a window on the other side lights the worktable.

REAR ENTRY: Allows direct passage from yard to both kitchen and to basement stairs, and provides space for ice box.

BED ROOMS: Have all the seclusion of rooms on a second floor; they are separated from the living quarters of the house by a double partition, enclosing closets and they are reached by a private hall, from which open the bath room and linen closet.

PLUMBING: Includes bath tub, lavatory, water closet, laundry tubs, kitchen sink, hot and cold water supply.

ELECTRIC OUTLETS: In proper places, available for iron, washing machine, vacuum cleaner, toaster, floor and table lamps, heater, etc.

63

HOUSE PLAN NO. 5B3

5B3

BY IGNORING THE VARIOUS STYLES, THIS HOUSE ACHIEVES THAT MOST ELUSIVE OF ARCHITECTURAL ASSETS, "STYLE"

IT WOULD BE DIFFICULT TO DESIGN AND PLAN A HOUSE WHICH OFFERS MORE FOR THE MONEY THAN THIS ONE

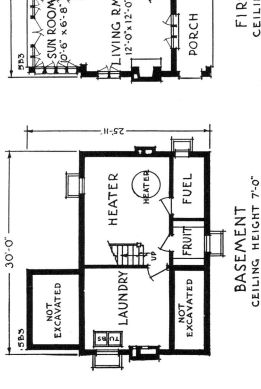

SECOND FLOOR
CEILING HEIGHT 7'-0"

FIRST FLOOR
CEILING HEIGHT 8'-6"

Note—For guidance in reading floor plans, see explanation on page 14

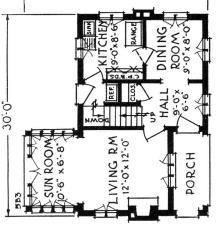

BASEMENT
CEILING HEIGHT 7'-0"

EXTERIOR

STYLE: American Domestic. Story-and-a-half type.

SIZE OF LOT REQUIRED: From 38 to 40 feet in width.

CONSTRUCTION: Brick exterior walls on masonry foundations.

FINISH: Hard burned water struck brick; dormer window shingled; roof shingled.

PORCHES: Entrance porch contained within the main body of the house, 5' 0" x 12' 6" helping to reduce cost of building. Sun room opening off living room.

CHIMNEYS: Two outside brick chimneys, one for heater and kitchen range flues, the other containing the fireplace flue.

DECORATIVE FEATURES: Homelike in character, and the outgrowth of straightforward planning with good proportions and a most appropriate use of building materials. The bath room dormer window moulds naturally into the single pitch of the main roof. A long flower box on the porch adds color and acts as a screen.

COLOR SCHEME SUGGESTED: Walls red brick with wide white mortar joints. Roof stained gray-green. Exterior finish and shutters painted white.

ALTERNATE EXTERIORS: This same basic plan with different exteriors may be found on Pages 60, 72, 80, 82 and 84, House Plan Nos. 5A1, 5B7, 5B13, 5A21 and 5A24.

INTERIOR

NUMBER OF ROOMS: 5 Main rooms, Sun-room, Bathroom and 4 Closets.

SIZE OF ROOMS:

First Floor

Living Room	12' 0" x 12' 0"
Dining Room	9' 0" x 8' 0"
Sun Room	10' 6" x 6' 8"
Kitchen	9' 0" x 8' 6"

Second Floor

Bed Room	12' 0" x 10' 0"
Bed Room	9' 0" x 10' 0"
Bath Room	6' 8" x 5' 6"

BASEMENT: Fully excavated with the exception of the portion directly under the entrance porch and sun room. It contains Laundry, Heater-room, Fruit-room and Fuel-bins.

PLAN TYPE: Living room running from front to rear including sun room. Stairs in center of the house.

DESIGNED TO FACE: South or East. For other facings, plans should be reversed.

FIREPLACE: One open fireplace in living room, with attractive Colonial mantel.

VENTILATION: 33 casement windows, triple windows in living room; 2 outside doors; French doors opening out of sun room.

WALL SPACES: Ample for large pieces of furniture.

CUBIC CONTENTS: Approximately 13,300 cubic feet.

SPECIAL FEATURES

LIVING ROOM: Combined with the sun room, making one large room of excellent proportions. Its many casement windows insure abundance of air in the warm months, and a sunny, well lighted room during the winter season.

DINING ROOM: Across the hall from the living room; the two casement windows insure a light, cheerful room.

HALL AND STAIRWAY: Flooded with light from windows in lower hall and on the stair landing; large coat closet in hall.

KITCHEN: The range, sink, cupboards and work table are compact and well placed. Two exposures insure a well lighted and ventilated room.

REAR ENTRY: Allows direct passage from yard to both kitchen and to basement stairs, and provides convenient space for ice box.

LINEN CLOSET: In the well-lighted upper hall.

PLUMBING: Includes bath tub, lavatory, water closet, laundry tubs, kitchen sink, and hot and cold water supply.

ELECTRIC OUTLETS: In the proper places, available for iron, washing machine, vacuum cleaner, toaster, floor and table lamps, heaters, etc., if any or all of them are desired.

5A4

APPROPRIATE DESIGN AND HONEST CONSTRUCTION HERE SERVE TO PERPETUATE BUNGALOW TRADITION AND POPULARITY

A SMALL, INEXPENSIVE HOUSE CAN BE ATTRACTIVE AND COMFORTABLE WHEN SKILLFULLY DESIGNED AND PLANNED

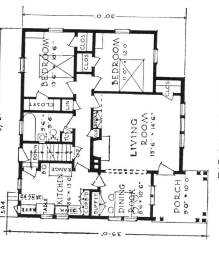

BEDROOM
13'6" x 11'6"

BEDROOM
11'0" x 12'0"

CLOS

CLOS

CLOS

CLOSET

CLOSET

LIN

DOWN

KITCHEN
8'6" x 13'0"

RANGE

REF

TABLE

CUP'D

BUFFET

CUPBOARD

LIVING
ROOM
15'6" x 14'6"

DINING
ROOM
8'6" x 10'6"

PORCH
9'0" x 10'0"

30'-0"

37'-2"

5A4

5A4

39'-0"

FIRST FLOOR
CEILING HEIGHT 8' 4"

Note—For guidance in reading floor plans, see explanation on page 14

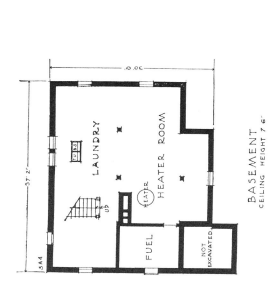

LAUNDRY

HEATER ROOM

HEATER

FUEL

NOT EXCAVATED

30'-0"

37'-2"

5A4

BASEMENT
CEILING HEIGHT 7' 6"

EXTERIOR

STYLE: Colonial Adaptation. Bungalow type.

SIZE OF LOT REQUIRED: From 43 to 48 feet in width.

CONSTRUCTION: Wood frame on masonry foundations.

FINISH: Wide wood siding for walls. Shingled roof.

PORCHES: Front entrance porch 9' 0" x 10' 0".

CHIMNEY: One inside brick chimney containing heater and fireplace flues.

DECORATIVE FEATURES: Good proportions and well designed details. Brick porch floor laid in interesting pattern. The triple window in living room with its flower box adds character.

COLOR SCHEME SUGGESTED: White painted siding; roof shingles stained brown-green; frames pearl-gray and sash white.

ALTERNATE EXTERIOR: This same basic plan with different exterior can be found on Page 50, House Plan No. 6A28.

INTERIOR

NUMBER OF ROOMS: 5 Main rooms, Bath-room and 6 Closets.

SIZE OF ROOMS:

Living Room	15' 6" x 14' 6"
Dining Room	8' 6" x 10' 6"
Kitchen	8' 6" x 13' 0"
Bed Room	13' 6" x 10' 6"
Bed Room	11' 0" x 12' 0"
Bath Room	5' 6" x 9' 6"

BASEMENT: Under entire house, containing Laundry, Heater-room and Fuel-bins.

PLAN TYPE: Living room and dining rooms running across front of the house.

DESIGNED TO FACE: In any direction. Plans may be reversed if desired.

FIREPLACE: One large brick fireplace in living room.

VENTILATION: 15 windows with double hung sash, located for cross ventilation; 2 outside doors.

WALL SPACES: Ample for large pieces of furniture.

CUBIC CONTENTS: Approximately 22,000 cubic feet.

SPECIAL FEATURES

THE FRONT BED ROOM: May be opened into the living room so as to provide a library. Closet-bed in this room would give an extra bed room.

BOOK CASE: Built-in in the living room. It has two small glazed doors above, two long panelled doors below and a wide seat under which is a drawer.

SIDEBOARD: Built-in in the dining room, with glazed doors above and panelled doors below.

KITCHEN: Has windows on two sides. The sink has cupboards on one side and is located under a double window. Ice box is in kitchen, but has outside icing door. There is a built-in ironing board.

LINEN CLOSET: In back hall, and towel closet and medicine cabinet in bath room.

BROOM CLOSET: In the back hall.

PLUMBING: Includes bath tub, water closet, lavatory, kitchen sink, laundry tubs and hot and cold water supply.

ELECTRIC OUTLETS: In the proper place, available for iron, washing machine, vacuum cleaner, toaster, floor and table lamps, heaters, etc., if any or all of them are desired.

5A6

RETAINS THE RARE QUALITY OF REPOSE CHARACTERISTIC OF COLONIAL WORK

HERE IS FOUND REFINEMENT NICELY BLENDED WITH PRACTICABILITY, RESULTING IN A HOUSE OF GREAT MERIT

Architects' Small House Service Bureau

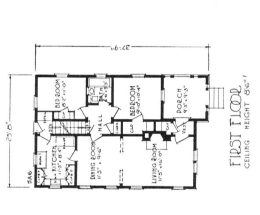

SECOND FLOOR
CEILING HEIGHT 7'6"

FIRST FLOOR
CEILING HEIGHT 8'6"

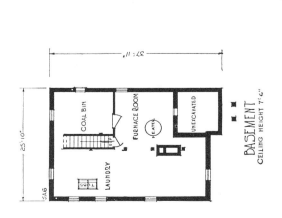

BASEMENT
CEILING HEIGHT 7'6"

Note—For guidance in reading floor plans, see explanation on page 14

EXTERIOR

STYLE: Germantown Colonial Adaptation. Bungalow type.

SIZE OF LOT REQUIRED: From 35 to 40 feet in width.

CONSTRUCTION: Frame construction on masonry foundation, cement base course.

FINISH: Wide clapboarded walls; shingled roof and dormer.

PORCHES: The entrance porch is also the living porch. It measures 9' 3" x 9' 3".

CHIMNEY: One inside brick chimney toward the front containing heater and fireplace flues.

DECORATIVE FEATURES: The trellises on each side of the entrance are attractive and may or may not be used to train vines over. The semi-circular louvre in the roof of the porch breaks the line and adds interest. The entrance and the rest of house are unified by the so-called "Germantown hood." The windows are well grouped and of good proportion.

COLOR SCHEME SUGGESTED: Cream white clapboards, sage green shutters, variegated green shingles for roof, white trim.

ALTERNATE EXTERIORS: This same basic plan, with different exterior, may be found on Page 62, House Plan No. 5A2.

INTERIOR

NUMBER OF ROOMS: 5 Finished rooms, 1 Unfinished room on second floor, Bath-room and 4 Closets.

SIZE OF ROOMS:

Living Room	11' 5" x 16' 0"
Dining Room	11' 5" x 9' 6"
Kitchen	11' 5" x 8' 4"
Bed Room	9' 10" x 10' 4"
Bed Room	8' 2" x 11' 0"
Bath Room	6' 6" x 5' 3"

BASEMENT: Under entire house, containing Laundry, Furnace-room and Coal-bin.

PLAN TYPE: Living room extending across front of house.

DESIGNED TO FACE: South or East. For other facings, plans should be reversed.

FIREPLACE: Large open fireplace with good-looking wood mantel in living room.

VENTILATION: 15 windows, with double hung sash; louvre in porch roof to admit free circulation of air; 2 outside doors.

WALL SPACES: Ample for large pieces of furniture.

CUBIC CONTENTS: Approximately 22,800 cubic feet.

SPECIAL FEATURES

LIVING ROOM AND DINING ROOM: Practically one large room, separated only by cased opening. The rear of these rooms is beautifully light having 6 windows; the open fireplace is the outstanding feature; a door from the dining room to the bed room hall gives good circulation.

KITCHEN: Small, light and compact, has ample cupboard space and a worktable directly under a window.

REAR ENTRY: Allows direct communication from out-of-doors to both kitchen and to basement; contains ice box.

BED ROOM HALL: Opens from dining room, into bed rooms, bath room and linen closet. Stairs ascend from it.

BED ROOMS: Each faces in two directions, and each has a closet; bath room equally convenient to both.

VESTIBULE: Opens from porch into living room; it contains a hat and coat closet.

STORAGE SPACE: In second floor, under eaves.

PLUMBING: Includes bath tub, lavatory, water closet, laundry tubs, kitchen sink, hot and cold water supply.

ELECTRIC OUTLETS: Properly placed, available for iron, washing machine, vacuum cleaner, toaster, floor and table lamps, heaters, etc., if any or all of them are desired.

House Plan No. 5B6

Architects' Small House Service Bureau

5B6.

ROMANTIC IN CHARACTER, HAVING ITS ORIGIN IN THE SMALL FARM HOUSES OF SUNNY ITALY

THERE IS A STRONG APPEAL IN THIS DESIGN TO THE BUILDER WHO IS LOOKING FOR INDIVIDUALITY IN HIS HOME

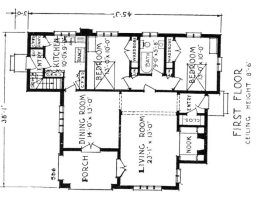

BASEMENT
CEILING HEIGHT 7'-0"

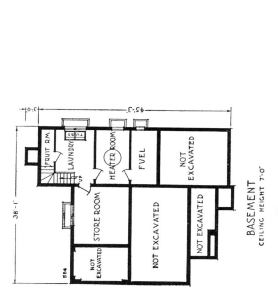

FIRST FLOOR
CEILING HEIGHT 8'-6"

Note—For guidance in reading floor plans, see explanation on page 14

EXTERIOR

STYLE: Italian Adaptation. Bungalow type.

SIZE OF LOT REQUIRED: From 45 to 50 feet in width.

CONSTRUCTION: Hollow tile walls on masonry foundations.

FINISH: Trowelled finish stucco; mission tile roof.

PORCHES: Living porch conveniently arranged so that it is reached from both living room and dining room. Small entrance stoop.

CHIMNEY: One massive chimney with one flue.

DECORATIVE FEATURES: The general form is unusual and the treatment of the ingle nook and chimney is delightful, and impressive. The break in the roof around the chimney softens the outline. The arched entrance doorway, well proportioned gables, close cornice, casement windows with solid outside blinds, combine interesting details, all of which contribute to a successful whole and a happy blending of the various units.

COLOR SCHEME SUGGESTED: Cream colored stucco for walls and chimney; dull red tile mission roof; the exterior woodwork stained a grayish-brown tone.

ALTERNATE EXTERIORS: None.

INTERIOR

NUMBER OF ROOMS: 5 Main rooms, Ingle-nook, Bathroom and 5 Closets.

SIZE OF ROOMS:

Living Room	23' 1" x 13' 0"
Dining Room	14' 0" x 13' 0"
Kitchen	10' 0" x 9' 0"
Bed Room	13' 0" x 10' 0"
Bed Room	13' 0" x 10' 0"
Bath Room	9' 0" x 5' 8"

BASEMENT: Partially excavated but of ample size to meet all demands; contains Laundry, Heater-room, Store-room, Fruit-storage and Fuel-bins.

PLAN TYPE: Especially adapted bungalow plan.

DESIGNED TO FACE: East. For other facings, plans should be reversed.

FIREPLACE: One unusual open fireplace in ingle nook with mantel, side seats and built-in bookcases.

VENTILATION: 22 casement windows in banks of four, three and two to an opening; 2 pairs of full length casement doors, opening onto garden porch; 2 outside doors; narrow arched ventilators in the gable ends for free circulation of air under roof.

WALL SPACES: Ample for large pieces of furniture.

CUBIC CONTENTS: Approximately 24,800 cubic feet.

SPECIAL FEATURES

LIVING ROOM: For a house of this size, a room 23 feet long is unusual. It is reached through a front entry containing a generous coat closet. An ingle nook, containing fireplace, seats and bookcase, is the outstanding feature.

DINING ROOM: Opening out of the living room and facing the garden, seen through a large bank of casement windows. It also opens onto the garden porch.

KITCHEN: Well planned and equipped with working space under a triple window. A storage pantry is provided and plenty of cupboards.

REAR ENTRY: Allows direct passage from yard both to kitchen and to basement stairs and provides excellent place for ice box.

BED ROOMS: These rooms are secluded from the living portion of the house by a private hall. Linen closets open from this hall as does the bath room.

PLUMBING: Includes bath tub, lavatory, water closet, laundry tubs, kitchen sink and hot and cold water supply.

ELECTRIC OUTLETS: In the proper places, available for iron, washing machine, vacuum cleaner, toaster, floor and table lamps, heaters, etc., if any or all of them are desired.

House Plan No. 5B7

5B7

FORERUNNERS OF THIS MODERN HOUSE ARE FOUND IN THE SOUTHERN COLONIES, BUILT DURING THE REIGNS OF THE GEORGES OF ENGLAND
TO PEOPLE OF REFINED TASTE WHO APPRECIATE A STRAIGHTFORWARD, CONSERVATIVE DESIGN, THIS HOUSE IS RECOMMENDED

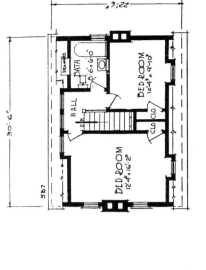

BASEMENT
CEILING HEIGHT 7'-5"

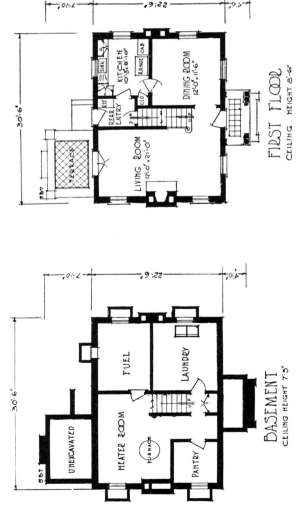

FIRST FLOOR
CEILING HEIGHT 8'-6"

SECOND FLOOR
CEILING HEIGHT 8'-6"

Note—For guidance in reading floor plans, see explanation on page 14

EXTERIOR

STYLE: Southern Colonial Adaptation. Story-and-a-half type.

SIZE OF LOT REQUIRED: From 38 to 40 feet in width.

CONSTRUCTION: Brick on masonry foundations.

FINISH: Brick for walls, gables and chimneys; walls may be stucco or siding if preferred.

PORCHES: Front entrance porch with flat roof; open terrace at rear of living room.

CHIMNEYS: Two outside brick chimneys, each with two flues.

DECORATIVE FEATURES: The house possesses just sufficient architectural elements to relieve it from plainness. The symmetrical arrangement of windows and clean-cut dormers; the porch with its turned columns and wall pilasters; and the right sense of materials give it a most engaging exterior, from every point of view.

COLOR SCHEME SUGGESTED: Broken tones of red brick for the walls; green roof, white paint for the woodwork, and green shutters.

ALTERNATE EXTERIORS: This same basic plan with different exteriors may be found on Pages 60, 76, 82 and 84, House Plan Nos. 5A1, 5B10, 5A21 and 5A24.

INTERIOR

NUMBER OF ROOMS: 5 Main rooms, Bath-room and 3 Closets.

SIZE OF ROOMS:

First Floor

Living Room	12' 0" x 21' 0"
Dining Room	12' 0" x 11' 6"
Kitchen	10' 3" x 8' 10"

Second Floor

Bed Room	12' 4" x 16' 2"
Bed Room	12' 4" x 9' 10"
Bath Room	8' 6" x 6' 0"

BASEMENT: Under entire house, containing Laundry, Heater-room, Storage and Fuel-bins.

PLAN TYPE: Living room running from front to rear; stairs in the center of house.

DESIGNED TO FACE: South and East. For other facings, plans should be reversed.

FIREPLACE: Fine open fireplace in living room, with wood mantel.

VENTILATION: 15 windows with double hung sash; pair French doors opening onto terrace, 2 outside doors.

WALL SPACES: Ample for large pieces of furniture.

CUBIC CONTENTS: Approximately 16,600 cubic feet.

SPECIAL FEATURES

LIVING ROOM: Commodious and comfortable, equally delightful in both winter and summer. Light on three sides, insuring cross ventilation.

COMPACT AND DIRECT PLAN: Little space is wasted in a hall which is merely an entry with the stairway directly opposite the front door. The wide openings into living room and dining room make an ideal first floor arrangement.

KITCHEN: Contains the usual complete equipment and a broom closet. Its working features are compact and well placed, and the two exposures insure a well ventilated room.

REAR ENTRY: Allows direct passage from yard to both kitchen and to basement stairs, and provides space for refrigerator.

BED ROOMS: One especially large room with light on three sides, and one good sized room with plenty of wall space.

BATH ROOM: Extra large for a small house; placed directly over kitchen, cutting plumbing costs. Contains built-in drawer for linen and a medicine cabinet.

PLUMBING: Includes bath tub, lavatory, water closet, kitchen sink, laundry tubs and hot and cold water supply.

ELECTRIC OUTLETS: In the proper places, available for iron, washing machine, vacuum cleaner, toaster, floor and table lamps, heater, etc., if any or all are desired.

HOUSE PLAN NO. 5A8

A DERIVATIVE OF THE BUNGALOW—SUCCESSFUL FROM BOTH ARTISTIC AND UTILITARIAN STANDPOINTS

A HOUSE TO CHALLENGE ADMIRATION FOR IT MEETS MODERN REQUIREMENTS IN A RATIONAL MANNER

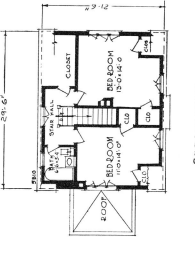

SECOND·FLOOR
CEILING HEIGHT 7'-6"

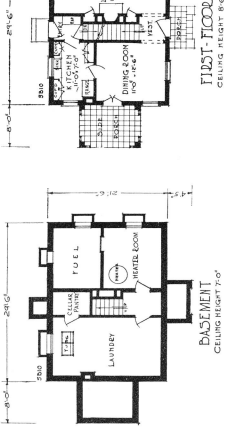

FIRST·FLOOR
CEILING HEIGHT 8'-6"

BASEMENT
CEILING HEIGHT 7'-0"

Note—For guidance in reading floor plans, see explanation on page 14

EXTERIOR

STYLE: Dutch Colonial Adaptation. Story-and-a-half type.

SIZE OF LOT REQUIRED: From 43 to 48 feet in width. Could be accommodated on a 40 foot lot if side porch were placed at the rear.

CONSTRUCTION: Wood frame with brick veneer, on masonry foundations.

FINISH: Walls, wire cut face brick veneer; dormer, wide wood siding; shingled roof.

PORCHES: Side porch providing excellent place to sit and to have one's meals in pleasant weather. Sheltered entrance stoop.

CHIMNEY: Two brick chimneys, one inside and one exterior.

DECORATIVE FEATURES: The well proportioned gambrel roof with its sloping dormers across the front and its Colonial hooded doorway form a harmonious combination of well designed units.

COLOR SCHEME SUGGESTED: Red brick with rough white mortar joints. Roof gray slate color; woodwork and doors white; shutters painted a gray blue.

ALTERNATE EXTERIORS: This same basic plan with different exteriors may be found on Pages 60, 64, 72, 80, 82 and 84. House Plan Nos. 5A1, 5B3, 5B7, 5B13, 5A21 and 5A24.

INTERIOR

NUMBER OF ROOMS: 5 Main rooms, Bath-room and 5 Closets.

SIZE OF ROOMS:

First Floor

Living Room	11' 6" x 20' 0"
Dining Room	11' 0" x 12' 6"
Kitchen	11' 0" x 7' 0"

Second Floor

Bed Room	13' 0" x 14' 0"
Bed Room	11' 0" x 14' 0"
Bath Room	6' 6" x 5' 4"

BASEMENT: Under entire house, containing Laundry, Heater-room, Cellar-pantry and Fuel-bins.

PLAN TYPE: Living room running from front to rear. Central staircase.

DESIGNED TO FACE: South, West or North. For East facing, plans should be reversed.

FIREPLACE: One large fireplace on inside wall of living room with well designed mantel.

VENTILATION: 9 double hung windows; 12 casement windows; 1 pair French doors, opening onto porch; 2 outside doors. Louvres in gable ends for free circulation of air under roof.

WALL SPACES: Ample for large pieces of furniture.

CUBIC CONTENTS: Approximately 17,600 cubic feet.

SPECIAL FEATURES

LIVING ROOM: Extending the full depth of the house with well placed windows on three sides, insuring abundance of air and sunshine. Bookcases on each side of fireplace making a balanced composition.

DINING ROOM: Placed opposite living room, and separated from it by a small entrance hall. Windows on two sides and opens onto attractive porch with brick columns and trellised panels.

KITCHEN: Rectangular shape, cross ventilation. Modern fixtures placed in practical manner.

REAR ENTRY: Allows direct passage from yard to both kitchen and to basement stairs and provides space for refrigerator.

BED ROOMS: Two spacious rooms with two closets for each. Windows on two sides.

BATH ROOM: Placed directly over kitchen, insuring minimum plumbing costs. Contains built-in medicine cabinet.

ADDITIONAL STORAGE CLOSET: Large space opening off the upstairs hall.

PLUMBING: Includes bath tub, lavatory, and water closet, laundry tubs, kitchen sink, and hot and cold water supply.

ELECTRIC OUTLETS: In the proper places, available for iron, washing machine, vacuum cleaner, toaster, floor and table lamps, heaters, if any or all are desired.

HOUSE PLAN NO. 5B11

5B11

A SUCCESSFUL COMBINATION OF NEW ENGLAND CLASSIC DETAILS WITH THE MODIFIED PATIO PLAN OF SPAIN

AN HONEST BUNGALOW TYPE EMBODYING RIGID ECONOMY, GOOD PROPORTION AND THE GRACE THAT DISTINGUISHES THE ARCHITECTURE OF THE EARLY REPUBLIC

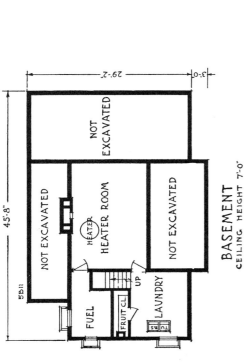

BASEMENT
CEILING HEIGHT 7'-0"

FIRST FLOOR
CEILING HEIGHT 8'-6"

Note—For guidance in reading floor plans, see explanation on page 14

EXTERIOR

STYLE: Combined Colonial and Classic. Bungalow type.

SIZE OF LOT REQUIRED: About 55 feet in width if placed on inside lot; will go on a corner lot 40 to 45 feet in width on one street.

CONSTRUCTION: Wood frame on masonry foundations.

FINISH: Wide wood siding. Roof shingled.

PORCHES: Two broad porches 19' 6" in length. The front porch is recessed within the main walls and projects slightly in front.

CHIMNEY: One interior chimney containing the heater and fireplace flues.

DECORATIVE FEATURES: The projection of the front porch diversifies the main exterior and is supported on columns of a simple but attractive design. The long, sloping roof line tends to tie the house and the ground together. The windows are well placed and of good proportion.

COLOR SCHEME SUGGESTED: Outside walls, doors and frames should be painted white, shutters and roof shingles green, and the chimney red.

ALTERNATE EXTERIORS: None.

INTERIOR

NUMBER OF ROOMS: 5 Main rooms, Bath-room and 2 Closets, all on one floor.

SIZE OF ROOMS:

Living Room	19' 6" x 13' 6"
Dining Room	12' 0" x 11' 0"
Kitchen	8' 6" x 9' 4"
Bed Room	12' 0" x 9' 0"
Bed Room	12' 0" x 9' 0"
Bath Room	8' 2" x 5' 0"

BASEMENT: Partially excavated; containing Laundry, Heater-room, Fruit-closet and Fuel-bins.

PLAN TYPE: Bungalow with living room as central feature.

DESIGNED TO FACE: East, North or South. For West facing, plans should be reversed.

FIREPLACE: One large open fireplace in living room.

VENTILATION: 11 windows with double hung sash; 3 pairs French doors, 2 from living room to terrace, 1 from dining room to porch; 2 outside doors. Circular windows in gable ends to admit air under roof.

WALL SPACES: Ample for large pieces of furniture.

CUBIC CONTENTS: Approximately 19,900 cubic feet.

SPECIAL FEATURES

LIVING ROOM: The nucleus of the plan, it is large and well shaped, opens into every part of the house, and yet has not the appearance of a thoroughfare. The French doors on each side of the fireplace make an attractive wall treatment and offer a pleasant vista from the front porch.

DINING ROOM: The spaciousness of a dining room combined with the convenience of a dining alcove. Opens, by French doors, onto front porch.

KITCHEN: Unusually compact and well arranged; excellent light and ventilation; stairs directly to cellar. Large cupboards.

REAR ENTRY: Large enough to contain ice box and to serve as a kitchen porch. Has double windows as well as door.

BEDROOM HALL: From which bedrooms and bath room open. Insures privacy.

PLUMBING: Includes bath tub, lavatory, water closet, laundry tubs, kitchen sink, hot and cold water supply.

ELECTRIC OUTLETS: In proper places, available for iron, washing machine, vacuum cleaner, toaster, floor and table lamps, heaters, etc., if any or all of them are desired.

HOUSE PLAN No. 5B13

5B13

THE STEEPLY PITCHED GABLES, AMPLE WALL SPACE AND CLOSE EAVES SUGGEST THE COTTAGES OF ENGLAND
THE RECTANGULAR PLAN ASSURES ECONOMICAL BUILDING COSTS AND ITS ARRANGEMENT GIVES REAL SERVICE

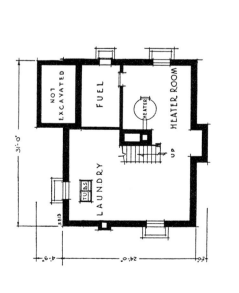

SECOND FLOOR
CEILING HEIGHT 8'-0"

BED ROOM
11'-6" x 17'-0"

HALL

CLOS.

CLOS.

BED ROOM
11'-6" x 13'-3"

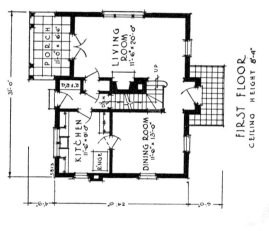

FIRST FLOOR
CEILING HEIGHT 8'-4"

PORCH
11'-0" x 6'-6"

LIVING ROOM
11'-6" x 20'-0"

KITCHEN
11'-6" x 9'-0"

DINING ROOM
11'-6" x 13'-0"

RANGE

31'-0"

24'-0"

9'-0"

BASEMENT
CEILING HEIGHT 7'-6"

NOT EXCAVATED

FUEL

LAUNDRY

TUBS

HEATER ROOM

HEATER

31'-0"

24'-0"

9'-0"

Note—For guidance in reading floor plans, see explanation on page 14

INTERIOR

NUMBER OF ROOMS: 5 Main rooms, Bath-room and 4 Closets.

SIZE OF ROOMS:

First Floor

Living Room	11' 6" x 20' 0"
Dining Room	11' 6" x 13' 0"
Kitchen	11' 6" x 9' 0"

Second Floor

Bed Room	11' 6" x 13' 3"
Bed Room	11' 6" x 17' 0"
Bath Room	7' 8" x 5' 0"

BASEMENT: Under entire house, containing Laundry, Heater-room, Storage-space and Fuel-bins.

PLAN TYPE: Living room running from front to rear; stairs in center of house.

DESIGNED TO FACE: West or North. For other facings, plans should be reversed.

FIREPLACE: One large open fireplace in the inside wall of the living room. Attractive wood mantel.

VENTILATION: 16 windows with double hung sash; 2 outside doors and full length casement windows opening onto porch.

WALL SPACES: Excellent spaces for large pieces of furniture.

CUBIC CONTENTS: Approximately 18,000 cubic feet.

SPECIAL FEATURES

LIVING ROOM: Extends full length of lower floor, with windows on three sides and opens onto the garden porch.

DINING ROOM: Opens off the hall directly across from the living room, and has direct communication with the kitchen.

KITCHEN: Possesses all the qualifications essential to the modern kitchen.

REAR ENTRY: Serves the kitchen and the basement and also provides a place for the refrigerator.

BED ROOMS: Have cross ventilation from three sides and each has a large closet.

LINEN CLOSET: In the upstairs hall well located in relation to bedrooms and bath room.

PLUMBING: Includes bath tub, lavatory and water closet, laundry tubs, kitchen sink and hot and cold water supply.

ELECTRIC OUTLETS: In the proper places, available for iron, washing machine, vacuum cleaner, toaster, floor and table lamps, heaters, etc., if any or all of them are desired.

EXTERIOR

STYLE: Georgian. Story-and-a-half type.

SIZE OF LOT REQUIRED: From 40 to 50 feet in width.

CONSTRUCTION: Brick for exterior walls on masonry foundations.

FINISH: Stiff mud or tapestry brick; roof, slate or shingled.

PORCHES: Garden porch 11' 0" x 6' 6", arranged to be screened for summer, or enclosed with glass for winter use. Front entrance stoop, sheltered by the projection of the main roof.

CHIMNEY: Central brick chimney containing flues for heater and fireplace. Separate flue for kitchen range.

DECORATIVE FEATURES: The ingenious extension of the main roof over the entrance doorway is interesting and softens the general outline, helping to produce a low effect. Dormer windows just the right size and scale.

COLOR SCHEME SUGGESTED: Brick should be deep tones of reds or browns. The roof should be a slate color; the doors, sash and blinds painted an apple green or a mahogany brown, and dormers painted white.

ALTERNATE EXTERIORS: This same basic plan with different exteriors may be found on Pages 60, 64, 72, 76, 82 and 84, House Plan Nos. 5A1, 5B3, 5B7, 5B10, 5A21 and 5A24.

Architects' Small House Service Bureau

Northwestern Division

A HAPPY MEDIUM BETWEEN THE MODERATE SIZE HOUSE AND THE BUNGALOW, FOLLOWING THE GENERAL LINES OF THE DUTCH COLONIAL STYLE

IT IS ECONOMICAL IN CONSTRUCTION, BUT NOTHING HAS BEEN OMITTED TO MAKE IT PRACTICAL

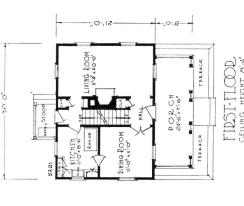

SECOND·FLOOR
CEILING HEIGHT 8'-0"

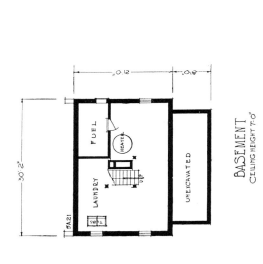

FIRST·FLOOR
CEILING HEIGHT 8'-4"

Note—For guidance in reading floor plans, see explanation on page 14

BASEMENT
CEILING HEIGHT 7'-0"

EXTERIOR

STYLE: Modified Dutch Colonial. Story-and-a-half type.

SIZE OF LOT REQUIRED: From 35 to 40 feet in width.

CONSTRUCTION: Wood frame on masonry foundations, cement base course.

FINISH: Wood siding for walls; shingled roof.

PORCHES: Living porch across the front, 24' 6" x 7' 6"; rear stoop under main roof.

CHIMNEY: One inside brick chimney, containing the heater and fireplace flues.

DECORATIVE FEATURES: Cutting in the roof is a pleasing variation from the projecting dormers; the mass of the house is shapely, the height reduced by bringing the roof down with a generous projection of the eaves; the porch columns are graceful and spaced so that they give the appearance of strength without being heavy in themselves. The lattice invites vines.

COLOR SCHEME SUGGESTED: Outside walls, doors and window frames painted white; front door and shutters green; roof stained brown or green.

ALTERNATE EXTERIORS: This same basic plan with different exteriors may be found on Pages 60, 64, 76, 80 and 84, House Plan Nos. 5A1, 5B3, 5B10, 5B13 and 5A24.

INTERIOR

NUMBER OF ROOMS: 5 Main rooms, Bath-room and 6 Closets.

SIZE OF ROOMS:

First Floor

Living Room	11' 3" x 20' 0"
Dining Room	11' 0" x 11' 0"
Kitchen	11' 0" x 8' 6"

Second Floor

Bed Room	11' 2" x 16' 6"
Bed Room	11' 2" x 10' 6"
Bath Room	7' 3" x 5' 6"

BASEMENT: Under the main portion of the house, containing Laundry, Heater-room, and Fuel-bins.

PLAN TYPE: Living room running from front to rear; stairway in center of the house.

DESIGNED TO FACE: North or West. For other facings, plans should be reversed.

FIREPLACE: One large open fireplace in center of inside wall of living room.

VENTILATION: 12 windows, with double hung sash; 3 pairs of casement windows in dormers; 2 outside doors; louvres in gable ends to permit free circulation of air under roof.

WALL SPACES: Ample for large pieces of furniture.

CUBIC CONTENTS: Approximately 17,500 cubic feet.

SPECIAL FEATURES

FIRST FLOOR SPACE: The plan hinges around a large central chimney; it is flush with the sides of the living room; its depth is made use of for a coat closet in the hall and for a broom closet in rear hall, and for a closet for the living room; there are doors from the hall to the dining room for privacy; the stairs are well lighted by windows in second story hall.

SECOND FLOOR SPACE: Surprisingly commodious with adequate stair hall from which the two bed rooms, bath room and linen closet open. The bed rooms are large, each with a closet and each with windows on two sides.

KITCHEN: Its full equipment is compact and well placed; two exposures insure a light and well ventilated room.

REAR STOOP AND ENTRY: The main roof is brought down to shelter the stoop and provide a place for the ice box. It will be most useful for a summer kitchen. Basement may be reached directly from out-of-doors through the entry.

PLUMBING: The bath room is over the kitchen, a thrifty arrangement; the fixtures include bath tub, lavatory, water closet, laundry tubs, kitchen sink, hot and cold water supply.

ELECTRIC OUTLETS: Properly placed, available for iron, washing machine, vacuum cleaner, toaster, floor and table lamps, heaters, etc., if any or all of them are desired.

HOUSE PLAN NO. 5A24

A CHARMING COMBINATION OF A COLONIAL FRONT WITH AN ENGLISH ROOF IN A SMALL FORMAL HOUSE

A STRAIGHTFORWARD PLAN THAT UTILIZES THE SPACE WITHOUT WASTE, AND PROVIDES ALL DESIRED CONVENIENCES

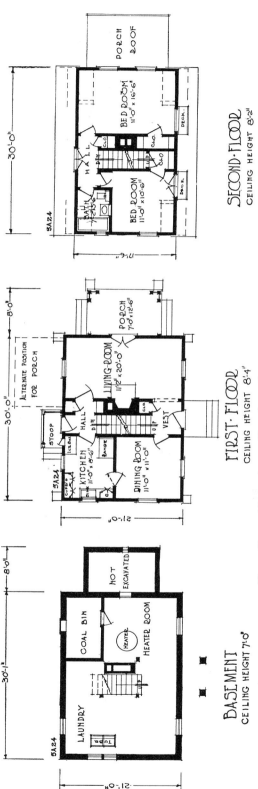

SECOND·FLOOR
CEILING HEIGHT 8'-2"

BED ROOM 11'-0" x 16'-6"

HALL

BATH 7'-2" x 5'-6"

BED ROOM 11'-0" x 10'-6"

DECK

DECK

CLO

CLO

CLO

5A24

30'-0"

17'-6"

FIRST·FLOOR
CEILING HEIGHT 8'-4"

LIVING·ROOM 11'-2" x 20'-0"

PORCH 7'-0" x 12'-6"

HALL

VEST

KITCHEN 11'-0" x 8'-6"

DINING ROOM 11'-0" x 11'-0"

STOOP

CLO

RANGE

CUPBD

ICE BOX

ALTERNATE POSITION FOR PORCH

5A24

30'-0"

8'-0"

21'-0"

BASEMENT
CEILING HEIGHT 7'-0"

COAL BIN

NOT EXCAVATED

HEATER ROOM

HEATER

LAUNDRY

TUBS

5A24

30'-1"

8'-0"

21'-0"

Note—For guidance in reading floor plans, see explanation on page 14

EXTERIOR

STYLE: Combined Colonial and English. Story-and-a-half type.

SIZE OF LOT REQUIRED: From 35 to 48 feet in width if placed as illustrated; from 26 to 39 feet in width if the gable end is placed toward street with stoop at the side.

CONSTRUCTION: Wood frame on masonry foundations.

FINISH: Wood shingles, wood siding, or stucco for walls; shingled roof; wood frontispiece and trellis.

PORCHES. Entrance stoop; living porch, 7'0" x 12'6", which may be placed at the side or in the rear as indicated by the dotted lines; rear stoop.

CHIMNEY: One inside brick chimney containing the heater and fireplace flues.

DECORATIVE FEATURES: Designs like this, with white walls, dark roof and quaint blinds in harmonizing color, produce a striking effect as far away as the house can be seen; yet the detail is so well conceived that it can be looked at, even touched with the hand without becoming coarse and ugly; the purity of Colonial detail is evident in the first story, and the steeply pitched roof with resulting end gable are English in character.

COLOR SCHEME SUGGESTED: Walls and trim painted white; blinds bottle green; roof stained variegated greens and browns.

ALTERNATE EXTERIORS: This same basic plan, with different exteriors may be found on Pages 60, 64, 76, 80 and 82. House Plan Nos. 5A1, 5B3, 5B10, 5B13 and 5A21.

INTERIOR

NUMBER OF ROOMS: 5 Main rooms, Bath-room and 6 Closets.

SIZE OF ROOMS:

First Floor

Living Room	11' 2" x 20' 0"
Dining Room	11' 0" x 11' 0"
Kitchen	11' 0" x 8' 6"

Second Floor

Bed Room	11' 0" x 16' 6"
Bed Room	11' 0" x 10' 6"
Bath Room	7' 2" x 5' 6"

BASEMENT: Under the main portion of the house, containing Laundry, Heater-room and Fuel-bins.

PLAN TYPE: Living room running from front to rear; stairway in the center of the house.

DESIGNED TO FACE: North or West. For other facings, plans should be reversed.

FIREPLACE: One large open fireplace in center of inside wall of living room.

VENTILATION: 10 windows with double hung sash; 6 casement windows in dormers; pair of French doors opening from living room onto the porch; 2 outside doors; louvres in gable ends for free circulation of air under roof.

WALL SPACES: Ample for large pieces of furniture.

CUBIC CONTENTS: Approximately 17,500 cubic feet.

SPECIAL FEATURES

LIVING ROOM: Everything that its name implies; it is large, sunny, and has the two necessities of a year 'round house, the porch for summer use, and the fireplace to gather 'round in winter; it has the unusual advantage of being accessible three ways; from the vestibule, from the rear hall and from the porch, a surprisingly useful feature.

KITCHEN: Invites the housekeeper's interest; it is step-saving, light and contains all the fixtures she could possibly need just where she wants them. The stoop is not only for passage to the kitchen and to the basement, it is sufficiently screened from view to allow one to use it as a summer kitchen; the ice box is iced from outside.

BED ROOMS: Both rooms have windows on two sides, and each has its own closet. The bath room, provided with a built-in medicine cabinet, is but a step from each.

SPECIAL CLOSETS: On the first floor are a coat closet in the vestibule, a broom closet and also a general catch-all off the living room; on the second floor, a linen closet.

PLUMBING: The bath room is over the kitchen, a thrifty arrangement; the fixtures include bath tub, lavatory, water closet, laundry tubs, kitchen sink and hot and cold water supply.

ELECTRIC OUTLETS: Properly placed, available for iron, washing machine, vacuum cleaner, toaster, floor and table lamps, heater, etc., if any or all of them are desired.

85

5A28

A HOUSE WHERE THE SIMPLEST SPANISH MOTIVES HAVE BEEN USED IN THE SIMPLEST POSSIBLE WAY
EASY AND SIMPLE TO CONSTRUCT, ADAPTABLE TO BOTH WARM AND COLD CLIMATES, AND FULL OF TRADITIONAL ATMOSPHERE

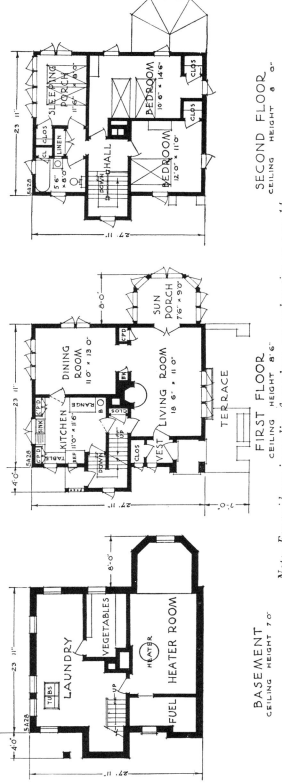

BASEMENT
CEILING HEIGHT 7'0"

FIRST FLOOR
CEILING HEIGHT 8'6"

SECOND FLOOR
CEILING HEIGHT 8'0"

Note—For guidance in reading floor plans, see explanation on page 14

EXTERIOR

STYLE: Spanish Adaptation. Full two-story type.

SIZE OF LOT REQUIRED: From 41 to 46 feet in width.

CONSTRUCTION: Wood frame on masonry foundations, carried above grade; may be solid masonry.

FINISH: Stucco with brick or stucco second story sill course; Spanish tile roof.

PORCHES: Recessed entrance porch; and large sun porch, 7' 6" x 9' 0", which is fully enclosed and is really part of the living room.

CHIMNEY: One central brick chimney, containing the heater, fireplace and kitchen range flues.

DECORATIVE FEATURES: Simplicity, enriched by the grouping of windows, arched entrance and hospitable tile roof, with wide projecting eaves, casting a deep shadow. Square outline relieved by the projection of the stair enclosure and by the tile capped buttress. The circular headed lattice provided for clinging vines serves as a pleasing balance for the entrance.

COLOR SCHEME SUGGESTED: Cream colored stucco with floated finish for walls; red brick sill course; variegated tile roof; exterior woodwork painted a dull blue.

ALTERNATE EXTERIORS: This same basic plan, with different exteriors, may be found on Pages 88, 92, 94, 96, 98 and 100, House Plan Nos. 5A29, 5A33, 5A34, 5A36, 5A38 and 5A43.

INTERIOR

NUMBER OF ROOMS: 5 Main rooms, Bath-room, Sleeping Porch, Sun Porch and 7 Closets.

SIZE OF ROOMS:

First Floor

Living Room	18' 6" x 11' 0"
Dining Room	11' 0" x 13' 0"
Kitchen	11' 0" x 11' 6"

Second Floor

Bed Room	12' 0" x 11' 0"
Bed Room	10' 6" x 14' 6"
Bath Room	5' 6" x 8' 0"
Sleeping Porch	11' 6" x 8' 0"

BASEMENT: Under entire house, containing Laundry, Heater-room, Vegetable-storage, and Fuel-bins.

PLAN TYPE: Living room running across the front of the house. Stairs at one side.

DESIGNED TO FACE: South or West. For other facings, plans should be reversed.

FIREPLACE: The fireplace in the living room has a dignified wood mantel, and arched recess above, carrying out the spirit of the design.

VENTILATION: 27 casement windows, in main house; 8 casement windows in sun porch; 2 outside doors.

WALL SPACES: Ample for large pieces of furniture.

CUBIC CONTENTS: Approximately 20,800 cubic feet.

SPECIAL FEATURES

ENTRANCE VESTIBULE: Good sized vestibule and well-lighted coat closet.

LIVING ROOM AND SUN ROOM: Are so arranged on a long axis that they increase the open, spacious effect of the room. At the left of the cased opening leading into the dining room is a built-in bookcase, with glazed doors, and at the right, opening into the living room, is a closet with solid door, that will be convenient for storage.

STAIRS: Are convenient to every room in the house.

KITCHEN: A model of economical planning; has direct passage to stairs and to front door; refrigerator iced from outside; broom closet at foot of stairs.

REAR ENTRY: Enabling one to go directly to basement from outside and providing entrance to kitchen.

BED ROOMS AND SLEEPING PORCH: Two large airy rooms and a generous sleeping porch, with six windows and a closet.

LINEN CLOSET AND BATH ROOM CLOSET: Large linen closet in upper hall, and closet with drawers and a medicine cabinet in the bath room.

PLUMBING: Includes bath tub, lavatory, water closet, laundry tubs, kitchen sink, water supply.

ELECTRIC OUTLETS: Properly placed, available for iron, washing machine, vacuum cleaner, toaster, floor and table lamps, heater, etc.

Architects' Small House Service Bureau

Northwestern Division

5A29

BORROWING AGAIN FROM THE DUTCH COLONISTS BUT USING THE VERY AMERICAN DORMER WINDOW TO COMPLETE THE DESIGN

A HOUSE WITHOUT A TRACE OF AFFECTATION, AND OBVIOUSLY ONE THAT WILL BE IN HARMONY WITH THE LIFE WITHIN AND ABOUT IT

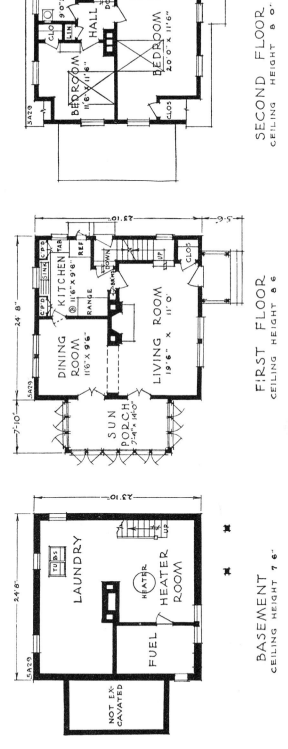

SECOND FLOOR
CEILING HEIGHT 8'0"

FIRST FLOOR
CEILING HEIGHT 8'6"

BASEMENT
CEILING HEIGHT 7'6"

Note—For guidance in reading floor plans, see explanation on page 14

EXTERIOR

STYLE: Modified Dutch Colonial. Story-and-a-half type.

SIZE OF LOT REQUIRED: From 37 to 43 feet in width.

CONSTRUCTION: Wood frame on masonry foundations, brick base course.

FINISH: Wood siding for walls; roof shingled.

PORCHES: Entrance porch; and glazed-in sun porch, 7' 4" x 14' 0".

CHIMNEY: One interior brick chimney containing the heater, fireplace and kitchen range flues.

DECORATIVE FEATURES: The sun porch gives additional width to the house; the gambrel roof and the wide dormers, front and back add charm to the composition.

COLOR SCHEME SUGGESTED: Siding painted white and roof shingles stained variegated green; shutters and door apple green; window frames white.

ALTERNATE EXTERIORS: This same basic plan with different exteriors can be found on Pages 86, 88, 92, 94, 96, 98 and 100, House Plan Nos. 5A28, 5A29, 5A33, 5A34, 5A36, 5A38 and 5A43.

INTERIOR

NUMBER OF ROOMS: 5 Main rooms, Bath-room and 5 Closets.

SIZE OF ROOMS:

First Floor

Living Room	19' 6" x 11' 0"
Dining Room	11' 6" x 9' 6"
Kitchen	11' 6" x 9' 6"

Second Floor

Bed Room	20' 0" x 11' 6"
Bed Room	11' 6" x 11' 6"
Bath Room	9' 0" x 7' 6"

BASEMENT: Under main portion of house, containing Laundry, Heater-room, Vegetable-storage, and Fuel-bins.

PLAN TYPE: Living room running across front of the house.

DESIGNED TO FACE: South or East. For other facings, plans should be reversed.

FIREPLACE: One large open fireplace in living room, with wide wood mantel shelf.

VENTILATION: 14 windows with double hung sash, 12 casement windows in sun porch, louvre in gable ends to ventilate attic.

WALL SPACES: Ample for large pieces of furniture.

CUBIC CONTENTS: Approximately 18,500 cubic feet.

SPECIAL FEATURES

THE STAIRWAY: Ascends from the end of the living room and no space is wasted by stair hall.

THE FIRST FLOOR: Opens up in impressive fashion; living room, dining room and sun room are practically one great big room.

KITCHEN: Is well planned with light and ventilation on two sides. Refrigerator is in kitchen but has an outside icing door. Direct access to front door and stairs.

BASEMENT STAIRS: Descend from a landing leading from the side entrance two steps below the kitchen floor level.

BED ROOMS: Each have a closet and light and air from two sides; the front bedroom has two closets.

LINEN CLOSET: In the upper hall.

BROOM CLOSET: In the kitchen.

COAT CLOSET: At right of the entrance door.

PLUMBING: Includes bath tub, lavatory, water closet, kitchen sink, laundry tubs and hot and cold water supply.

ELECTRIC OUTLETS: In the proper places available for iron, washing machine, vacuum cleaner, toaster, floor and table lamps, heaters, etc., if any or all of them are desired.

Architects' Small House Service Bureau

Northwestern Division

TRANSLATING THE FORMS OF AN OLD DUTCH FARMHOUSE INTO A HOME OF VARIED BEAUTY AND CONTINUING PLEASURE

NO WASTE OF SPACE OR MATERIALS, WHICH MEANS REAL SERVICE TO THOSE ABOUT TO INVEST THEIR MONEY IN A HOME

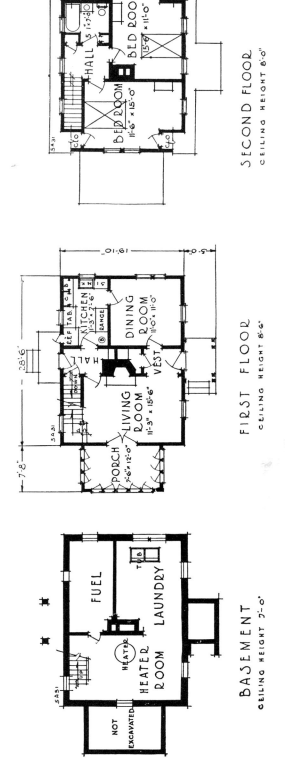

SECOND FLOOR
CEILING HEIGHT 8'-0"

FIRST FLOOR
CEILING HEIGHT 8'-6"

BASEMENT
CEILING HEIGHT 7'-0"

Note—For guidance in reading floor plans, see explanation on page 14

EXTERIOR

STYLE: Dutch Colonial Adaptation. Story-and-a-half type.

SIZE OF LOT REQUIRED: From 30 to 35 feet in width if sun porch is toward street; from 42 to 47 feet in width if entrance stoop is toward street.

CONSTRUCTION: Wood frame on masonry foundations, brick base course.

FINISH: Design shows wide wood siding; may be shingles or stucco. Roof shingled.

PORCHES: Glazed-in sun porch, 7' 6" x 12' 0". Covered entrance stoop with brick flooring; rear open platform.

CHIMNEY: One brick chimney with heater and fireplace flues.

DECORATIVE FEATURES: The gambrel roof and large dormer window. The commodious glazed porch and the covered entrance doorway.

COLOR SCHEME SUGGESTED: White siding, variegated green roof and bottle green blinds and door.

ALTERNATE EXTERIORS: This same basic plan with different exteriors can be found on Pages 38, 52 and 92, House Plan Nos. 6A15, 6A31 and 5A33.

INTERIOR

NUMBER OF ROOMS: 5 Main rooms, Bath-room and 8 Closets.

SIZE OF ROOMS:

First Floor

Living Room	11' 3" x 15' 6"
Dining Room	11' 0" x 11' 0"
Kitchen	11' 3" x 7' 6"

Second Floor

Bed Room	15' 6" x 11' 0"
Bed Room	11' 6" x 15' 0"
Bath Room	5' 1" x 7' 0"

BASEMENT: Under the entire house, containing Laundry, Heater-room, and Fuel-bins.

PLAN TYPE: Living room running from front to back, stairway at one end of living room.

DESIGNED TO FACE: Front corner of living room toward the Southwest.

FIREPLACE: One large open fireplace in the inside wall of the living room.

VENTILATION: 16 windows with double hung sash; 11 casement windows in sun porch; 2 outside doors.

WALL SPACES: Ample for large pieces of furniture.

CUBIC CONTENTS: Approximately 17,000 cubic feet.

SPECIAL FEATURES

THE OPEN STAIRWAY: Which ascends from the living room is a space saving arrangement.

VESTIBULE: Is provided with deep coat closet.

KITCHEN: Is compact, well lighted by windows on two sides and equipped with built-in cupboards and table. Refrigerator is in this room, but has outside icing door.

BASEMENT STAIRS: Descend from rear hall near back entrance and go under main stairs.

BED ROOMS: Are light and airy, and each has two closets and cross ventilation.

LINEN CLOSET: At the head of the stairs, in the upper hall, and towel closet in bath room.

MEDICINE CABINET: In the bath room.

PLUMBING: Includes bath tub, lavatory, water closet, kitchen sink, laundry tubs and hot and cold water supply.

ELECTRIC OUTLETS: In the proper places, available for iron, washing machine, vacuum cleaner, toaster, floor and table lamps, heaters, etc., if any or all of them are desired.

OLD ENGLAND SOUNDS AN EMPHATIC NOTE IN THIS QUAINT AND CHARMING HOME

A HOUSE WITH A WEALTH OF ROOM FOR ITS SIZE, DESIGNED AND PLANNED SO THAT IT WILL BE REASONABLE TO BUILD

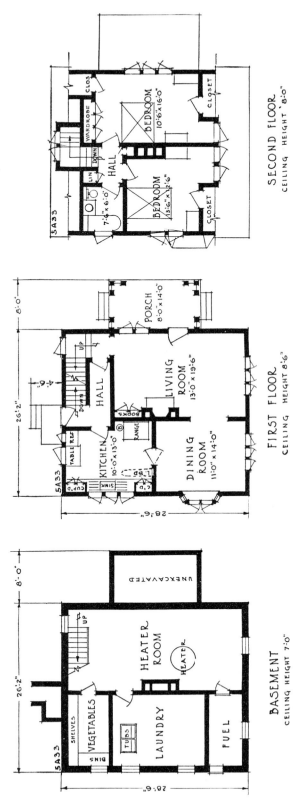

BASEMENT
CEILING HEIGHT 7'-0"

FIRST FLOOR
CEILING HEIGHT 8'-6"

SECOND FLOOR
CEILING HEIGHT 8'-0"

Note—For guidance in reading floor plans, see explanation on page 14

EXTERIOR

STYLE: English Domestic. One-and-a-half story type.

SIZE OF LOT REQUIRED: From 39 to 44 feet in width. House can be faced in either of two ways with respect to the street.

CONSTRUCTION: Wood frame on masonry foundations.

FINISH: Stucco walls; roof shingled.

PORCHES: Living porch opening from living room, 8' 0" x 14'0".

CHIMNEY: One interior chimney, containing heater, fireplace and kitchen range flues.

COLOR SCHEME SUGGESTED: Cream white stucco walls with variegated stained roof.

DECORATIVE FEATURES: Lattices on corners of porch make excellent braces for vines.

ALTERNATE EXTERIORS: This same basic plan, with different exteriors can be found on Pages 38, 52 and 90, House Plan Nos. 6A15, 6A31 and 5A31.

INTERIOR

NUMBER OF ROOMS: 5 Main rooms, Bath-room and 6 Closets.

SIZE OF ROOMS:

	First Floor		
Living Room	13' 0" x 19' 6"		
Dining Room	11' 0" x 14' 0"		
Kitchen	10' 0" x 13' 0"		

	Second Floor		
Bed Room	13' 6" x 12' 6"		
Bed Room	10' 6" x 16' 0"		
Bath Room	7' 6" x 6' 0"		

BASEMENT: Under entire house, containing Laundry, Heater-room, Vegetable-storage and Fuel-bins.

PLAN TYPE: Living room and dining room dividing the front.

DESIGNED TO FACE: Outside corner of living room toward southwest.

FIREPLACE: One large open fireplace in living room.

VENTILATION: 26 casement windows, arranged for cross ventilation; 2 outside doors.

WALL SPACES: Ample for large pieces of furniture.

CUBIC CONTENTS: 22,700 cubic feet.

SPECIAL FEATURES

STORAGE SPACE IN ATTIC: Reached through a scuttle in second floor hall.

DELIVERY OF ICE DIRECT TO ICE BOX: Without entering the house.

CUPBOARDS AND DRESSERS: In the kitchen.

BUILT-IN IRONING AND PRESSING BOARD: In the kitchen.

BAY WINDOW: In the dining room.

BUILT-IN BOOK CASE: In the living room.

LINEN CLOSET: In the second floor hall.

BUILT-IN WARDROBE: In the main bedroom.

PLUMBING: Includes bath tub, water closet, lavatory, kitchen sink, laundry tubs and hot and cold water supply.

ELECTRIC OUTLETS: In the proper places, available for iron, washing machine, vacuum cleaner, toaster, floor and table lamps, heaters, etc., if any or all of them are desired.

HOUSE PLAN NO. 5A34

Architects' Small House Service Bureau

TO CATCH AND REPRODUCE THE CHARM OF A EUROPEAN STYLE AND STILL CONFORM TO AMERICAN REQUIREMENTS IS AN ACHIEVEMENT

PROVING THAT A SMALL HOUSE CAN BE PRACTICAL, ECONOMICAL AND AT THE SAME TIME HAVE GOOD DESIGN

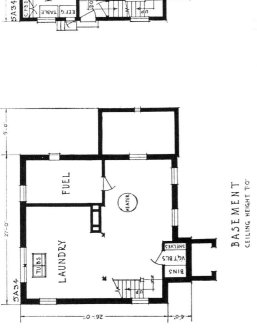

BASEMENT
CEILING HEIGHT 7'0"

FIRST FLOOR
CEILING HEIGHT 8'6"

SECOND FLOOR
CEILING HEIGHT 8'-0"

Note—For guidance in reading floor plans, see explanation on page 14

EXTERIOR

STYLE: Reflection of English forms. Story-and-a-half type.

SIZE OF LOT REQUIRED: From 41 to 46 feet in width.

CONSTRUCTION: Wood frame on masonry foundations; cement base course.

FINISH: Wood siding for walls; moulded wood trim for doorway; shingled roof.

PORCHES: Glazed-in living porch 8' 0" x 13' 0" opening off living room; entrance stoop.

CHIMNEY: One inside brick chimney, containing the furnace, fireplace and kitchen range flues.

DECORATIVE FEATURES: The roof plays an important part in the design; the ridge pole is very high, which makes it possible to get rooms on the second floor; the long sweep of the roof is interrupted by the four window dormer and by the high-pitched gable over the vestibule. The doorway is the focal point of interest on the first floor.

COLOR SCHEME SUGGESTED: Siding painted white; trim cream color; roof stained variegated brown greens.

ALTERNATE EXTERIORS: This same basic plan, with different exteriors, may be found on Pages 86, 88, 92, 96, 98 and 100, House Plan Nos. 5A28, 5A29, 5A33, 5A36, 5A38 and 5A43.

INTERIOR

NUMBER OF ROOMS: 5 Main rooms, Bath-room, and 7 Closets.

SIZE OF ROOMS:

First Floor

Living Room	22' 0" x 13' 0"
Dining Room	13' 0" x 11' 0"
Kitchen	12' 6" x 9' 6"

Second Floor

Bed Room	19' 0" x 10' 0"
Bed Room	14' 6" x 11' 0"
Bath Room	6' 0" x 7' 6"

BASEMENT: Under the entire house, containing Laundry, Heater-room, Vegetable-storage and Fuel-bins.

PLAN TYPE: Living room running across the front of the house; stairs at one side, going up the side wall.

DESIGNED TO FACE: South or West. For other facings, plans should be reversed.

FIREPLACE: One large open fireplace in center of inside wall of living room. Wood mantel.

VENTILATION: 22 windows with double hung sash; 2 outside doors; semi-circular windows in gable ends for free circulation of air under roofs.

WALL SPACES: Ample for large pieces of furniture.

CUBIC CONTENTS: Approximately 25,500 cubic feet.

SPECIAL FEATURES

ENTRANCE VESTIBULE: An added convenience, containing a hat and coat closet.

LIVING ROOM: A large, well-lighted room, with exposures on three sides; the window which lights the stair landing is really in this room, as the stairs are open; the wide trimmed opening into the dining room adds to the apparent size of both rooms, and the rear windows in the dining room give a fourth outlook to the living room.

KITCHEN: Equipped with all modern conveniences for doing work with the fewest steps and least labor; direct passage from kitchen to front door and to stairway. Outside icing for ice box.

SIDE ENTRY: Serves the kitchen and basement with direct passage out-of-doors; handy closet provided for brooms, etc.

SECOND FLOOR: Besides the two light, airy bed rooms and the bath room, there is a linen closet, an extra hall closet and a large storage room over the porch.

PLUMBING: Includes bath tub, lavatory, water closet, laundry tubs, kitchen sink, hot and cold water supply.

ELECTRIC OUTLETS: Properly placed, available for iron, washing machine, vacuum cleaner, toaster, floor and table lamps, heaters, etc., if any or all of them are desired.

HOUSE PLAN NO. 5A36

Architects' Small House Service Bureau

COMBINING THE MANY DESIRES OF THE HOME BUILDER AND SECURING FOR HIM THE QUALITIES HE UNCONSCIOUSLY ADMIRES

A HOUSE ESPECIALLY ADAPTED FOR A NARROW LOT, MEETING THE DEMAND FOR COMPACTNESS OF PLAN AND RIGID ECONOMY

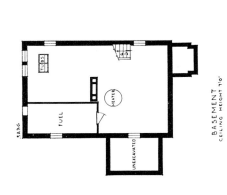

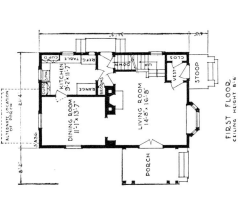

SECOND FLOOR
CEILING HEIGHT 8'0"

BED ROOM
11'-11" x 12'-2"

BED ROOM
14'-8" x 16'-8"

ROOF

5A36

FIRST FLOOR
CEILING HEIGHT 8'-6"

KITCHEN
9'-2" x 11'-7"

DINING ROOM
11'-1" x 13'-7"

LIVING ROOM
14'-8" x 16'-8"

PORCH

STOOP

VEST

CLOS

5A36

ALTERNATE LOCATION
OF PORCH

BASEMENT
CEILING HEIGHT 7'-0"

FUEL

HEATER

UNEXCAVATED

5A36

Note—For guidance in reading floor plans, see explanation on page 14

EXTERIOR

STYLE: American Suburban. Two-story type.

SIZE OF LOT REQUIRED: From 30 to 35 feet in width.

CONSTRUCTION: Wood frame on masonry foundations, cement base course and brick steps.

FINISH: Wood siding with corner boards and moulded cornice; roof shingled.

PORCHES: Living porch at the side, opening off the living room; may be placed at rear as shown by dotted lines on the plan; entrance porch, sheltered by projecting hood over doorway.

CHIMNEY: One inside brick chimney, containing the heater, fireplace and kitchen range flues.

DECORATIVE FEATURES: The excellent use of plain surfaces serves to enhance the proportions of the windows, doors and cornice; the unique roofs over the bay and entrance add an attractive note, and tie these features into the front wall. The chimney, coming in the center of the ridge, balances nicely and does not cut up the side elevation nor detract from the roof lines.

ALTERNATE EXTERIORS: This same basic plan with different exteriors may be found on Pages 86, 92, 94, 98 and 100, House Plan Nos. 5A28; 5A33; 5A34; 5A38 and 5A43.

INTERIOR

NUMBER OF ROOMS: 5 Main rooms, Bath-room and 7 Closets.

SIZE OF ROOMS:

First Floor

Living Room	14' 8" x 16' 8"
Dining Room	11' 1" x 13' 7"
Kitchen	9' 2" x 11' 7"

Second Floor

Bed Room	14' 8" x 16' 8"
Bed Room	11' 11" x 12' 2"
Bath Room	8' 0" x 8' 0"

BASEMENT: Under the entire house, containing Laundry, Heater-room, Storage and Fuel-bins.

PLAN TYPE: Living room running across the front of the house, stairs at one side.

DESIGNED TO FACE: East or South. For other facings, plans should be reversed.

FIREPLACE: One large open fireplace in living room in the center of the inside wall. Colonial mantelpiece.

VENTILATION: 15 windows with double hung sash; 1 pair of French doors, opening onto porch; 2 outside doors; louvers in gable ends to permit free circulation of air under roof.

WALL SPACES: Ample for large pieces of furniture.

CUBIC CONTENTS: Approximately 20,500 cubic feet.

SPECIAL FEATURES

ENTRANCE VESTIBULE: An added convenience, containing a hat and coat closet.

LIVING ROOM: A large, airy room with exposures on three sides; the window which lights the stair landing is really in this room as the stairs are open. The wide cased opening into the dining room adds to the apparent size of both rooms, and the rear window in the dining room gives a fourth source of light and ventilation to the living room.

KITCHEN: Designed and equipped with every convenience for doing work with the fewest steps and the least labor; direct passage to front door and stairway.

SIDE ENTRY: Serves the kitchen and basement with direct passage out-of-doors. Handy broom closet provided.

SECOND FLOOR: Each bed room has windows on two sides; both have ample closet; owner's room has two closets; large linen closet in hall, convenient to bed rooms and to bath room.

PLUMBING: Includes bath tub, lavatory, water closet, laundry tubs, kitchen sink, hot and cold water supply.

ELECTRIC OUTLETS: Properly placed, available for iron, washing machine, vacuum cleaner, toaster, floor and table lamps, heaters, etc., if any or all of them are desired.

House Plan No. 5A38

Architects' Small House Service Bureau

Northwestern Division

THERE IS STAUNCHNESS ABOUT THE OLD DUTCH HOUSES THAT IS COMPELLING, MAKING THEM WORTHY INSPIRATIONS FOR MODERN DWELLINGS
GOOD DESIGN DOES NOT INCREASE BUILDING COST, BUT IT DOES ENHANCE THE VALUE OF THE HOUSE WHEN BUILT

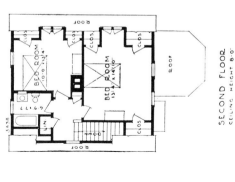

SECOND FLOOR
CEILING HEIGHT 8'-0"

BED ROOM
10'-0" x 14'-4"

BED ROOM
13'-4" x 14'-10"

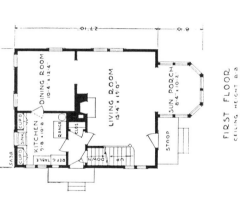

FIRST FLOOR
CEILING HEIGHT 8'-8"

KITCHEN
9'-8" x 10'-8"

DINING ROOM
10'-4" x 12'-4"

LIVING ROOM
15'-4" x 19'-0"

SUN PORCH
8'-4" x 10'-2"

STOOP

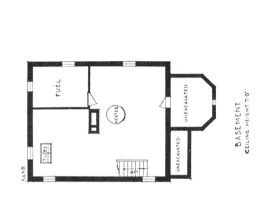

BASEMENT
CEILING HEIGHT 7'-0"

FUEL

HEATER

UNEXCAVATED

UNEXCAVATED

Note—For guidance in reading floor plans, see explanation on page 14

EXTERIOR

STYLE: Dutch Colonial Adaptation. Story-and-a-half type.

SIZE OF LOT REQUIRED: From 30 to 35 feet in width.

CONSTRUCTION: Wood frame on masonry foundations, brick base course.

FINISH: Wide wood siding or may be built of shingles. Roof shingled.

PORCHES: Enclosed sun porch, 8' 4" x 10' 2". Brick front stoop with hooded doorway; side stoop.

CHIMNEY: One inside brick chimney containing the heater, fireplace and kitchen range flues.

DECORATIVE FEATURES: The five sided sun porch with attractive railing. The fine six panelled front door and the excellence of window spacing. The attractive gambrel roofs on main body of the house and the dormer.

COLOR SCHEME SUGGESTED: White siding; blue green door and shutters and louvre slats; roof stained brown or green.

ALTERNATE EXTERIORS: This same basic plan with different exteriors can be found on Pages 86, 88, 92, 94, 96 and 100, House Plan Nos. 5A28, 5A29, 5A33, 5A34, 5A36 and 5A43.

INTERIOR

NUMBER OF ROOMS: 5 Main rooms, Bath-room and 8 Closets.

SIZE OF ROOMS:

First Floor

Living Room	15' 4" x 19' 0"
Dining Room	10' 4" x 12' 4"
Kitchen	9' 8" x 10' 8"

Second Floor

Bed Room	13' 4" x 14' 10"
Bed Room	10' 0" x 13' 4"
Bath Room	6' 9" x 7' 7"

BASEMENT: Under the main portion of the house, containing Laundry, Heater-room, Fuel-bins.

PLAN TYPE: Living room running across the front of the house with stairway at one side.

DESIGNED TO FACE: South or West. For other facings, plans should be reversed.

FIREPLACE: One brick fireplace in the living room, has wood trim.

VENTILATION: 23 windows with double hung sash, 4 casement windows; 2 outside doors; louvres in gable for ventilation of attic space.

WALL SPACES: Ample for large pieces of furniture.

CUBIC CONTENTS: Approximately 16,500 cubic feet.

SPECIAL FEATURES

LIVING ROOM: Sun porch and dining room are thrown together by wide cased openings, giving the impression of spaciousness.

SIDE HALL: Gives easy access from the kitchen to front of the house. The side stoop and the cellar stairs open off this hall.

COAT CLOSET: In the side hall.

KITCHEN: Is a model of compact arrangement. The sink is under a window with built-in cupboards on each side. The refrigerator has a door for outside icing.

BED ROOMS: Owner's room extra large with three closets and windows on two sides. The second bedroom has cross ventilation and two closets.

LINEN CLOSET: In the upper hall.

BROOM CLOSET: In the upper hall.

PLUMBING: The bath room is over the kitchen, a thrifty arrangement; the fixtures include bath tub, water closet, lavatory, kitchen sink, laundry tubs and hot and cold water supply.

ELECTRIC OUTLETS: In proper place, available for iron, washing machine, vacuum cleaner, toaster, floor and table lamps, heaters, etc., if any or all are desired.

Architects' Small House Service Bureau

Northwestern Division

ENTIRELY MODERN IN PLAN, BUT RESTING UPON FIRM FOUNDATIONS OF ENGLISH COTTAGE PRECEDENT
EASY TO LIVE IN, AND A DELIGHT TO POSSESS

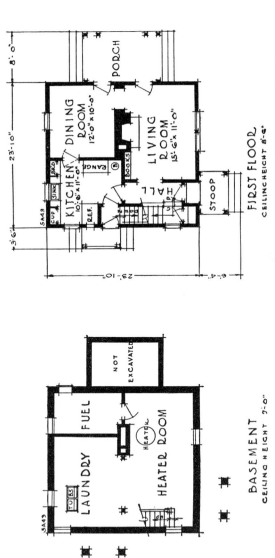

SECOND FLOOR
CEILING HEIGHT 8'-0"

BED ROOM 13'-0" x 10'-0"
BED ROOM 15'-0" x 10'-0"
HALL
9'-6" x 5'-0"
CLOS.

FIRST FLOOR
CEILING HEIGHT 8'-6"

KITCHEN 10'-6" x 11'-0"
DINING ROOM 12'-0" x 10'-0"
LIVING ROOM 15'-6" x 11'-0"
PORCH
HALL
STOOP

BASEMENT
CEILING HEIGHT 7'-0"

LAUNDRY
FUEL
NOT EXCAVATED
HEATER ROOM

Note—For guidance in reading floor plans, see explanation on page 14

EXTERIOR

STYLE: English Cottage Adaptation. Story-and-a-half type.

SIZE OF LOT REQUIRED: From 37 to 42 feet in width; if porch were placed at the rear, from 29 to 34 feet in width.

CONSTRUCTION: Frame construction on masonry foundations, cement base course.

FINISH: Wide clapboards; roof shingled. Stucco could also be used if preferred.

PORCHES: A covered entrance stoop, and a living porch, which can be reached both from the dining room and from the living room.

CHIMNEY: One interior brick chimney, with 2 flues, one for heater and one for living room fireplace.

DECORATIVE FEATURES: The pleasing relation of the various units to each other and to the whole make a decorative house, without the addition of "ornaments." The shutters tend to lower the height of the roof and give length to the house; the porches are supported on graceful columns and pilasters.

COLOR SCHEME SUGGESTED: White walls and trim; apple green shutters; variegated green and brown roof shingles.

ALTERNATE EXTERIORS: This same basic plan, with different exteriors, may be found on Pages 86, 88, 92, 94, 96 and 98. House Plan Nos. 5A28, 5A29, 5A33, 5A34, 5A36 and 5A38.

INTERIOR

NUMBER OF ROOMS: 5 Main rooms, Bath-room and 4 Closets.

SIZE OF ROOMS:

First Floor

Living Room	15' 6" x 11' 0"
Dining Room	12' 0" x 10' 0"
Kitchen	10' 6" x 11' 0"

Second Floor

Bed Room	15' 0" x 10' 0"
Bed Room	13' 0" x 10' 0"
Bath Room	9' 6" x 5' 0"

BASEMENT: Under entire house, containing Laundry, Heater-room, and Fuel-bins.

PLAN TYPE: Living room extending across the front of the house. Stairs at one side.

DESIGNED TO FACE: West or North. For other facings, plans should be reversed.

FIREPLACE: One large open fireplace in living room.

VENTILATION: 12 windows with double hung sash; 2 French doors; 2 outside doors; louvre in gable end to admit circulation of air under roof. Good attic ventilation tends to keep the second story cooler in hot weather.

WALL SPACES: Ample for large pieces of furniture.

CUBIC CONTENTS: Approximately 16,000 cubic feet.

SPECIAL FEATURES

LIVING ROOM: Of livable dimensions, with inviting fireplace and built-in bookcase, connects with the porch by a French door.

HALL AND VESTIBULE: A small vestibule opening into the hall gives protection from bad weather. On the stair landing in the hall is a closet. The hall communicates directly with the living room, the rear entry and the kitchen.

DINING ROOM: Convenient to the kitchen; can be supplemented by porch for summer use, direct access is afforded by a French door.

KITCHEN: Small, well-lighted and compact. Refrigerator iced from outside.

REAR ENTRY: Gives direct access to kitchen, to front hall and to basement stairs.

BED ROOMS: Well ventilated, having windows on 2 sides; each has a closet.

BATH ROOM AND LARGE STORE CLOSET open at opposite ends of the hall.

STORAGE SPACE IN ATTIC reached by stairs, ascending from second floor hall closet.

PLUMBING: Includes bath tub, lavatory, water closet, laundry tubs, kitchen sink, hot and cold water supply.

ELECTRIC OUTLETS: Properly placed, available for iron, washing machine, vacuum cleaner, toaster, floor and table lamps, heaters, etc.

101

House Plan No. 5A47

Architects' Small House Service Bureau

Northwestern Division

IN PERFECT ACCORD WITH THE IMPORTED CHAR[]

A HOUSE WHICH IS A BEAUTIFUL AND P[]

[]T STANDS CONFESSED A MODERN HOUSE

[] THE FAMILY WHO LIVE IN IT

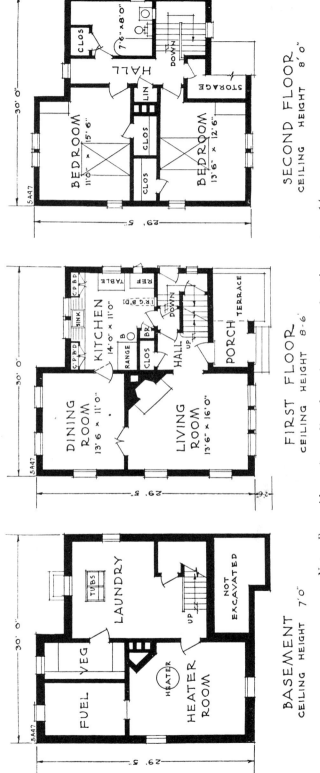

BASEMENT
CEILING HEIGHT 7'0"

FUEL | VEG
HEATER ROOM
LAUNDRY — TUBS
UP
NOT EXCAVATED

FIRST FLOOR
CEILING HEIGHT 8'-6"

DINING ROOM 13'6" x 11'0"
KITCHEN 14'0" x 11'0"
C'P'B'D — SINK
C'P'B'D — TABLE
REF
LIVING ROOM 13'6" x 16'0"
RANGE
B
CLOS
BR
HALL
UP
DOWN
PORCH
TERRACE

SECOND FLOOR
CEILING HEIGHT 8'0"

BEDROOM 11'0" x 15'6"
CLOS — 7'6" x 8'0"
HALL
CLOS
LIN
CLOS
CLOS
BEDROOM 13'6" x 12'6"
DOWN
STORAGE

Note—For guidance in reading floor plans, see explanation on page 14

EXTERIOR

STYLE: English Domestic. Two-story type.

SIZE OF LOT REQUIRED: From 35 to 40 feet in width.

CONSTRUCTION: Wood frame, with brick veneer for outside walls on masonry foundation.

FINISH: Rough texture brick veneer, for walls; shingled roof.

PORCH: Covered entrance porch with open brick terrace bounded by solid brick railing.

CHIMNEY: One inside brick chimney, containing the heater, fireplace and kitchen range flues.

DECORATIVE FEATURES: The design holds closely to the letter as well as to the spirit of English detail. The steep pitch of the roofs, the well proportioned gable ends, with close eaves, ample wall spaces and grouped windows and graceful arched entrance, give the house a real character; flower boxes along the terrace wall will further enhance the generally excellent appearance.

COLOR SCHEME SUGGESTED: Walls in broken colors of reds and browns; roof stained a brownish green; the exterior woodwork painted white or mahogany brown.

ALTERNATE EXTERIORS: None.

INTERIOR

NUMBER OF ROOMS: 5 Main rooms, Bath-room and 7 Closets.

SIZE OF ROOMS:

First Floor

Living Room	13' 6" x 16' 0"
Dining Room	13' 6" x 11' 0"
Kitchen	14' 0" x 11' 0"

Second Floor

Bed Room	13' 6" x 12' 6"
Bed Room	11' 0" x 15' 6"
Bath Room	7' 6" x 8' 0"

BASEMENT: Under main portion of the house, containing Laundry, Heater-room, Vegetable-storage, and Fuel-bins.

PLAN TYPE: Living room and dining room run continuously from front to back.

DESIGNED TO FACE: South or East. For other facings, plans should be reversed.

FIREPLACE: One open fireplace in living room.

VENTILATION: 21 windows with double hung sash; 2 outside doors.

WALL SPACES: Ample for large pieces of furniture.

CUBIC CONTENTS: Approximately 21,800 cubic feet.

SPECIAL FEATURES

LIVING ROOM: Generously proportioned, with 5 windows and a hospitable corner fireplace; the wide openings which separate it from the hall and dining room make the first floor seem spacious.

STAIR HALL: Ample size and most convenient; coat closet provided; direct passage from kitchen to both the stairs and the front door; hall lighted by window on stair landing.

KITCHEN: Contains the usual complete equipment, with a built in ironing board and broom closet; the refrigerator is iced from the outside.

BED ROOMS: Each is a corner room, with windows on two sides, and each has a spacious closet.

UNUSUAL CLOSET SPACE: Besides the linen closet in the upstairs hall, handy for bed rooms, and bath room there is a large storage closet. In the bath-room, there is a large closet, with drawers; also a medicine cabinet.

PLUMBING: The bath room is directly over the kitchen, thus saving plumbing costs; fixtures include bath tub, lavatory, water closet, laundry tubs, kitchen sink, hot and cold water supply.

ELECTRIC OUTLETS: Properly placed, available for iron, washing machine, vacuum cleaner, heaters floor and table lamps, toaster, etc.

Architects' Small House Service Bureau

Northwestern Division

AN AMERICAN BUNGALOW ADAPTED TO EXTREMES IN CLIMATIC CONDITIONS

ECONOMICAL, BOTH IN SIZE AND CONSTRUCTION, SUGGESTING COMFORT AND EASY MAINTENANCE

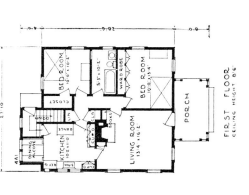

FIRST FLOOR
CEILING HEIGHT 8·6

BASEMENT
CEILING HEIGHT 8·0

Note—For guidance in reading floor plans, see explanation on page 14

EXTERIOR

STYLE: American Bungalow. One-story type.

SIZE OF LOT REQUIRED: From 33 to 38 feet in width.

CONSTRUCTION: Wood frame on masonry foundation, cement base course.

FINISH: Wood siding for walls, shingled roof.

PORCHES: Living porch 8' 0" x 14' 0", so placed that it does not cut off the air and sunlight from the rooms; serves as protection to entrance, making vestibule unnecessary.

CHIMNEY: One inside brick chimney, containing furnace and fireplace flues.

DECORATIVE FEATURES: The American porch was the opening wedge to outdoor life; the porch of this house carries an engaging social atmosphere; it was designed to fit the house, and its well-spaced columns with trellis between and the blank wall space invite its use as an out-of-door living room.

ALTERNATE EXTERIORS: This is one of four designs developed from the same plan; the only differences being the location of the porch, and the direction in which the plan is faced; for the three different exteriors, see Pages 110, 114, 126, House Plan Nos. 4A6, 4A8 and 4A13.

INTERIOR

NUMBER OF ROOMS: 4 Main rooms, Dining Alcove, Bath-room and 4 Closets.

SIZE OF ROOMS:
Living Room   13' 4" x 16' 2"
Kitchen   10' 2" x 11' 0"
Bed Room   10' 0" x 13' 4"
Bed Room   10' 0" x 10' 2"
Bath Room   5' 3" x 10' 2"

BASEMENT: Under the main part of the house, containing Laundry, Heater-room, Vegetable-storage and Fuel-bins.

PLAN TYPE: Living room and kitchen running from front to rear.

DESIGNED TO FACE: East or North. For other facings, plans should be reversed.

FIREPLACE: One large open fireplace with wide wood mantel shelf. Built-in bookcases on one side and one end of chimney; lower part of the end case could be used to store paper and kindling.

VENTILATION: 13 windows with double hung sash; 2 outside doors.

WALL SPACES: Ample for large pieces of furniture.

CUBIC CONTENTS: Approximately 18,000 cubic feet.

SPECIAL FEATURES

ALL CORNER ROOMS: Having windows on two sides; it is easy to get from one room to another, and yet there is privacy for the bed rooms and bath room, which are entirely shut off from the living quarters; easy communication makes for ease of living and economy of space.

DINING ALCOVE: Occupies a bay opening off the kitchen; doubly pleasant with two windows at the head of a built-in table and side seats. It serves all the purposes of a regular dining room; linen may be kept under the seats, and china in the cupboards above.

KITCHEN: A well-lighted kitchen, thoroughly modern, provided with many labor-saving devices; refrigerator so placed that it may be iced from outside.

BATH ROOM: Conveniently placed between the bed rooms, and provided with four large built-in drawers and a medicine closet.

LINEN CLOSET AND ADDITIONAL HANGING CLOSET: Opening off the private bed room hall.

PLUMBING: Includes bath tub, lavatory, water closet, laundry tubs, kitchen sink, hot and cold water supply.

ELECTRIC OUTLETS: Properly placed, available for iron, washing machine, vacuum cleaner, toaster, floor and table lamps, heaters, etc., if any or all of them are desired.

House Plan No. 4B1

4B1

ITALIAN IN CHARACTER AND A TYPE OF HOUSE PECULIARLY ADAPTED TO THE NEEDS OF HOME-BUILDERS IN THE WEST

AN ACHIEVEMENT OF LIVABLENESS, COMPLETENESS AND EXTREME ECONOMY

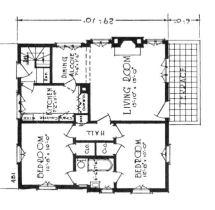

BASEMENT
CEILING HEIGHT 7'-0"

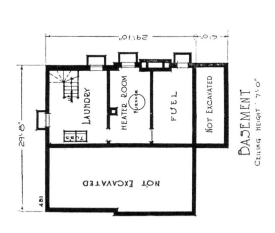

FIRST FLOOR
CEILING HEIGHT 7'-6"

Note—For guidance in reading floor plans, see explanation on page 14

EXTERIOR

STYLE: Italian influence. Bungalow type.

SIZE OF LOT REQUIRED: From 40 to 45 feet in width.

CONSTRUCTION: Hollow terra cotta tile walls on concrete foundations.

FINISH: Trowelled finish stucco walls; mission tile roof.

PORCHES: Open terrace with tiled or concrete floor extends across the front of the living room, with front door opening onto it.

CHIMNEYS: Outside chimney, projecting beyond main walls with ornamental insert of tile at the top. Kitchen chimney in rear.

DECORATIVE FEATURES: The low, pleasant proportions of the house fit it into the landscape. The relation of wall surfaces to roof is excellent. The overhanging entrance hood with its sturdy brackets, the old fashioned solid blinds and the batten door with wrought iron strap hinges contribute to the success of the design.

COLOR SCHEME SUGGESTED: Cream colored stucco with trowelled finish. Red mission tile roof; exterior woodwork stained silver gray.

ALTERNATE EXTERIORS: None.

INTERIOR

NUMBER OF ROOMS: 4 Main rooms, Dining Alcove, Bath-room and 3 Closets.

SIZE OF ROOMS:

Living Room	15' 10" x 15' 0"
Dining Alcove	7' 6" x 7' 6"
Kitchen	7' 2" x 11' 9"
Bed Room	12' 8" x 10' 0"
Bed Room	12' 8" x 10' 0"
Bath Room	6' 6" x 7' 6"

BASEMENT: Little more than half excavated; contains Laundry, Heater-room and Fuel-bins.

PLAN TYPE: Bed rooms running from front to rear, with living room and dining alcove on the opposite side. Central door.

DESIGNED TO FACE: West or North. For other facings, plans should be reversed.

FIREPLACES: One large open fireplace in the living room with mantel in keeping with the design.

VENTILATION: 23 casement windows, arranged in banks of 3, 2 and 1. Louvres in gable ends for free circulation of air under the roof.

WALL SPACES: Ample for large pieces of furniture.

CUBIC CONTENTS: Approximately 15,800 cubic feet.

SPECIAL FEATURES

LIVING ROOM: Larger than one might expect to find in so small a house and has the advantage of two outlooks. It carries out the promise of unusual charm given by the exterior.

DINING ALCOVE: Well lighted by triple windows; and conveniently placed between the kitchen and living room. It possesses all the advantages of a dining room.

KITCHEN: The most modern type, designed and equipped to lighten housework.

REAR ENTRY: The kitchen and the basement stairs are reached direct from outside and space is provided for refrigerator.

BED ROOMS: Reached by a private hall containing a linen closet. The rooms are of equal size; each has its closet and each has cross ventilation with windows on two sides.

PLUMBING: Includes bath tub, lavatory, water closet, laundry tubs, kitchen sink, hot and cold water supply.

ELECTRIC OUTLETS: In proper places, available for iron, washing machine, vacuum cleaner, toaster, floor and table lamps, heaters, etc., if any or all of them are desired.

House Plan No. 4B2

4B2

THIS DESIGN EMBODIES THE DIGNITY AND GOOD BREEDING OF THE NEW ENGLAND TOWN HOUSE

IT IS NOT ONLY AN EXCELLENT COLONIAL TYPE, BUT IT IS ECONOMICAL IN ITS GENERAL ARRANGEMENT AND WOULD LOOK WELL. PLACED NEAR THE STREET ON A NARROW LOT

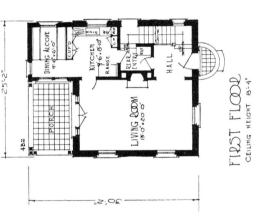

SECOND FLOOR
CEILING HEIGHT 7'-6"

BALCONY FLOOR

BEDROOM 13'-4"x10'-1"

BEDROOM 13'-4"x10'-1"

BATH 9'-6"x6'-0"

WARDROBE

HALL

LINEN

CLOSET

25'-2"

30'-0"

4B2

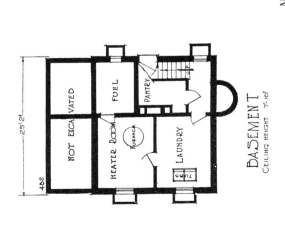

FIRST FLOOR
CEILING HEIGHT 8'-4"

DINING ALCOVE 9'-6"x6'-0"

KITCHEN 9'-6"x8'-10"

CUP'D

RANGE

REAR ENTRY

LIVING ROOM 13'-0"x20'-0"

PORCH

HALL

UP

25'-2"

30'-0"

4B2

Note—For guidance in reading floor plans, see explanation on page 14

BASEMENT
CEILING HEIGHT 7'-10"

NOT EXCAVATED

FUEL

PANTRY

HEATER ROOM

FURNACE

LAUNDRY

25'-2"

4B2

EXTERIOR

STYLE: New England Colonial. Two-story type.

SIZE OF LOT REQUIRED: Will go on a lot 35 feet in width.

CONSTRUCTION: Brick exterior walls on concrete foundations, cement base course.

FINISH: Stiff mud brick for walls, moulded wood entrance doorway and main cornice and shingled roof.

PORCHES: Opening off the living room is a beautiful columned porch tied into the house by a well-turned balustrade. Brick paved semi-circular entrance steps.

CHIMNEY: One chimney in center of house, containing the heater, fireplace and kitchen range flues.

DECORATIVE FEATURES: The design is not dependent upon broken lines and many gables for its interest and beauty. The proportions of the whole house; the shape, placing and divisions of the windows; and the decorative treatment of the doorway, brick corner quoins and cornice give the house its distinctive qualities.

COLOR SCHEME SUGGESTED: Wall variegated red brick, with roof shingles stained brownish green; exterior woodwork painted white, blinds apple green.

ALTERNATE EXTERIORS: This same basic plan, with different exteriors, may be found on Pages 134 and 136, House Plan Nos. 4A21 and 4A23.

INTERIOR

NUMBER OF ROOMS: 4 Main rooms, Dining Alcove, Bath-room and 2 Closets.

SIZE OF ROOMS:

First Floor

Living Room	13' 0" x 20' 0"
Kitchen	9' 6" x 8' 10"
Dining Alcove	9' 6" x 6' 0"

Second Floor

Bed Room	13' 4" x 10' 1"
Bed Room	13' 4" x 10' 0"
Bath Room	8' 0" x 6' 0"

BASEMENT: Under the main portion of the house containing Laundry, Heater-room, Storage-pantry and Fuel-bins.

PLAN TYPE: Living room running from front to back; stairs going up along outside wall on one side.

DESIGNED TO FACE: North, East or South. For West facing, plans should be reversed.

FIREPLACE: One large open fireplace on inside wall of living room; fine Colonial mantel.

VENTILATION: 14 windows with double hung sash; pair of French doors from living room to porch; 2 outside doors.

WALL SPACES: Ample for large pieces of furniture.

CUBIC CONTENTS: Approximately 15,400 cubic feet.

SPECIAL FEATURES

LIVING ROOM: The proportions and size make it convenient for the varied uses to which it is apt to be put; it is large enough for entertaining but not so large that a few people will feel lost in it.

DINING ALCOVE: Lighted from three sides, overlooking the garden and porch; equipped with built-in table and side benches.

KITCHEN: The working space, sink and china cupboards are placed on outside wall near the light; a combination china cabinet forms the wall between the kitchen and the dining alcove.

STAIR HALL AND REAR ENTRY: Easy access from front hall to kitchen and from rear entry to the kitchen and the basement stairs, making it possible enter basement from house or from yard without going through kitchen.

BED ROOMS: Two of equal size, each with a closet and windows on two sides.

LINEN CLOSET: In upstairs hall; bath room opens off this hall; it is directly over the kitchen, which reduces plumbing costs.

PLUMBING: Includes bath tub, lavatory, water closet, laundry tubs, kitchen sink and water supply.

ELECTRIC OUTLETS: In proper places, available for iron, washing machine, vacuum cleaner, toaster, floor and table lamps, heater, etc.

Architects' Small House Service Bureau

Northwestern Division

4A6

A DEMURE HOMESTEAD, RECALLING THE COLONIAL HOUSES OF CONNECTICUT

A HOUSE THAT BY ITS STERLING QUALITIES DOES HONOR TO ITS OWNER'S TASTE, JUDGMENT AND GOOD SENSE

FIRST FLOOR
CEILING HEIGHT 8'0"

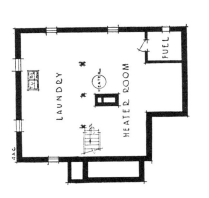

BASEMENT
CEILING HEIGHT 8'0"

Note—For guidance in reading floor plans, see explanation on page 14

EXTERIOR

STYLE: Connecticut Colonial Adaptation. Story-and-a-half type.

SIZE OF LOT REQUIRED: From 38 to 43 feet in width.

CONSTRUCTION: Frame construction on masonry foundation, cement base course.

FINISH: Wide clapboards for walls; shingled roof.

PORCHES: Entrance porch and sun room, 11' 6" x 7' 9", incorporated within the main walls, and under main roof; also side porch, near kitchen.

CHIMNEY: One interior brick chimney, containing heater and living room fireplace flues.

DECORATIVE FEATURES: The pointed roof of the entrance porch is softened by the arched doorway, with its moulded band and key-stone. The bank of casement windows in the sun porch is nicely proportioned; the addition of a dining alcove extension is successfully achieved; it is a pleasing and natural continuation of the main house.

COLOR SCHEME SUGGESTED: White walls and trim, and chimney stack; dark variegated green roof shingles; dark green band around chimney cap.

ALTERNATE EXTERIORS: This same basic plan with different exteriors, may be found on Pages 104, 114 and 126, House Plan Nos. 4A1, 4A8, and 4A13.

INTERIOR

NUMBER OF ROOMS: 4 Main rooms, Dining Alcove, Bath-room and 4 Closets.

SIZE OF ROOMS:

Living Room	16' 2" x 13' 4"
Kitchen	11' 0" x 10' 2"
Bed Room	10' 0" x 13' 4"
Bed Room	10' 0" x 10' 2"
Bath Room	5' 3" x 10' 2"

BASEMENT: Under entire house, containing Laundry, Heater-room and Fuel-bins.

PLAN TYPE: Living room and kitchen extending across the entire front.

DESIGNED TO FACE: North or West. For other facings, plans should be reversed.

FIREPLACE: One large open fireplace in inside wall of living room.

VENTILATION: 12 windows with double hung sash; 8 casement windows; 2 outside doors; 2 small windows in gable ends to admit circulation of air in attic.

WALL SPACES: Ample for large pieces of furniture.

CUBIC CONTENTS: Approximately 19,000 cubic feet.

SPECIAL FEATURES

ENTRY AND VESTIBULE: With hat and coat closet.

LIVING ROOM: Is really one with the sun room; it has a fireplace with built-in bookcase on one side and small closet or cupboard on the other. Doors opening directly into kitchen and into bedroom hall.

KITCHEN AND DINING ALCOVE: Convenient and complete kitchen equipment, just a step to dining alcove, which has built-in table and seats; under seats there are linen presses and above, china cupboards.

REAR ENTRY AND STOOP: Provide kitchen and basement and bed room hall with egress without passing through living room.

BED ROOMS AND BED ROOM HALL: Hall communicates with all parts of house, and opens into both bed rooms and into bath room. It has a deep storage closet near kitchen. Both bed rooms have closet space and two outlooks.

ATTIC STORAGE SPACE: Reached by stairs in main hall; ventilated and lighted by small windows.

PLUMBING: Includes bath tub, lavatory, water closet, laundry tubs, kitchen sink, hot and cold water supply.

ELECTRIC OUTLETS: Properly placed; available for iron, washing machine, vacuum cleaner, toaster, floor and table lamps, heater, etc., if any or all of them are desired.

111

HOUSE PLAN NO. 4B6

4B6

THE COLONISTS FROM SPAIN TRANSPLANTED THIS STYLE OF HOUSE FROM THE MOTHERLAND TO AMERICA

THIS HOUSE, WHILE INTENDED FOR A WARM CLIMATE, IS ESPECIALLY ADAPTED TO WESTERN, SOUTHWESTERN AND PACIFIC COAST LOCATIONS

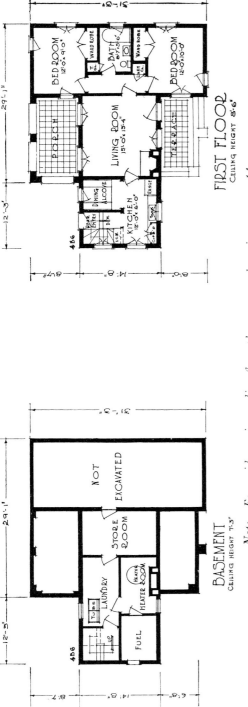

BASEMENT
CEILING HEIGHT 7'-3"

NOT EXCAVATED

STORE ROOM

LAUNDRY

HEATER ROOM

TUBS

FUEL

UP

FIRST FLOOR
CEILING HEIGHT 8'-6"

BED ROOM 12'-0"x9'-0"

WARD ROBE

BATH 8'7"x5'6"

WARD ROBE

LINEN CL.

BED ROOM 12'-0"x10'-0"

PORCH

LIVING ROOM 15'-0"x13'-4"

TERRACE

DINING ALCOVE

REAR ENTRY

KITCHEN 12'-0"x6'-0"

RANGE

SINK

Note—For guidance in reading floor plans, see explanation on page 14

EXTERIOR

STYLE: Spanish-American. Bungalow type.

SIZE OF LOT REQUIRED: From 50 to 60 feet in width.

CONSTRUCTION: Hollow tile walls on concrete foundations.

FINISH: Trowelled stucco for walls; variegated mission tile roof; wood doors and shutters.

PORCHES: Living porch opening off the living room in the rear; if enclosed with glass it can be used as a summer dining room and converted into a sun room for winter use. Entrance terrace, with hood over door for shelter.

CHIMNEY: One chimney in front wall, three flues, terminating in terra cotta chimney pots; serves both kitchen and living room.

DECORATIVE FEATURES: The charm of this house is created by the chaste and simple outline of the walls, the low pitched roofs and the unique placing of the windows in relation to the gable and chimney; all members of the design pull together and make a well balanced whole.

COLOR SCHEME SUGGESTED: Light pink stucco walls, trowelled finish; brown, red and yellow tile laid in irregular form for roof; weathered pine color for woodwork with turquoise blue shutters.

ALTERNATE EXTERIORS: None.

INTERIOR

NUMBER OF ROOMS: 4 Main rooms, Dining Alcove, Bath-room and 4 Closets.

SIZE OF ROOMS:

Living Room	15' 0" x 13' 4"
Kitchen	12' 0" x 6' 0"
Dining Alcove	5' 8" x 6' 10"
Bed Room	12' 0" x 10' 0"
Bed Room	12' 0" x 9' 0"
Bath Room	8' 7" x 5' 6"

BASEMENT: Only partially excavated, but includes ample Laundry, Heater-room, Store-room and Fuel-bins.

PLAN TYPE: Living room so placed that it serves as an axis for the balance of the house.

DESIGNED TO FACE: North, South or East. For West facing, plans should be reversed.

FIREPLACE: One large open fireplace in the living room, with mantel in keeping with the style of the house.

VENTILATION: 19 casement windows, opening in; 2 pairs of full length casement windows from living room to porch; 2 outside doors; louvres in gable ends to permit free circulation of air under roof.

WALL SPACES: Ample for large pieces of furniture.

CUBIC CONTENTS: Approximately 13,700 cubic feet.

SPECIAL FEATURES

LIVING ROOM: Entered directly from front door; all parts of the house are easily reached from this room. It is altogether delightful with its view of the garden through the full length windows opening onto the porch.

DINING ALCOVE: Overlooks the garden; it may be reached from the living room without entering the kitchen, if a door is cut through the living room wall.

KITCHEN: Faces the street and yet is in close communication with the rear yard; it has every convenience of a well equipped modern kitchen; windows on two sides, one group directly over sink.

REAR ENTRY: Contains the basement stairs, and provides passage direct from basement and from kitchen to yard.

BED ROOM WING: Contains a private hall, leading to two bed rooms, the bath room and a linen closet; the bedrooms are unusual in that they have windows on three sides; each has a closet, there is an extra closet in the bathroom.

PLUMBING: Includes bath tub, lavatory, water closet, kitchen sink, laundry tubs and hot and cold water supply.

ELECTRIC OUTLETS: In proper places, available for iron, washing machine, vacuum cleaner, toaster, floor and table lamps, heaters, etc., if any or all of them are desired.

HOUSE PLAN NO. 4A8

4A8

THE CONSERVATIVE DIGNITY OF THIS DERIVATIVE OF NEW ENGLAND COLONIAL HOUSES HAS REAL CHARM

IT COMBINES THE MOST WELCOME ATTRIBUTES OF A HOME, COMFORT, CONVENIENCE AND ECONOMY

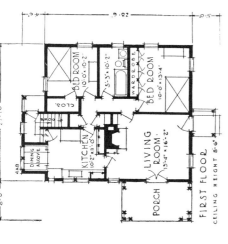

Note—For guidance in reading floor plans, see explanation on page 14

EXTERIOR

STYLE: New England Colonial Adaptation. Bungalow type.

SIZE OF LOT REQUIRED: From 40 to 45 feet in width.

CONSTRUCTION: Wood frame on masonry foundation, cement base course.

FINISH: Wide clapboard siding; shingled roof.

PORCHES: A covered entrance porch, and a living porch which opens from the living room; a small porch at the back, under the main roof.

CHIMNEY: One interior brick chimney, containing heater and living room fireplace flues. Capped with terra cotta chimney pots.

DECORATIVE FEATURES: By extending the main roof and the front wall of the house to embrace the living porch, a feeling of length has been achieved; the entrance porch roof gives the necessary variety to the roof line, and there remains little to be wished for in the way of decoration; this little is found in the lattices at the porch corners and forming the sides of the entrance. They could have vines trained over them, and make of the house a "rose embowered cottage."

COLOR SCHEME SUGGESTED: Colonial yellow walls; white trim; green blinds; and variegated greens for roof shingles.

ALTERNATE EXTERIORS: This same basic plan with different exteriors, may be found on Pages 104, 110, and 126, House Plan Nos. 4A1; 4A6; and 4A13.

INTERIOR

NUMBER OF ROOMS: 4 Main rooms, Dining Alcove, Bath-room and 4 Closets.

SIZE OF ROOMS:

Living Room	13' 4" x 16' 2"
Kitchen	10' 2" x 11' 0"
Bed Room	10' 0" x 13' 4"
Bed Room	10' 0" x 10' 2"
Bath Room	5' 3" x 10' 2"

BASEMENT: Under entire house, containing Laundry, Heater-room and Fuel-bins.

PLAN TYPE: Living room and kitchen running from front to back.

DESIGNED TO FACE: East or North. For other facings, plans should be reversed.

FIREPLACE: One large open fireplace in end wall of living room.

VENTILATION: 12 windows with double hung sash; 1 pair French doors; 2 outside doors; 2 small windows in gable end to admit circulation of air under roof.

WALL SPACES: Ample for large pieces of furniture.

CUBIC CONTENTS: Approximately 18,000 cubic feet.

SPECIAL FEATURES

LIVING ROOM: Is well lighted, and opens by French doors onto the porch. It has a good-looking mantelpiece of wood, flanked on one side by a built-in bookcase and on the other by a built-in closet, or if desired, this could be a china cupboard. It has doors leading to kitchen and to bed room hall.

KITCHEN: Practical, with every convenience within easy reach; the ice box has outside icing door.

DINING ALCOVE: Has double window, looking over garden; built-in table and seats with cupboards above them.

REAR ENTRY AND KITCHEN PORCH: Giving direct access to kitchen and to basement stairs; porch will be a great convenience for the housewife when preparing meals or preserving in hot weather.

BED ROOMS: Well shut off from living portion of the house, but accessible. Each has cross ventilation and closet space; the bath room is equally convenient to both.

PLUMBING: Includes bath tub, lavatory, water closet, laundry tubs, kitchen sink, hot and cold water supply.

ELECTRIC OUTLETS: Properly placed, available for iron, washing machine, vacuum cleaner, toaster, floor and table lamps, heater, etc., if any or all of them are desired.

4B8

ITALIAN AND SPANISH FORMS PLEASANTLY COMBINED TO CREATE A PRACTICAL ONE STORY HOUSE

WHILE PRIMARILY A WESTERN TYPE OF HOUSE, IT IS WELL SUITED TO ALMOST ANY SECTION OF THE COUNTRY

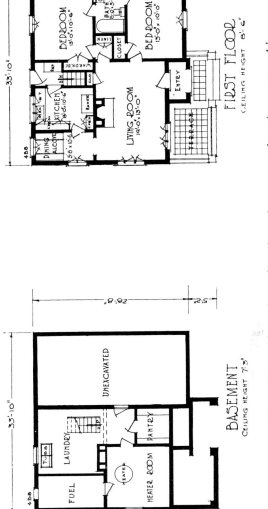

BASEMENT
CEILING HEIGHT 7'5"

FIRST FLOOR
CEILING HEIGHT 8'6"

Note—For guidance in reading floor plans, see explanation on page 14

EXTERIOR

STYLE: Italian in character. Bungalow type.

SIZE OF LOT REQUIRED: From 40 to 45 feet in width.

CONSTRUCTION: Hollow terra cotta tile on masonry foundations.

FINISH: Floated stucco for walls; mission tile roof.

PORCHES: Enclosed entry and open terrace with posts and railing. The absence of a porch roof insures a light and bright living room.

CHIMNEY: One inside brick chimney, stucco covered above the roof, containing the heater, fireplace and kitchen range flues.

DECORATIVE FEATURES: The combination of hip and single pitch roofs is admirable. The arched and buttressed projection is strong and emphasizes the entrance. The tile "roofed" chimney, with its terra cotta chimney pots, adds a finishing touch to the design.

COLOR SCHEME SUGGESTED: Walls light pink, roof variegated reds, browns and grays; exterior woodwork stained to produce the effect of weathered pine; shutters painted a light blue.

ALTERNATE EXTERIORS: None.

INTERIOR

NUMBER OF ROOMS: 4 Main rooms, Dining Alcove, Bath-room and 4 Closets.

SIZE OF ROOMS:

Living Room	19' 0" x 13' 0"
Dining Alcove	5' 8" x 10' 6"
Kitchen	8' 0" x 10' 6"
Bed Room	13' 0" x 10' 6"
Bed Room	13' 0" x 10' 0"
Bath Room	8' 0" x 5' 6"

BASEMENT: Only partially excavated, but large enough for Laundry, Heater-room, Storage-pantry and Fuel-bins.

PLAN TYPE: Living room and dining alcove running from front to back; central entrance; bed rooms run from front to back.

DESIGNED TO FACE: South or East. For other facings, plans should be reversed.

FIREPLACE: One large fireplace in center of inside wall of living room, with beautiful mantel.

VENTILATION: 23 casement windows arranged in banks of threes and twos; 2 outside doors; louvres in gable ends to permit free circulation of air under roof.

WALL SPACES: Ample for large pieces of furniture.

CUBIC CONTENTS: Approximately 17,100 cubic feet.

SPECIAL FEATURES

LIVING ROOM: The dominating room of the house, spacious in size, and well lighted with a bank of windows on two sides; there is a convenient closet in this room.

DINING ALCOVE: In a secluded corner, close to the kitchen, and overlooking the garden on one side, has windows on two sides, built-in table and side seats with china cupboards above.

KITCHEN: Ample proportions, with excellently arranged sink, worktable, cupboards, dressers and range. Bank of three windows over the sink.

REAR ENTRY: Enabling one to go directly down to the basement from the outside; place for the ice box with cupboards above.

BED ROOMS: Two exposures for each room, good sized closets and a linen closet in the small private hall.

PLUMBING: Includes bath tub, lavatory, water closet, laundry tubs, kitchen sink and hot and cold water supply.

ELECTRIC OUTLETS: In proper places, available for iron, washing machine, vacuum cleaner, toaster, floor and table lamps, heaters, etc., if any or all of them are desired.

House Plan No. 4B9

Mountain Division

Architects' Small House Service Bureau

4B9

IN THE DAYS OF CALIFORNIA'S EARLY HISTORY, THE MISSION PADRES FROM SPAIN BUILT THIS TYPE OF HOUSE
THERE IS AN IRRESISTIBLE CHARM CREATED BY THE GROUPED ARCHES, DIGNIFYING THE SPANISH MISSION BUNGALOW ABOVE THE ORDINARY SMALL HOUSE

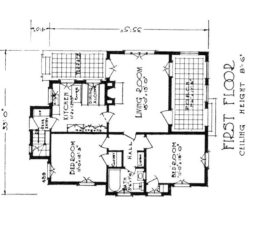

BASEMENT

CEILING HEIGHT 7'3"

33'0"

35'5"

FIRST FLOOR

CEILING HEIGHT 8'6"

33'0"

35'5"

Note—For guidance in reading floor plans, see explanation on page 14

EXTERIOR

Style: Spanish Mission Adaptation. Bungalow type.

Size of Lot Required: From 40 to 45 feet in width.

Construction: Hollow tile walls on masonry foundation.

Finish: Floated stucco walls; roofed with wood shingles.

Porches: Front living porch, 7' 6" x 17' 6" contained within the walls of the house. Side paved or tiled open terrace, opening from the living room.

Chimney: One inside brick chimney covered with stucco above roof, and topped with terra cotta chimney pots.

Decorative Features: The design, although devoid of mere ornament, possesses unusual merit. The fine contour of the wall lines, and the successful breaking of the mass by graceful arched openings filled in with an iron balustrade to indicate the porch, and left open to emphasize the entrance, makes it outshine the average bungalow.

Color Scheme Suggested: Walls light pink; roof stained Venetian red; sash and doors painted silver gray; balance of exterior woodwork stained a weathered pine color.

Alternate Exteriors: None.

INTERIOR

Number of Rooms: 4 Main rooms, Bath-room and 3 Closets.

Size of Rooms:

Living Room	18' 0" x 13' 0"
Kitchen	11' 2" x 12' 3"
Bed Room	11' 0" x 13' 0"
Bed Room	11' 0" x 12' 3"
Bath Room	5' 6" x 7' 6"

Basement: Although not fully excavated, the Laundry, Heater-room, Store-room and Fuel-bins are ample.

Plan Type: Centralized living room, with bed rooms running from front to rear on one side.

Designed to Face: West or North. For other facings, plans should be reversed.

Fireplace: One large open fireplace in living room, with beautiful mantel.

Ventilation: 25 casement windows, arranged in pairs; French doors to terrace; 2 outside doors; louvres in gable ends to admit free circulation of air under roof.

Wall Spaces: Ample for large pieces of furniture.

Cubic Contents: Approximately 18,000 cubic feet.

SPECIAL FEATURES

Living Room: Large enough for the members of the household to congregate in comfort and entertain their guests. The cheerful fireplace in the center of the inside wall is nicely balanced with openings leading to the kitchen on one side and to the terrace on the other.

Dining Alcove: Built-in table with side benches and china closet is shown in the kitchen; the pair of casement windows in the wall adjoining this feature would give ample light if the alcove were enclosed by partitions.

Kitchen: Installed with every convenience for doing the work with the fewest steps and least labor.

Rear Entry: Allows direct passage both to kitchen and to the basement stairs, and provides space for ice box with cupboards above.

Bed Rooms: All the privacy of second floor rooms as they open off a private hall containing a linen closet. Each room has two exposures, insuring good ventilation, and each has a large closet.

Plumbing: Includes bath tub, lavatory, water closet, laundry tubs, kitchen sink, hot and cold water supply.

Electric Outlets: In the proper places, available for iron, washing machine, vacuum cleaner, toaster, floor and table lamps, heaters, etc., if any or all of them are desired.

Architects' Small House Service Bureau

Mountain Division

4B10

LIKE THE VILLAS OF ITALY, THIS HOUSE IS BOTH DIGNIFIED AND DISTINCTIVE IN APPEARANCE

ALTHOUGH ITS DIMENSIONS ARE SMALL, THE BOLDNESS OF THE STYLE IS OBTAINED BY PLAIN WALL SURFACES, RECESSED PORCH AND WROUGHT IRON EMBELLISHMENTS

SECOND FLOOR
CEILING HEIGHT 7'-6"

30'-7"   22'-0"

BEDROOM 11'6" x 18'-0"
BEDROOM 9'0" x 13'-2"
BATH 7'-2" x 6'-0"
BALCONY
CLO. LINEN CLO. CLO.
HALL

FIRST FLOOR
CEILING HEIGHT 8'-6"

30'-7"   9'-0"   22'-0"

TERRACE
LIVING ROOM 18'-0" x 13'-0"
DINING ALCOVE
KITCHEN 9'-0" x 9'-2"
HALL
PORCH
ENTRY
CUPB'DS

Note—For information about securing working plans for this house, see page 14

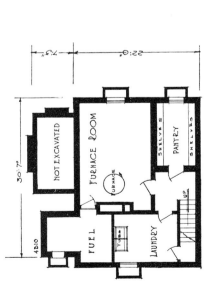

BASEMENT
CEILING HEIGHT 7'-5"

30'-7"   7'-5"   22'-0"

NOT EXCAVATED
FURNACE ROOM
FURNACE
PANTRY SHELVES SHELVES
FUEL
LAUNDRY
UP

EXTERIOR

STYLE: Italian Villa. Two-story type.

SIZE OF LOT REQUIRED: From 38 to 40 feet in width.

CONSTRUCTION: Hollow tile walls on masonry foundations.

FINISH: Stucco walls; tiled roof.

PORCHES: Front porch built within the main body of the house; paved garden terrace opening off living room.

CHIMNEY: One central brick chimney with stucco finish above roof, serves fireplace, furnace and kitchen range flues.

DECORATIVE FEATURES: By concentrating upon pronounced features with a sparing use of detail, there is created for this house a real individuality; the main entrance is emphasized by the arched opening and by the tall window and wrought iron balcony. The service entrance is made a feature of the design, and tied to the house by a well-shaped console over the gate.

COLOR SCHEME SUGGESTED: Cream colored stucco with floated finish for the walls; variegated tile roof; exterior woodwork painted dull blue.

ALTERNATE EXTERIORS: None.

INTERIOR

NUMBER OF ROOMS: 4 Main rooms, Dining Alcove, Bath-room and 6 Closets.

SIZE OF ROOMS:

	First Floor
Living Room	18' 0" x 13' 0"
Kitchen	9' 0" x 9' 2"

	Second Floor
Bed Room	11' 6" x 18' 0"
Bed Room	9' 0" x 13' 2"
Bath Room	7' 9" x 6' 0"

BASEMENT: Under entire house, containing Laundry, Heater-room, Storage-pantry, and Fuel-bins.

PLAN TYPE: Living room running across the house; stairs starting from central hall and running parallel with the front wall.

DESIGNED TO FACE: West or North. For other facings, plans should be reversed.

FIREPLACE: Large open fireplace on inside end of living room; well designed mantel with bookcase adjoining.

VENTILATION: 26 casement windows arranged in banks of four, three, two and one; one pair of French doors, opening onto terrace; 2 outside doors.

WALL SPACES: Ample for large pieces of furniture.

CUBIC CONTENTS: Approximately 20,000 cubic feet.

SPECIAL FEATURES

LIVING ROOM: A large and spacious room with a beautiful fireplace and group of four windows on the wall facing it.

KITCHEN: Ample size with every detail known to the modern kitchen equipment, and is splendidly lighted.

DINING ALCOVE: Opening off the kitchen are a built-in table, wall benches and recessed china closet, offering every advantage of a dining room, and yet taking up very little floor space.

REAR ENTRY: Serves the kitchen and basement with direct access out-of-doors, and provides space for ice box with storage cabinet above.

BED ROOMS: Owner's bed room extends full depth of house, with light on three sides. A window seat and three closets are provided and a wrought iron balcony overlooking the entrance. The smaller room has a large closet, and a wrought iron balcony opening through French doors, overlooking the garden.

PLUMBING: Includes bath tub, lavatory, water closet, laundry tubs, kitchen sink, hot and cold water supply.

ELECTRIC OUTLETS: In proper places, available for iron, washing machine, vacuum cleaner, toaster, floor and table lamps, heater, etc., if any or all of them are desired.

121

HOUSE PLAN NO. 4A11

MARYLAND, VIRGINIA AND THE CAROLINAS ABOUND IN THIS PARTICULARLY RESTFUL AND HOME-LIKE STYLE
EXPRESSIVE OF THE HOSPITALITY OF THE NATIVE STATES, THIS HOUSE HAS ALSO THE ADVANTAGE OF BEING MOST COMPACT AND EASILY ADMINISTERED

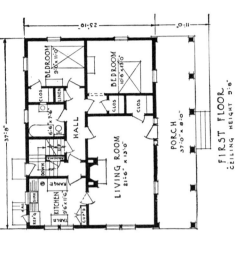

FIRST FLOOR
CEILING HEIGHT 9'-6"

BASEMENT
CEILING HEIGHT 7'-6"

Note—For guidance in reading floor plans, see explanation on page 14

EXTERIOR

Style: Adaptation of Southern Colonial. Story-and-a-half type.

Size of Lot Required: From 43 to 48 feet in width.

Construction: Frame construction on masonry foundations.

Finish: Wide siding and shingled roof.

Porch: A living porch extending the entire breadth of the house, 37' 0" x 8' 0".

Chimney: One interior brick chimney, containing heater and fireplace flues, and capped by terra cotta chimney pots.

Decorative Features: The entrance doorway with its surrounding side lights and transom, is the main point of interest; the porch columns are delicate yet strong enough to be substantial. The lattice under the porch is decorative in itself, or it would be admirable support for vines. A simple moulding finishes the top of the porch.

Color Scheme Suggested: White walls and **trim**, green shutters and variegated shingles.

Alternate Exterior: None.

INTERIOR

Number of Rooms: 4 Main rooms, Bath-room and 5 Closets.

Size of Rooms:

Living Room	21' 6" x 13' 0"
Kitchen	9' 6" x 11' 6"
Bed Room	10' 6" x 13' 0"
Bed Room	9' 0" x 11' 0"
Bath Room	6' 6" x 7' 6"

Basement: Under entire house, containing Laundry, Heater-room, Closet, Vegetable-room and Fuel-bins.

Plan Type: Living room and one of the bed rooms running across the front of the house.

Designed to Face: South or East. For other facings, plans should be reversed.

Fireplace: Large open fireplace in living room.

Ventilation: 14 windows with double hung sash; 2 of them unfinished, being on second floor; 2 outside doors.

Wall Space: Ample for large pieces of furniture.

Cubic Contents: Approximately 23,500 cubic feet.

SPECIAL FEATURES

Living Room: That easily meets a dual demand; is also used as the dining room, the table being set near the door into the kitchen. A large coat closet at the right of the front door prevents one from missing an entrance hall. The large fireplace is the chief decoration. Plenty of doors and windows for circulation of both people and air.

Kitchen: Thoroughly modern and compact; outside icing for refrigerator. Work-table under double windows.

Rear Entry: Giving direct access, not only to kitchen and to basement, but also to bed room hall.

Bed Rooms: Of good size, each with a closet and each with windows on two sides.

Closets: A linen closet and broom closet on the main floor, in addition to bed room closets, and a large storage closet in basement.

Plumbing: Includes bath tub, lavatory, water closet, laundry tubs, kitchen sink, and hot and cold water supply.

Electric Outlets: In proper places, available for iron, washing machine, vacuum cleaner, toaster, floor and table lamps, heaters, etc., if any or all of them are desired.

Architects' Small House Service Bureau

Mountain Division

4B11

FROM ENGLAND IN GEORGIAN DAYS WE DRAW MOTIVES THAT NEVER LOSE THEIR HOLD UPON OUR AFFECTIONS

MONEY IS NOT WASTED ON MEANINGLESS ORNAMENTATION OR ONE INCH OF SPACE LOST WITHIN THE FOUR STRAIGHT WALLS OF THIS DIGNIFIED BUNGALOW

BED ROOM
9'0"x12'0"

HALL

BED ROOM
9'0"x12'0"

DINING
ALCOVE

KITCHEN
7'6"x10'0"

BATH.
5'6"x6'6"

LIVING ROOM
17'0"x12'0"

TILE
PORCH

FIRST FLOOR
CEILING HEIGHT 8'-6"

Note—For guidance in reading floor plans, see explanation on page 14

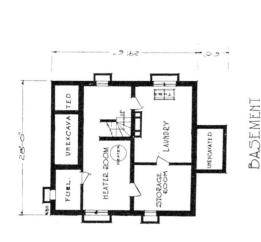

FUEL.

UNEXCAVATED

HEATER ROOM
HEATER

STORAGE
ROOM

LAUNDRY

UNEXCAVATED

BASEMENT
CEILING HEIGHT 7'-3"

EXTERIOR

STYLE: Colonial of James River and Chesapeake Bay. Bungalow type.

SIZE OF LOT REQUIRED: From 35 to 40 feet in width.

CONSTRUCTION: Brick walls carried full height of the gable; masonry foundations.

FINISH: Brick walls, wood porch; roof shingled; may be wood siding or stucco if desired.

PORCHES: Two porches, front and rear; the covered entrance porch, with tile floor, is 10' 0" x 6' 0", and will be cool and inviting. The rear porch is recessed within the walls of the house and serves the double purpose of a sitting porch and as an entrance into the kitchen and basement.

CHIMNEY: One inside brick chimney with three flues terminating in terra cotta chimney pots.

DECORATIVE FEATURES: The symmetrical arrangement of the perfectly proportioned windows; the relation of the sheltered porch to the whole mass; the columns and pilasters of the porch; and the close overhang of the gable rakes, carry out the indefinable feeling of good taste so obvious in this house.

COLOR SCHEME SUGGESTED: Walls in broken colors of reds and brown; roof stained a brownish green; the exterior woodwork painted white and the blinds an apple green.

ALTERNATE EXTERIORS: None.

INTERIOR

NUMBER OF ROOMS: 4 Main rooms, Dining Alcove, Bath-room and 3 Closets, all on one floor.

SIZE OF ROOMS:
Living Room   17' 0" x 12' 0"
Kitchen   7' 6" x 10' 0"
Bed Room   9' 0" x 12' 0"
Bed Room   9' 0" x 12' 0"
Bath Room   5' 6" x 6' 6"

BASEMENT: Under the main portion of house, containing a Laundry, Heater-room, Storage-room and Fuel-bins.

PLAN TYPE: Living room and one bed room running across the front of the house.

DESIGNED TO FACE: West or North. For other facings, plan should be reversed.

FIREPLACE: One large open fireplace in living room, with wood mantel.

VENTILATION: 20 casement windows; 2 outside doors; attractive round windows in gable ends for free circulation of air under roof.

WALL SPACES: Ample for large pieces of furniture.

CUBIC CONTENTS: Approximately 19,000 cubic feet.

LIVING ROOM: Pleasing shape with windows on two sides. It has a well balanced inside wall with a fireplace in the center and doors leading into rear hall and kitchen on each.

SPECIAL FEATURES

LIVING ROOM: Pleasing shape with windows on two sides. It has a well balanced inside wall with a fireplace in the center and doors leading into rear hall and kitchen on each.

KITCHEN: Contains the necessary equipment of the modern kitchen, properly located in relation to each other. The kitchen is reached from the rear porch.

DINING ALCOVE: At one end of the kitchen, facing the garden, is the popular and labor-saving built-in table, with a bench on each side, and a china cabinet above them. Most convenient for serving from the kitchen. If it is desired to serve some of the meals in one end of the living room, the kitchen is conveniently placed to permit such an arrangement.

BED ROOMS: Open off a private hall, as does the linen closet and also the bath-room. The bed rooms are lighted on two sides and each is provided with good sized closet.

PLUMBING: Includes bath tub, lavatory, water closet, laundry tubs, kitchen sink and hot and cold water supply.

ELECTRIC OUTLETS: In the proper places, available for iron, washing machine, vacuum cleaner, toaster, floor and table lamps, heaters, etc., if any or all of them are desired.

Architects' Small House Service Bureau

4A13

NOT A SLAVISH FOLLOWING OF A TRADITIONAL STYLE, BUT REMINISCENT IN ITS LINES OF PENNSYLVANIA DUTCH PREDECESSORS

A SUCCESSFUL HOUSE NEEDS A PLEASING, WELL DESIGNED EXTERIOR AS WELL AS A GOOD, PRACTICAL PLAN

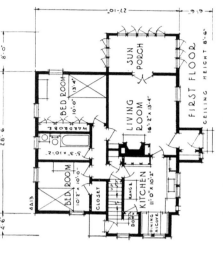

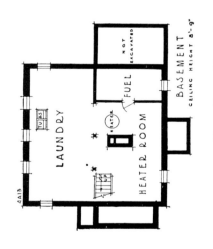

BASEMENT
CEILING HEIGHT 8'-9"

FIRST FLOOR
CEILING HEIGHT 8'-6"

Note—For guidance in reading floor plans, see explanation on page 14

EXTERIOR

STYLE: Pennsylvania Colonial Adaptation. Bungalow type.

SIZE OF LOT REQUIRED: Will go on a lot of varying sizes, depending upon facings; from 45 to 50 feet in width if placed as shown in illustration; if sun room is placed to front, will go on lot 37 to 42 feet in width.

CONSTRUCTION: Wood frame on masonry foundations on solid footings below the frost line.

FINISH: Wide wood siding for walls; roof shingled.

PORCHES: Sun porch with casement windows opening off living room; entrance vestibule with hooded roof protecting stoop.

CHIMNEY: One central brick chimney containing the heater, living room fireplace and kitchen range flues.

DECORATIVE FEATURES: Design brings out natural beauty of wood. The wide siding gives a splendid texture to the walls. A so-called Germantown hooded roof, broken to emphasize the entrance, recalls the old Pennsylvania Dutch houses.

COLOR SCHEME SUGGESTED: Siding painted white, door and window trim cream white, blinds blue-green, roof variegated greens.

ALTERNATE EXTERIORS: This is one of four designs developed from the same plan, the only difference being the location of the porch, and the direction in which the plan is faced. For the three different exteriors, see Pages 104, 110 and 114, House Plan Nos. 4A1; 4A6 and 4A8.

INTERIOR

NUMBER OF ROOMS: 4 Main Rooms, Dining Alcove, Bath-room and 4 Closets.

The second floor may be finished off if desired to provide a good sized bed room with large closet and plenty of storage space.

SIZE OF ROOMS:

Living Room	16' 2" x 13' 4"
Kitchen	11' 0" x 10' 2"
Bed Room	10' 0" x 13' 4"
Bed Room	10' 2" x 10' 0"
Bath Room	5' 3" x 10' 2"

BASEMENT: Under main portion of house; containing Laundry, Heater-room and Fuel-bins.

PLAN TYPE: Living room and kitchen running across the front of the house.

DESIGNED TO FACE: The house should be placed so that living room and sun porch have southern exposure.

FIREPLACE: One large open fireplace in living room, with Colonial mantelpiece.

VENTILATION: 11 windows with double hung sash; 11 casement windows in sun porch; 2 outside doors; windows in attic for free circulation of air under roof.

WALL SPACES: Ample for large pieces of furniture.

CUBIC CONTENTS: Approximately 19,000 cubic feet.

SPECIAL FEATURES

ALL THE ROOMS are so placed as to afford ease of communication, which makes for ease of living and an economy of space.

ENTRANCE VESTIBULE: An added convenience, containing a well lighted hat and coat closet.

LIVING ROOM: In combination with the glazed in sun porch is a most livable room. There are built-in bookcases on each side of the fireplace.

KITCHEN: Faces the street; the working space extends across the front wall under two windows with a continuous counter shelf from dresser to work-table. Fully equipped. Ice box may be iced from outside. Dining alcove included.

REAR ENTRY: To kitchen and to basement stairs, direct from outside.

BED ROOMS: Reached by private hall opening off living room and kitchen. Cross ventilation assured by windows on two sides. Closet for each room and a linen closet at the foot of the stairs, convenient to all parts of the house.

SPACE FOR ROOMS IN SECOND FLOOR: The ridge of the roof is high enough to permit a good sized bed room, hall and storage closet to be placed on a second floor, if it is desired to finish it off. Stairs are provided.

PLUMBING: Includes bath tub, lavatory, water closet, laundry tubs, kitchen sink, water supply.

ELECTRIC OUTLETS: In proper places, available for iron, washing machine, vacuum cleaner, toaster, floor and table lamps, heaters, etc.

127

Architects' Small House Service Bureau

Northwestern Division

4A15

A HOUSE WHICH SUGGESTS THE RESTFULNESS OF THE EARLY HOMES IN NEW NETHERLANDS

IT IS INDIVIDUAL IN DESIGN AND A SUITABLE BACKGROUND FOR AMERICAN HOME LIFE

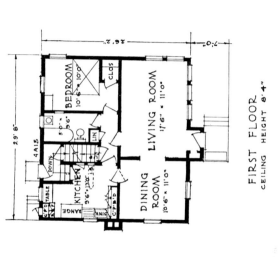

BEDROOM
12'0" x 14'6"

HALL

STORAGE   CLOS

DOWN

4A15

SECOND FLOOR
CEILING HEIGHT 8'0"

BEDROOM
10'6" x 10'0"

CLOS

KITCHEN
9'6" x 13'6"

LIN

DOWN

RANGE

DINING
ROOM
10'6" x 11'0"

LIVING ROOM
17'6" x 11'0"

FIRST FLOOR
CEILING HEIGHT 8'4"

CLOS

TUBS

LAUNDRY

VEG

HEATER

HEATER ROOM   FUEL

BASEMENT
CEILING HEIGHT 7'0"

Note—For guidance in reading floor plans, see explanation on page 14

EXTERIOR

STYLE: Dutch Colonial Adaptation. Story-and-a-half type.

SIZE OF LOT REQUIRED: From 35 to 40 feet in width.

CONSTRUCTION: Wood frame on masonry foundations, cement base course.

FINISH: Wide wood siding; may be shingles or stucco. Roof shingled.

PORCH: Entrance stoop of cement or brick.

CHIMNEY: One outside brick chimney containing the heater and kitchen range flues.

DECORATIVE FEATURES: Hooded entrance with sawn brackets, overhanging eaves and seat of Dutch precedent.

COLOR SCHEME SUGGESTED: Cream colored siding with dark green front door.

ALTERNATE EXTERIORS: This same basic plan with different exteriors can be found on Pages 32, 36 and 132, House Plan Nos. 6A11, 6A12 and 4A16.

INTERIOR

NUMBER OF ROOMS: 4 Main rooms, Bath-room and 3 Closets. Unfinished room in the attic.

SIZE OF ROOMS:

Living Room	17' 6" x 11' 0"
Dining Room	10' 6" x 11' 0"
Kitchen	9' 6" x 13' 0"
Bed Room	10' 6" x 10' 0"
Bath Room	5' 0" x 9' 6"

BASEMENT: Under entire house, containing Laundry, Heater-room, Fuel-bins and Vegetable-storage.

PLAN TYPE: Living room and dining room running across the front of the house.

FIREPLACE: None.

DESIGNED TO FACE: North or West. For other facings, plans should be reversed.

VENTILATION: 12 windows with double hung sash, 2 outside doors, 8 windows in attic.

WALL SPACES: Ample for large pieces of furniture.

CUBIC CONTENTS: Approximately 17,200 cubic feet.

SPECIAL FEATURES

LOCATION OF WINDOWS IN LIVING ROOM: Arranged to make this room serve the purpose of sun room.

EXTRA BED ROOM: May be obtained in the attic, as shown by second floor plan. Two closets are provided and windows for cross ventilation.

STORAGE ROOM: Large space on second floor lighted by three windows.

FRENCH DOORS: Between living room and dining room permit these rooms to be thrown together.

KITCHEN: Equipped with labor saving devices. Built-in cupboards, ironing board and broom closet. The ice box has a door for outside icing and a cupboard above.

LINEN CLOSET: In rear hall, close to bath room; coat closet in vestibule.

PLUMBING: Includes bath tub, water closet, lavatory, kitchen sink, laundry tubs and hot and cold water supply.

ELECTRIC OUTLETS: In proper places for iron, washing machine, vacuum cleaner, toaster, floor and table lamps, heaters, etc., if any or all of them are desired.

129

House Plan No. 4B15

Architects' Small House Service Bureau

4B15

IN COLONIAL TIMES THIS STYLE OF HOUSE WAS CALLED A "COTTAGE"; TODAY IT IS KNOWN AS A BUNGALOW

NOT AN EVERYDAY TYPE OF BUNGALOW, HOWEVER, BUT A WELL PROPORTIONED HOUSE OFFERING A GOOD RETURN FOR EVERY DOLLAR INVESTED IN IT

BASEMENT
CEILING HEIGHT 7'-2"

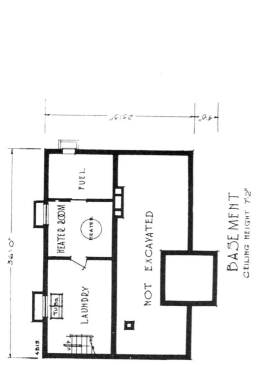

FIRST FLOOR
CEILING HEIGHT 8'-0"

Note—For guidance in reading floor plans, see explanation on page 14

EXTERIOR

STYLE: Colonial Adaptation. Bungalow type.

SIZE OF LOT REQUIRED: From 41 to 46 feet in width.

CONSTRUCTION: Wood frame on masonry foundations.

FINISH: Wide wood siding; roof shingled.

PORCH: Entrance porch, partly projecting and partly recessed. Its slender boxed columns and wall pilasters, its classic cornice and pediment make this porch the outstanding feature of the design.

DECORATIVE FEATURES: In addition to the charming porch, the house is distinguished by the dignity and simplicity of its various members. There is sufficient wall space to carry the large window openings. The roof pitch is well studied, resulting in pleasing gable ends. The cornice projection is right, and the chimney bold, yet unobtrusive.

COLOR SCHEME SUGGESTED: Wall siding painted white; roof stained green, window and door frames painted a pale gray with sash painted white; dark red chimneys.

ALTERNATE EXTERIORS: None.

INTERIOR

NUMBER OF ROOMS: 4 Main rooms, Dining Alcove, Bath-room and 3 Closets, all on one floor.

SIZE OF ROOMS:

Living Room	17' 0" x 13' 0"
Dining Alcove	8' 0" x 8' 6"
Kitchen	9' 0" x 9' 0"
Bed Room	12' 0" x 10' 6"
Bed Room	10' 0" x 10' 6"
Bath Room	5' 6" x 6' 8"

BASEMENT: Partially excavated, but of ample size to contain Laundry, Heater-room, and Fuel-bins.

PLAN TYPE: Living room running across the front of the house.

DESIGNED TO FACE: North or West. For other facings, plans should be reversed.

FIREPLACE: One large open fireplace on the inside wall of the living room, fine wood mantel.

VENTILATION: 21 casement windows arranged in banks of four, three, two and one to an opening. 2 outside doors; oriel windows in gable ends to admit free circulation of air under roof.

WALL SPACES: Ample for large pieces of furniture.

CUBIC CONTENTS: Approximately 15,800 cubic feet.

SPECIAL FEATURES

LIVING ROOM: Cheerful and well lighted with attractive group of windows facing the street and the side. The dining alcove is conveniently placed between the kitchen and living room, an arched beam opening makes the two rooms practically one.

KITCHEN: Faces the street; the working space extends across the front wall; the counter shelves on the two china cabinets provide a continuous shelf. Windows on two sides; china closet in dining alcove.

REAR ENTRY: Opening from the kitchen, in which the ice box is placed. The basement stairs may be reached through this passage from both the kitchen and the yard.

BED ROOMS: Facing the garden, providing exposures which will give them the morning sun. Reached by back hall from which the bath room and linen closet open. A closet is provided in each room.

PLUMBING: Includes bath tub, lavatory, water closet; laundry tubs, kitchen sink, hot and cold water supply.

ELECTRIC OUTLETS: In proper places available for iron, washing machine, vacuum cleaner, toaster, floor and table lamps, heaters, etc.

Design No. 4-B-15

House Plan No. 4A16

Architects' Small House Service Bureau

Northwestern Division

THE NEW ENGLANDER AND THE PENNSYLVANIA DUTCHMAN UNDERSTOOD THE ART OF COMBINING COMFORT WITH ECONOMY

THIS HOUSE IS BOTH COMFORTABLE TO LIVE IN AND ATTRACTIVE IN APPEARANCE, EACH ROOM IS CAREFULLY PLANNED TO GIVE MAXIMUM SERVICE

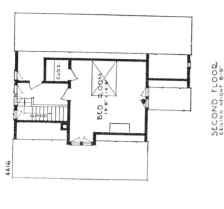

SECOND FLOOR
CEILING HEIGHT 8'-0"

FIRST FLOOR
CEILING HEIGHT 8'-4"

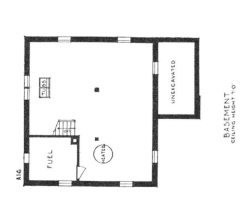

BASEMENT
CEILING HEIGHT 7'-0"

Note—For guidance in reading floor plans, see explanation on page 14

EXTERIOR

STYLE: Combination of New England and Pennsylvania Colonial. Story-and-a-half type.

SIZE OF LOT REQUIRED: From 35 to 40 feet in width.

CONSTRUCTION: Frame construction on masonry foundations, cement base course.

FINISH: Wood clapboard walls; shingled roof.

PORCHES: A small sheltered entrance porch, and a large glass-enclosed sun porch, opening into the living room.

CHIMNEY: One brick chimney with one flue, and terra cotta chimney pot.

DECORATIVE FEATURES: The grouping of the entrance porch and sun porch in one unit adds interest to the exterior. The columns and pilasters supporting the entrance are simple but in excellent taste. The bank of windows and the louvre in the pediment are well thought out. The overhang of the roof is sufficient to give a play of light and shade to the side of the house.

COLOR SCHEME SUGGESTED: White clapboards with white trim, door also white; green shutters; variegated roof shingles.

ALTERNATE EXTERIORS: This same basic plan with different exteriors, may be found on Pages 32, 36 and 128 House Plan Nos. 6A11, 6A12 and 4A15.

INTERIOR

NUMBER OF ROOMS: 4 Main rooms, 1 Unfinished room in Attic, Bath-room and 3 Closets.

SIZE OF ROOMS:

Living Room	11' 4" x 17' 6"
Dining Room	11' 4" x 11' 6"
Kitchen	9' 2" x 11' 6"
Bed Room	10' 2" x 10' 6"
Bath Room	5' 8" x 7' 9"

BASEMENT: Under entire house, containing Laundry, Heater-room, and Fuel-bins.

PLAN TYPE: Living room and dining room running across the front of the house.

DESIGNED TO FACE: North or West. For other facings, plans should be reversed.

FIREPLACES: None.

VENTILATION: 16 windows, with double hung sash, 8 casement windows; 2 outside doors, louvre in pediment for circulation of air in porch roof.

WALL SPACES: Ample for large pieces of furniture.

CUBIC CONTENTS: Approximately 18,200 cubic feet.

SPECIAL FEATURES

LIVING ROOM: Can easily be enlarged to take in the dining room and sun porch; making an ideal pace for entertaining. Convenient closet is provided in this room.

SUN PORCH: Is really an auxilliary living room, it serves many purposes equally well—sun room for winter, porch for summer.

KITCHEN: Good sized, and complete; out-door icing for ice box. Ample cupboard space.

REAR ENTRY: Stairs to kitchen and basement accessible directly from yard.

BED ROOM HALL runs back of the living room and gives direct access to kitchen from bed rooms, a most helpful arrangement for the housekeeper. Bath room and linen closet also open from this hall, as do the stairs to the incompleted second floor.

PLUMBING: Includes bath tub, lavatory, water closet, laundry tubs, kitchen sink, hot and cold water supply.

ELECTRIC OUTLETS: In proper places, available for iron, washing machine, vacuum cleaner, toaster, floor and table lamps, heaters, etc., if any or all of them are desired.

1 3 3

HOUSE PLAN NO. 4A21

Architects' Small House Service Bureau

4A21

A HAPPY COMBINATION OF NEW ENGLAND FORMALITY AND WESTERN FREEDOM OF STYLE

A MOST LIVABLE HOUSE, AND ONE THAT REFLECTS CREDIT ON ITS OWNER'S JUDGMENT

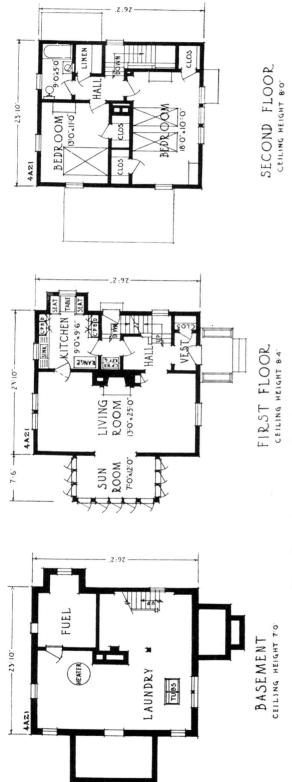

SECOND FLOOR
CEILING HEIGHT 8'·0"

FIRST FLOOR
CEILING HEIGHT 8'·4"

BASEMENT
CEILING HEIGHT 7'·0"

Note—For guidance in reading floor plans, see explanation on page 14

EXTERIOR

STYLE: Combination of New England Colonial and Prairie Style. Full two-story type.

SIZE OF LOT REQUIRED: From 40 to 45 feet in width.

CONSTRUCTION: Frame construction on masonry foundation, brick base course.

FINISH: Wide clapboards for first story, smooth siding or stucco for second story; and shingled roof.

PORCHES: Brick floored, semi-covered entrance porch; sun room 7' 0" x 12' 0", opening from living room.

CHIMNEY: One interior chimney, of brick, with 2 flues, taking care of heater, living room fireplace and kitchen range flues.

DECORATIVE FEATURES: The entrance stoop, brick floored, with its simple hood, supported on sturdy brackets, and sloping top, is the focal point of the front; the flower boxes on each side add a softening touch and the well panelled door, all make a distinctive group. The second story bank of windows is nicely proportioned to the wall space; the projection of the roof adds shadow and emphasizes the contrast between clapboards and siding.

COLOR SCHEME SUGGESTED: White walls, dark green door and shutters, variegated green roof shingles.

ALTERNATE EXTERIOR: This same basic plan with different exterior may be found on Page 136, House Plan No. 4A23.

INTERIOR

NUMBER OF ROOMS: 4 Main rooms, Dining Alcove, Bath-room and 5 Closets.

SIZE OF ROOMS:

First Floor

Living Room	13' 0" x 25' 0"
Kitchen	9' 0" x 9' 6"

Second Floor

Bed Room	18' 0" x 10' 0"
Bed Room	13' 0" x 11' 0"
Bath Room	9' 0" x 5' 0"

BASEMENT: Under entire house, containing Laundry, Heater-room and Fuel-bins.

PLAN TYPE: Living room running from front to back of the house.

DESIGNED TO FACE: East or South. For other facings, plans should be reversed.

FIREPLACE: One large fireplace in living room, with Colonial mantel.

VENTILATION: 14 windows, with double hung sash; 11 casement windows in sun porch; 2 outside doors.

WALL SPACES: Ample for large pieces of furniture.

CUBIC CONTENTS: Approximately 18,600 cubic feet.

SPECIAL FEATURES

LIVING ROOM: A room of excellent shape, with windows at each end; the fireplace and opening, without doors, into the sun porch, balance each other nicely. The chimney has a closet on one side, the lower part of which could be used to store paper and kindling; the upper for books. The door into the kitchen makes it possible to serve meals in this room if desired.

VESTIBULE AND ENTRANCE HALL: The closet in the vestibule is most useful in inclement weather; the hall gives direct passage to the living room and to the kitchen; the stairs ascend from it.

THE STAIRS: Have a landing half way up, with a window; a conservative type of staircase, making room for rear entry on first floor and for linen closet on second floor.

KITCHEN: Compact and convenient, ample cupboard space; the dining alcove is placed in a bay, well lighted, and has a built-in table with benches; part of the kitchen and yet separate.

BED ROOMS: Each has two exposures and a good sized closet; bath room and linen closet equally accessible to both.

PLUMBING: Includes bath tub, lavatory, water closet, laundry tubs, kitchen sink, water supply.

ELECTRIC OUTLETS: Properly placed, available for iron, washing machine, vacuum cleaner, toaster, floor and table lamps, heaters, etc.

Design No. 4-A-21

135

Architects' Small House Service Bureau

Northwestern Division

A HOME-LIKE MODERN DWELLING WITH JUST A SUGGESTION OF THE OLD WORLD

A NOVEL AND PERSONAL PLAN HAS BEEN DEVELOPED WHICH IS TRULY AMERICAN IN ITS COMPACTNESS AND ECONOMY

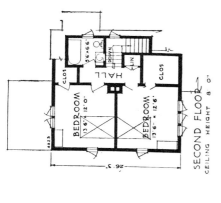

SECOND FLOOR
CEILING HEIGHT 8' 0"

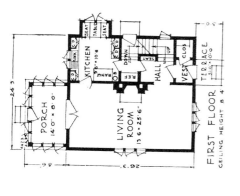

FIRST FLOOR
CEILING HEIGHT 8' 4"

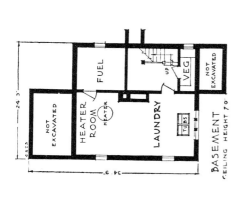

BASEMENT
CEILING HEIGHT 7' 0"

Note—For guidance in reading floor plans, see explanation on page 14

EXTERIOR

Style: English Half Timber. Two-story type.

Size of Lot Required: From 34 to 40 feet in width.

Construction: Wood frame on masonry foundations; brick steps.

Finish: Stucco with exposed timbers for walls; wood entrance hood and brackets; roof shingled.

Porches: Brick entrance terrace; living porch, 14' 0" x 8' 0" opening off living room.

Chimney: One inside brick chimney, covered with stucco above roof, contains the heater, fireplace and kitchen range flues.

Decorative Features: The form and outline are striking yet nothing bizarre is present. The timber work and hooded entrance suggest the homes of "Merrie England". Casement windows are also in keeping with the style.

Color Scheme Suggested: Cream colored walls with timbers stained dark brown; variegated brown stain for roof shingles.

Alternate Exteriors: This same basic plan, with different exteriors, may be found on Pages 108 and 134, House Plan No. 4B2 and 4A21.

INTERIOR

Number of Rooms: 4 Main rooms, Bath-room and 4 Closets.

Size of Rooms:

First Floor		
Living Room	13' 6" x 25' 6"	
Kitchen	9' 6" x 10' 6"	
Second Floor		
Bed Room	13' 6" x 12' 6"	
Bed Room	13' 6" x 12' 0"	
Bath Room	5' 6" x 6' 6"	

Basement: Under entire house, containing Laundry, Heater-room, Vegetable-storage and Fuel-bins.

Plan Type: Living room running from front to back of the house.

Designed to Face: East or South. For other facings, plans should be reversed.

Fireplace: One large fireplace in living room.

Ventilation: 20 casement windows, arranged to assure cross ventilation; 10 casement windows in porch; 2 outside doors.

Wall Spaces: Ample for large pieces of furniture.

Cubic Contents: Approximately 18,600 cubic feet.

SPECIAL FEATURES

Front Vestibule: Provides weather protection and a large coat closet. Opens directly into a well proportioned stair hall, lighted by a window on the stair landing.

Living Room: Extends full length of the house with windows on three sides. The room is so large that a table set at the garden end will answer all the needs of a dining room if dining alcove is not in use.

Kitchen: Designed to lighten labor and lessen steps. There is direct access to front entrance, stairs and living room.

Side Entry: The basement is reached without going through any part of the house, and an excellent space is provided for ice box.

Bed Rooms: Two large bed rooms, each with a closet of more than usual size. Commodious linen closet in upper hall.

Plumbing: Includes bath tub, lavatory, water closet, laundry tubs, kitchen sink, hot and cold water supply.

Electric Outlets: Properly placed, available for iron, washing machine, vacuum cleaner, toaster, floor and table lamps, heater, etc., if any or all of them are desired.

HOUSE PLAN NO. 3A1

Architects' Small House Service Bureau

Northwestern Division

A WELL DESIGNED WESTERN BUNGALOW OF GOOD PROPORTIONS AND ATTRACTIVE ROOF LINES
PLANNED TO GIVE A DEGREE OF COMFORT AND CONVENIENCE THAT ARE TRULY REMARKABLE IN SO SMALL A HOUSE

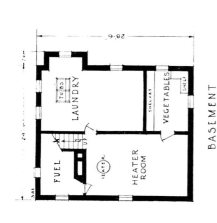

BASEMENT
CEILING HEIGHT 7'-0"

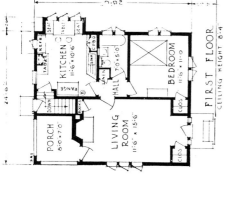

FIRST FLOOR
CEILING HEIGHT 8'-4"

Note—For guidance in reading floor plans, see explanation on page 11

EXTERIOR

STYLE: Western Bungalow. All rooms on one floor.

SIZE OF LOT REQUIRED: From 32 to 37 feet in width.

CONSTRUCTION: Wood frame on masonry foundations, cement base course.

FINISH: Wide wood siding for walls; may be shingles, stucco or brick; shingled roof.

PORCHES: Hooded entrance stoop; living porch at rear which can be screened or glazed inexpensively and used the year around.

CHIMNEY: One brick chimney, containing the heater and fireplace flues.

DECORATIVE FEATURES: The simple beauty of the house depends upon a few carefully considered details; in addition to the proportion of its mass and the nice placing of the windows and doors; the solid blinds and exposed rafter ends give a substantial effect.

COLOR SCHEME SUGGESTED: White walls and trim; blue blinds, variegated green stain on roof.

ALTERNATE EXTERIORS: None.

INTERIOR

NUMBER OF ROOMS: 3 Main rooms, Bath-room and 3 Closets.

SIZE OF ROOMS:

Living Room	11' 6" x 15' 6"
Kitchen	11' 6" x 10' 6"
Bed Room	11' 6" x 11' 0"

BASEMENT: Under the entire house, containing Laundry, Heater-room, Vegetable-storage and Fuel-bins.

PLAN TYPE: Living room running from front to back of the house.

DESIGNED TO FACE: North or East. For other facings, plans should be reversed.

FIREPLACE: One large open fireplace in the living room.

VENTILATION: 12 casement windows, 1 double hung window; louvres in gable ends to air the attic space and keep rooms below cooler in summer, and warmer in winter.

WALL SPACES: Ample for large pieces of furniture.

CUBIC CONTENTS: Approximately 13,500 cubic feet.

SPECIAL FEATURES

LIVING ROOM: Is unusually pleasant with light and air on three sides; triple casement windows, brick fireplace with panels above and adjoining built-in bookcase make the room most livable. The full length glazed entrance door and porch door afford glimpses of street and garden; there is a convenient coat closet at the left upon entering.

DINING ALCOVE: Provides all the advantages of a dining room; opens directly from the kitchen and has built-in table with seats at the sides.

KITCHEN: Compact and well-equipped with cupboards and work-table; direct delivery of ice to ice box without entering house.

DIRECT ENTRANCE TO BASEMENT: Stairs descend to basement from rear entry.

BED ROOM: Nice corner room opening off an inner hall, insuring privacy and quietness; cross ventilation and large closet; linen closet in the hall.

PLUMBING: Includes bath tub, lavatory, water closet, laundry tubs, kitchen sink and hot and cold water supply.

ELECTRIC OUTLETS: Properly placed, available for iron, washing machine, vacuum cleaner, toaster, floor and table lamps, heaters, etc., if any or all of them should be desired.

Design No. 3-A-1

139

HOUSE PLAN NO. 3B1

3B1

"DOWN EAST" COLONIAL COTTAGE RETAINING THE SPIRIT OF THE FAMOUS HOUSES ON CAPE COD
A MOST CONVENIENT MODERN HOUSE, DEPENDING FOR ITS BEAUTY UPON PROPORTION AND DETAILS, SPARINGLY EMPLOYED

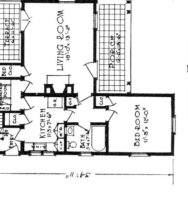

BASEMENT
CEILING HEIGHT 7'-0"

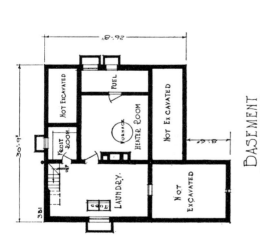

FIRST FLOOR
CEILING HEIGHT 8'-6"

Note—For guidance in reading floor plans, see explanation on page 14

EXTERIOR

STYLE: New England Colonial. Bungalow type.

SIZE OF LOT REQUIRED: From 40 to 45 feet in width.

CONSTRUCTION: Wood frame on masonry foundations.

FINISH: Wide wood lapsiding for walls. Shingled roof.

PORCHES: Living porch, 6' 0" x 18' 6", with the main roof extended to shelter it. Paved open terrace opening off the living room.

CHIMNEY: One brick chimney on inside wall containing heater, fireplace and kitchen range flues, and providing breast for kitchen range.

DECORATIVE FEATURES: There is a sweetness and simplicity about this design which make it likeable. It is Colonial in scale and the detail in consequence is slim, light and delicate, as befits wood, which is so easily worked and of so little weight. A house of small dimensions but of great beauty.

COLOR SCHEME SUGGESTED: Siding painted white; roof shingles stained brownish-green; shutters painted blue-green; door and window frames painted white.

ALTERNATE EXTERIORS: None.

INTERIOR

NUMBER OF ROOMS: 3 Main rooms, Breakfast-nook, Bath-room and 4 Closets.

SIZE OF ROOMS:

Living Room	18' 0" x 13' 2"
Kitchen	11' 3" x 7' 6"
Bed Room	11' 3" x 12' 0"
Bath Room	5' 4" x 7' 6"

BASEMENT: Not completely excavated under the entire house, but contains an ample Laundry, Heater-room, Fruit-room and Fuel-bins.

PLAN TYPE: Living room the dominating feature, with all the rooms of the house in direct communication with it.

DESIGNED TO FACE: West or North. For other facings, plans should be reversed.

FIREPLACE: One large open fireplace in the center of the inside wall of the living room; fine Colonial mantelpiece.

VENTILATION: 9 windows with double hung sash; pair of full length casement windows opening onto terrace; 2 outside doors; louvres in gable ends to permit free circulation of air under roof.

WALL SPACES: Ample for large pieces of furniture.

CUBIC CONTENTS: Approximately 12,600 cubic feet.

SPECIAL FEATURES

LIVING ROOM: The relation between the length and breadth of the room is excellent, with windows on three sides it will get the afternoon sun and be cheerful in all seasons of the year. A window-seat with built-in bookcases on each side is included; a closet opening off this room provides space for a wall-bed for the guest.

BREAKFAST NOOK: Equipped with built-in seats with hinged tops, a dining table, and an attractive china closet. It is accessible from both kitchen and living room.

KITCHEN: Very compact, designed and equipped to do away with extra steps for the housekeeper. It contains a large storage closet.

REAR ENTRY: Stairs to basement descend from here with direct passage from basement and from kitchen to the yard. Space for ice box with cupboard above is included.

BED ROOM: Placed in front of house, opening off an inside hall, with bath room and linen closet adjoining.

PLUMBING: Includes bath tub, lavatory, water closet, laundry tubs, kitchen sink and hot and cold water supply.

ELECTRIC OUTLETS: In proper places, available for iron, washing machine, vacuum cleaner, toaster, floor and table lamps, heaters, etc., if any or all of them are desired.

141

House Plan No. 3A2

Architects' Small House Service Bureau

THE PICTURESQUENESS AND HOME-LIKE ATMOSPHERE OF ENGLISH COTTAGES

HERE IS A HOUSE WHICH IS ATTRACTIVE, CONVENIENTLY PLANNED AND REASONABLE TO BUILD

BASEMENT
CEILING HEIGHT 7'-0"

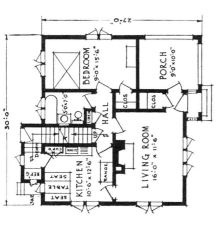

FIRST FLOOR
CEILING HEIGHT 8'-4"

SECOND FLOOR
CEILING HEIGHT 8'-0"

Note—For guidance in reading floor plans see explanation on page 14

EXTERIOR

Style: English Cottage. Story-and-a-half type.

Size of Lot Required: From 35 to 40 feet in width.

Construction: Wood frame on masonry foundations.

Finish: Stucco on metal lath; roof shingled.

Porch: Living porch 9' 0" x 10' 0", included under main roof. It has boxed railing and can be screened or glazed for all year around use, thereby adding one more room to the house.

Chimney: One brick chimney covered with stucco.

Decorative Features: While practically square in plan the clipped gable ends destroy the box-like appearance; the triple window in living room; eyebrow hood over the entrance stoop.

Color Scheme Suggested: Cream colored stucco, roof variegated shingles; wood work stained dark oak color.

Alternate Exteriors: This same basic plan with different exteriors can be found on Pages 144, 148 and 150, House Plan Nos. 3A3, 3A7 and 3A9.

INTERIOR

Number of Rooms: 3 Main rooms, Bath-room, and 3 Closets; unfinished room in attic.

Size of Rooms:

Living Room	16' 0" x 11' 6"
Kitchen	10' 6" x 12' 6"
Bed Room	9' 0" x 15' 6"
Bath Room	5' 0" x 7' 0"

Basement: Under entire house, containing Laundry, Heater-room, Vegetable-storage, Fuel-bins.

Plan Type: Living room and porch running across the front of the house.

Designed to Face: North or West. For other facings, plans should be reversed.

Fireplace: One brick fireplace with brick mantel facing and wood shelf.

Ventilation: 15 casement windows; 2 outside doors.

Wall Spaces: Ample for large pieces of furniture.

Cubic Contents: Approximately 17,000 cubic feet.

SPECIAL FEATURES

Extra Bed Room: In attic is provided as shown on second floor plan.

Eating Accommodations: In kitchen where built-in dining table and seats are provided, or the end of the living room can be used for this purpose.

Entrance Hall: With good sized coat closet.

Kitchen: Has cupboard spaces and plenty of light and air. Ice box in rear entry iced from outside.

Living Room: Has outlook from two sides. It is a room of pleasing proportions.

Stairs: Descend to basement from rear entry and space for stairs to second floor is provided over these.

Bed Room: Is a corner room opening from a private hall. Sunlight and air are assured by windows on two sides. It has a large closet.

Linen Closet: In the back hall.

Medicine Cabinet: In the bath room.

Plumbing: Includes bath tub, water closet, lavatory, kitchen sink, laundry tubs and hot and cold water supply.

Electric Outlets: In proper places, available for iron, washing machine, vacuum cleaner, toaster, floor and table lamps, heaters, if any or all are desired.

Design No. 3-A-2

143

Northwestern Division

House Plan No. 3A3

A SNUG THREE ROOM BUNGALOW REMINISCENT OF COLONIAL COTTAGES

THE PRACTICAL, ALMOST SQUARE PLAN, AND THE REFINEMENT OF DETAILS MAKE THIS HOUSE INEXPENSIVE TO BUILD

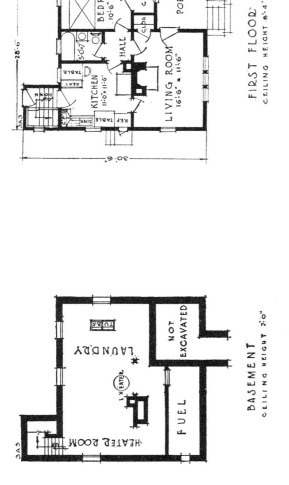

BASEMENT
CEILING HEIGHT 7'-0"

FIRST FLOOR
CEILING HEIGHT 8'-4"

Note—For guidance in reading floor plans, see explanation on page 14

EXTERIOR

STYLE: Cottage Bungalow. All rooms on one floor.

SIZE OF LOT REQUIRED: From 34 to 39 feet in width.

CONSTRUCTION: Wood frame on masonry foundation, concrete base course.

FINISH: Wide wood siding; may be shingles or stucco if preferred. Roof shingled.

PORCH: Corner living porch, 8' 0" x 11' 0".

CHIMNEY: One brick chimney, with heater, fireplace and kitchen range flues.

DECORATIVE FEATURES: The house is frankly kept very simple, four straight walls and a gable roof without meaningless projection of eaves and a lot of details crowded into a small building.

COLOR SCHEME SUGGESTED: Walls, trim and columns painted white, roof stained variegated green.

ALTERNATE EXTERIORS: This same basic plan with different exteriors can be found on Pages 142, 148 and 150, House Plan Nos. 3A2, 3A7 and 3A9.

INTERIOR

NUMBER OF ROOMS: 3 Main rooms, Bath-room, 2 Closets.

SIZE OF ROOMS:
Living Room   16' 6" x 11' 6"
Kitchen   11' 0" x 11' 6"
Bed Room   10' 6" x 11' 6"
Bath Room   5' 0" x 7' 0"

BASEMENT: Under entire house, containing Laundry, Heater-room, Fuel-bins.

PLAN TYPE: Living room across the front of the house.

DESIGNED TO FACE: North or West. For other facings, plans should be reversed.

FIREPLACE: One brick fireplace with wood trim.

VENTILATION: 11 windows with double hung sash; 1 casement window; 2 outside doors; louvres in gables ventilate space under roof in summer.

WALL SPACES: Ample for large pieces of furniture.

CUBIC CONTENTS: Approximately 13,900 cubic feet.

SPECIAL FEATURES

LIVING ROOM: Attractive proportions with light and air on three sides. The triple windows help to furnish the room.

COAT CLOSET: In living room close by the front door.

KITCHEN: Is well planned and modern in every way. It is large enough to get a built-in dining table and seat in one end. The ice box can be iced from outside.

BED ROOM: Has cross ventilation with windows on two sides. It has a large closet supplied with a window.

BATH ROOM AND BED ROOM: Lead from a small hall which gives privacy to these rooms. There is a built-in medicine cabinet in the bath room.

PLUMBING: Includes bath tub, water closet, lavatory, kitchen sink, laundry tubs and hot and cold water supply.

ELECTRIC OUTLETS: Properly placed, available for iron, washing machine, vacuum cleaner, toaster, floor and table lamps, heaters, etc., if any or all are desired.

145

HOUSE PLAN NO. 3A5

A BUNGALOW OF GOOD PROPORTIONS AND ONE THAT ELIMINATES THE HEAVY FEATURES SO COMMON IN THIS TYPE OF HOUSE

THIS ECONOMICAL PLAN OFFERS A LARGE AMOUNT OF COMFORT WITHIN A LIMITED FLOOR SPACE AND FOR LITTLE MONEY

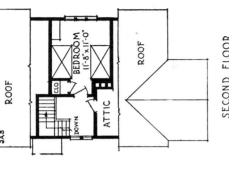

ROOF

ROOF

BEDROOM
11'-8" x 11'-0"

CLO

DOWN

ATTIC

SECOND FLOOR
CEILING HEIGHT 7'-0"

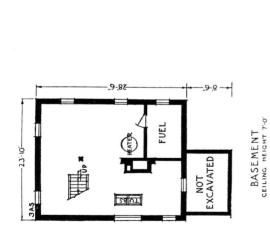

BEDROOM
11'-4" x 11'-0"

CLOS

UP

LIN

KITCHEN
7'10" x 12'-0"

REF.

DOWN

LIVING ROOM
11'-4" x 16'-4"

CLOS

VEST

SEAT

TABLE

SEAT

PORCH

FIRST FLOOR
CEILING HEIGHT 8'-4"

28'-6"

23'-10"

8'-6"

BASEMENT
CEILING HEIGHT 7'-0"

28'-6"

23'-10"

8'-6"

HEATER

FUEL

TUBS

UP

NOT EXCAVATED

Note—For guidance in reading floor plans, see explanation on page 14

EXTERIOR

STYLE: Western Bungalow type.

SIZE OF LOT REQUIRED: From 29 to 34 feet in width, depending upon city ordinances.

CONSTRUCTION: Wood frame on masonry foundations, cement base course.

FINISH: Wood siding for walls; shingled roof; walls may be stucco if desired.

PORCHES: Front entrance and living porch.

CHIMNEY: One inside brick chimney, containing the heater, fireplace and kitchen range flues.

DECORATIVE FEATURES: This house may be built in several different materials for its interest lies in its well proportioned wall spaces, its masses and its simple details; there has been no effort to invent something that a planing mill could not fabricate. In a home like this we please not only ourselves but our most critical friends.

COLOR SCHEME SUGGESTED: Walls and trim painted white: roof stained variegated greens and browns.

ALTERNATE EXTERIORS: None.

INTERIOR

NUMBER OF ROOMS: 3 Main rooms, Dining Alcove, Bath-room and 3 Closets.

SIZE OF ROOMS:

Living Room	11' 4" x 16' 4"
Kitchen	7' 10" x 12' 0"
Bed Room	11' 4" x 11' 0"
Bath Room	5' 4" x 6' 9"

BASEMENT. Under the main portion of the house, containing Laundry, Heater-room and Fuel-bins.

PLAN TYPE: Square with every room having two exposures.

DESIGNED TO FACE: North or West. For other facings, plans should be reversed.

FIREPLACE: One large open fireplace in the center of the inside wall of the living room; wood mantel-piece.

VENTILATION: 14 windows with double hung sash; 2 outside doors.

WALL SPACES: Ample for large pieces of furniture.

CUBIC CONTENTS: Approximately 15,000 cubic feet.

SPECIAL FEATURES

ADDITIONAL BED ROOM: There is space for another bed room with a closet and a storage closet on the upper floor, if it is desired to finish off the attic; stairs are provided to reach this second floor.

ENTRANCE VESTIBULE: Provided with coat closet; both living room and kitchen open direct from here, saving many steps.

DINING ALCOVE: Compact arrangement of built-in table and seats offering the advantages of a dining room, but taking up very little floor space.

KITCHEN: The sink, work-table, range and cupboards are placed where they will receive the best light and be most convenient.

BED ROOM: It has a large closet and windows on two sides.

EXTRA CLOSETS: There is a linen closet in the rear hall, a broom closet provided in the kitchen and a built-in medicine cabinet in the bath room.

PLUMBING: Includes bath tub, lavatory, water closet, laundry tubs, kitchen sink, hot and cold water supply.

ELECTRIC OUTLETS: Properly placed, available for iron, washing machine, vacuum cleaner, toaster, floor and table lamps, heater, etc., if any or all of them are desired.

147

HOUSE PLAN NO. 3A7

Architects' Small House Service Bureau

A LITTLE DWELLING THAT HAS WON FAVOR IN MANY PARTS OF THE UNITED STATES

HOSPITALITY HAS BEEN BUILT INTO THE EXTERIOR AND INTERIOR OF THIS LITTLE HOUSE   EVERY DETAIL HAS A REAL MEANING

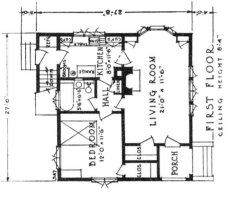

FIRST FLOOR
CEILING HEIGHT 8'-4"

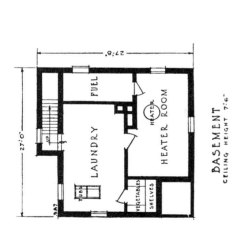

BASEMENT
CEILING HEIGHT 7'-6"

Note—For guidance in reading floor plans, see explanation on page 14

EXTERIOR

STYLE: Bungalow.
All rooms on one floor.

SIZE OF LOT REQUIRED: From 32 to 47 feet in width.

CONSTRUCTION: Wood frame on masonry foundations.

FINISH: Stucco; roof shingled.

PORCH: Small covered entrance porch.

CHIMNEY: One interior brick chimney, with stucco finish above roof, containing the heater, fireplace and kitchen range flues.

DECORATIVE FEATURES: Unusually simple in design, depending upon its good proportion and excellent scale for beauty. The triple window and deftly planned bay on one side add interest.

COLOR SCHEME SUGGESTED: Floated finish cream stucco; shingles stained dark brown.

ALTERNATE EXTERIORS: This same basic plan with different exteriors may be found on Pages 142, 144 and 150, House Plan Nos. 3A2, 3A3 and 3A9.

INTERIOR

NUMBER OF ROOMS: 3 Main rooms, Bath-room and 3 Closets.

SIZE OF ROOMS:

Living Room	21' 0" x 11' 6"
Kitchen	8' 0" x 11' 6"
Bed Room	12' 0" x 11' 6"
Bed Room	5' 6" x 6' 6"

BASEMENT: Under main portion of the house, containing Laundry, Heater-room, Vegetable-storage and Fuel-bins.

PLAN TYPE: Living room running across the front of the house.

DESIGNED TO FACE: South or West.
For other facings, plans should be reversed.

FIREPLACE: One brick fireplace in living room.

VENTILATION: 16 casement windows; 2 outside doors; attic space under roof is ventilated by louvres in gable ends.

WALL SPACES: Ample for large pieces of furniture.

CUBIC CONTENTS: Approximately 14,000 cubic feet.

SPECIAL FEATURES

LIVING ROOM: Unusually large, with built-in corner cupboards on each side of an attractive bay window; the room is large enough to hold a dining table, which can be set in one end if so desired.

EXTRA SLEEPING ACCOMMODATIONS: Can be obtained by installing a closet-bed in the large closet off the living room.

KITCHEN: Is supplied with plenty of cupboard space and a broom closet; the refrigerator is just outside the door in the rear entry.

BED ROOM: Is practically square with ideal place for double bed; windows on two sides, and a large closet.

LINEN CLOSET: In rear hall.

COAT CLOSET: In living room at the left of the entrance door.

PLUMBING: Includes bath tub, lavatory, water closet, kitchen sink, laundry tubs and hot and cold water supply.

ELECTRIC OUTLETS: Properly placed, available for iron, washing machine, vacuum cleaner, toaster, floor and table lamps, heaters, etc., if any or all of them are desired.

Architects' Small House Service Bureau

Northwestern Division

3A9

THE STYLE OF THIS HOUSE IS ENGLISH, ADAPTED TO AMERICAN IDEAS OF A HOME

THIS STORY-AND-A-HALF BUNGALOW WOULD ATTRACT NOTICE, EVEN IN A COLONY OF HOMES COSTING TWO OR THREE TIMES AS MUCH

SECOND FLOOR
CEILING HEIGHT 7'-8".

FIRST FLOOR
CEILING HEIGHT 8'-6"

BASEMENT
CEILING HEIGHT 7'-6"

Note—For guidance in reading floor plans, see explanation on page 14

EXTERIOR

STYLE: English Cottage. Story-and-a-half type.

SIZE OF LOT REQUIRED: From 35 to 40 feet in width, depending upon city ordinances.

CONSTRUCTION: Wood frame on masonry foundation, cement base course.

FINISH: Wood shingles for walls; roof shingled.

PORCHES: Front covered porch, 6' 0" x 12' 0", which shades and protects the entrance.

CHIMNEY: One interior brick chimney, containing the heater, fireplace and kitchen range flues.

DECORATIVE FEATURES: The picturesque roof lines and the excellent placing of the windows; there is not one feature without a structural value; take any one of them away, and something is lacking.

COLOR SCHEME SUGGESTED: Shingles stained a warm brown, with roof to match.

ALTERNATE EXTERIORS: This same basic plan with different exteriors may be found on Pages 138, 142, 144 and 148, House Plan Nos. 3A1, 3A2, 3A3 and 3A7.

INTERIOR

NUMBER OF ROOMS: 3 Main rooms, Bath-room and 3 Closets.

SIZE OF ROOMS:
Living Room   17' 6" x 13' 0"
Kitchen   8' 0" x 11' 0"
Bed Room   10' 6" x 13' 0"
Bath Room   5' 6" x 8' 0"

BASEMENT: Under entire house, containing Laundry, Heater-room, Vegetable-storage and Fuel-bins.

PLAN TYPE: Living room running across the front of the house.

DESIGNED TO FACE: South or West. For other facings, plans should be reversed.

FIREPLACE: One large open fireplace in the living room.

VENTILATION: 11 windows with double hung sash; 3 casement windows over dining alcove; 2 outside doors.

WALL SPACE: Ample for large pieces of furniture.

CUBIC CONTENTS: Approximately 16,500 cubic feet.

SPECIAL FEATURES

ON THE SECOND FLOOR: There is space to finish off a bed room, with windows for cross ventilation if desired; space has been provided for stairs to reach this floor.

THE DINING ALCOVE: With built-in seats and table occupies a bay off the living room. It has all the advantages of a dining room yet does not take up the same amount of space in the house.

KITCHEN: Is small, but fitted and planned efficiently. The ice box is in the rear entry, with door for outside icing.

BED ROOM: Is off by itself with cross ventilation and has a spacious closet.

LINEN CLOSET: In back hall, which gives privacy to bed room and bath room.

VESTIBULE: Provided with a large coat closet.

PLUMBING: Includes bath tub, lavatory, water closet, laundry tubs, kitchen sink, hot and cold water supply.

ELECTRIC OUTLETS: Properly placed, available for iron, washing machine, vacuum cleaner, toaster, floor and table lamps, heater, etc., if any or all of them are desired.

House Plan No. 3B9

Mountain Division

Architects' Small House Service Bureau

A BUNGALOW OF RUSTIC ROMANCE AND ECONOMY, EVEN NOW, AS IN THE DAYS OF THE FRONTIERSMEN

POSSESSING ALL THE REQUIREMENTS AND DELIGHTS OF A COMFORTABLE HOME IN THE MOUNTAINS OR COUNTRY

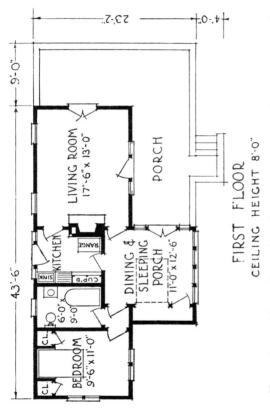

FIRST FLOOR

CEILING HEIGHT 8'-0"

Note—For guidance in reading floor plans, see explanation on page 14

Floor plan labels:
- BEDROOM 9'-6" x 11'-0"
- CL / CL
- KITCHEN
- SINK
- CUP'D.
- RANGE
- 6'-0" / 9'-0"
- LIVING ROOM 17'-6" x 13'-0"
- DINING & SLEEPING PORCH 11'-0" x 12'-6"
- PORCH
- 43'-6"
- 9'-0"
- 23'-2"
- 4'-0"

EXTERIOR

STYLE: Lake or Mountain Cottage. One-story type.

SIZE OF LOT REQUIRED: Inappropriate in a congested neighborhood; needs land around it to set it off.

CONSTRUCTION: From the foundation to the first floor level, irregular stone, laid at random; wood frame above; shingled, roof.

FINISH: Upper walls of random width, rough sawed boards.

PORCHES: Terrace porch designed for sitting in the open on one side; sheltered at one end. Does not cut off sunlight from living room.

CHIMNEY: One large, rough stone interior chimney, containing fireplace and kitchen range flues.

DECORATIVE FEATURES: Very charming in its general appearance, with long, low roof lines; its eaves, with exposed rafters, and its generous windows; the horizontal lines are accentuated so that it has the air of always having existed and being indigenous to a beautiful countryside.

COLOR SCHEME SUGGESTED: Walls stained a weathered oak color, roof shingles stained variegated browns and greens; foundations, local stone.

ALTERNATE EXTERIORS: None.

INTERIOR

NUMBER OF ROOMS: 3 Main rooms, Dining and Sleeping-porch, Bath-room and 3 Closets.

SIZE OF ROOMS:

Living Room	17' 6" x 13' 0"
Kitchen	7' 0" x 9' 0"
Bed Room	9' 6" x 11' 0"
Dining Room and Sleeping Porch	11' 0" x 12' 6"
Bath Room	6' 0" x 9' 0"

BASEMENT: While there is no excavation required, the first floor is sufficiently above grade so that one is not sleeping on the ground.

PLAN TYPE: The arrangement makes it possible to take advantage of the views from any room of the house; easy to get from room to room.

DESIGNED TO FACE: Can be placed in any direction of the compass.

FIREPLACE: One large open fireplace, of rough stone, with wood mantel shelf.

VENTILATION: 17 windows with double hung sash; 2 pairs of casement windows leading to porch and terrace; 2 outside doors; louvres in gable ends to permit free circulation of air under roofs.

WALL SPACES: Ample for large pieces of furniture.

CUBIC CONTENTS: Approximately 11,700 cubic feet.

SPECIAL FEATURES

THE MAIN FLOOR: Is reached from the open porch, four steps above grade.

THE LIVING ROOM: Is open on three sides, and has a ceiling of exposed rafters, which, in combination with the rough stone fireplace, are in keeping with the exterior.

KITCHEN: Most conveniently placed, and containing all the requirements usually found in town houses; it adjoins the bath room, reducing plumbing costs.

DINING AND SLEEPING PORCH: Entered directly from the kitchen as well as from living room and bed room. Its abundance of windows and its easy access to the bath room make it an ideal sleeping porch; a patented bed could be put in the bed closet provided; also has a clothes closet.

BED ROOM: Conveniently located in relation to bath room; contains two closets and two windows for cross ventilation.

PLUMBING: Includes bath tub, lavatory, water closet, laundry tubs, kitchen sink, hot and cold water supply.

ELECTRIC OUTLETS: Properly placed, available for iron, washing machine, vacuum cleaner; toaster, floor and table lamps, heaters, etc., if any or all of them are desired.

Design No. 3-B-9

153

What The Architects' Small House Service Bureau Has to Offer

A Real Service at a Moderate Cost

The Advantage of Using Carefully Prepared Plans and Documents, Combined with Professional Counsel and Building Advice

THE Architects' Small House Service Bureau offers as complete a plan service as can possibly be devised. Only from an individual practicing architect working out your own individual building problem, could you get anything more complete.

They furnish you "Working Drawings and Details," "Specifications," a "Quantity Survey," form of "Agreement Between Contractor and Owner," and an advisory and most helpful architectural service during the time your house is being built.

Working Drawings and Details

The "Working Drawings and Details" are the complete plans which the contractor must use in building. The plans are not of the "hit or miss" variety. They are not gotten out as an inducement to purchase certain building materials, supplies, or any form of home equipment. They are drawn accurately by the most skillful architects. They have been checked, re-checked, and back-checked. They have been made as accurate as is humanly possible to make them. They are designed to reduce the cost of good construction, wherever possible being so drawn as to permit the use of standard lengths of lumber and standard sizes of other materials, thereby avoiding waste. If need be, the Bureau can make minor changes in the drawings to meet your individual needs, and would charge you a nominal price for doing this added work, the charge depending upon how much time it takes to make the revisions.

Contractors have told the Bureau again and again that they have been able to build from their drawings more accurately and more quickly, and can build a better house than from so many of the inaccurate, undependable plans furnished today by untrained and inexperienced draftsmen.

The reason for this is that the Bureau's plans are painstakingly and intelligently studied and accurately drawn by accredited and experienced practicing architects. When the house is built it is a credit to the builder and he is proud to turn it over to the owner.

When a contractor has a thorough set of plans he can build quickly and accurately. Doing the work once and doing it right costs less and makes a better job than doing it wrong and doing it over again. An accurate set of plans not only saves you money but insures your house being well built.

Specifications

The "Specifications" cover a list of the various materials that the contractor is to use and the character of workmanship that is to be done in the building of your home. They give you the opportunity of definitely determining beforehand each kind of material that is to be used and the quality of workmanship that you require, overcoming the possibility of later misunderstandings or disputes. Of necessity, with so many local conditions controlling, these "Specifications" as first sent you cannot in all details be complete, though after consulting with your local architect or with some reliable local contractor and advice from The Architects' Small House Service Bureau, they can soon be made so. Through the use of a complete set of "Specifications" you know exactly what to expect as regards materials and workmanship during the building of your house, and the contractor knows just what he must do to fulfill his contract. Starting to build a home without a set of "Specifications" is like starting on a voyage on an unknown sea without a chart to steer by.

If you require special "Specifications" in addition to those that accompany your plans, the

Bureau will prepare them for you, asking you to pay a nominal fee for the necessary time and labor required in their preparation.

Quantity Survey

The "Quantity Survey" shows the quantity and size of each of the various materials required in the building of the house plan selected by you. This is a very unusual service to find with small house plans. Practicing architects rarely give this service. It has been added so as to give contractors a check on their estimates. Contractors say that these lists of materials have helped many times to see where they were overfiguring the quantities or under-figuring them. A list of materials such as this makes it possible for all contractors to figure on substantially the same basis. The contractor knows, with this list, the quantities of each material needed to complete the job, he does not find it necessary, therefore, to add an amount to protect himself against the possible contingency of his estimate being too low. If you build the house by day labor, the bill of materials acts as a buying list, its accuracy depending on how you utilize the materials. This "Quantity Survey" is in such form as to make it easily possible for anyone who uses it to get all needed information from it.

These three documents—complete working drawings, a definite set of specifications, and an accurate quantity survey—combine together to give the contractor confidence that he can build your house without making costly mistakes and so make it possible for him to build more economically. With this you get the benefits of reduced costs and at the same time a better building.

Form of Agreement

The fourth document furnished is the form of "Agreement Between Contractor and Owner." This is based on the standard legal forms used by The American Institute of Architects. It is the printed agreement that you sign with your contractor by which he promises to deliver to you your completed house in accordance with the specifications and by which you promise to pay him an agreed-upon sum. It is a carefully prepared document and is a necessary safeguard. There are no pitfalls in it. Each one knows what he has to do. This agreement form tops off the whole scheme of the Bureau's document service, and makes it complete, accurate and dependable in every way.

Service

There is one last thought to leave with you and a most important one. It is the service, and the real service, that stands behind the Architects' Small House Service Bureau. You know what service means. When you buy a motor car or a washing machine, the company selling it stands behind the sale to see that you get full value for your money. During the time your house is being built the Bureau would want and would expect to be helpful in rendering you such service as will insure, insofar as is possible to do, your getting a good building. They answer your questions about materials; tell you frankly and exactly what the value of any material or mechanical device you may wish to use may be. They are not financially interested in, nor prejudiced in favor of any material, device, or mechanical affair of any kind, but are interested in helping you secure full value for your investment. If you wish to have the Bureau give an alternate color scheme for the painting of your house to the one suggested with each house plan, they will do it. Do not hesitate to ask for any assistance of this kind. Of course there must be some limit to what they can do in this way with the low charge that is made for the complete service, but they have never had a client ask more of them than they were glad to give. They are pleased to help home-builders with their problems.

The prices for complete working drawings, specifications, quantity survey and form of agreement, including professional counsel and building advice, range from $15.50 to $35.50. You will find a complete list of prices on page 164.

Building Documents Supplied by The Bureau

THERE is illustrated on the following pages in considerably reduced size, a complete set of building documents prepared and furnished by The Architects' Small House Service Bureau. The Working Drawings and Details consist of three to five sheets of blue prints. These blue prints as they come to you measure 17 by 24 inches, and are bound together in a tough paper cover. Following the usual custom in architects' offices, these plans and elevations are drawn at the standard scale of one-quarter inch to the foot, with all important details of construction drawn at larger scale.

Study the completeness of these drawings, covering as they do all exterior, interior, foundation and framing details. You get as complete a set of drawings as you would secure if you employed an individual practicing architect to design your house. All drawings have been checked, re-checked and double-checked to insure their being as accurate as it is humanly possible to make them.

Window and door schedules are shown. Dimensions are clear and accurate. Notes cover special items. In fact all data, professional and technical, is given to insure your home being erected just as it has been planned.

Accompanying each plan is a set of "Specifications." You also receive a "Quantity Survey," listing the quantity of each material required in construction. In addition we supply you with form of "Agreement Between Contractor and Owner."

All plans are carefully bound and delivered in good condition. In fact you receive four complete and separate documents when you use the Bureau service. *First*, "Working Drawings and Details"; *second*, "Specifications"; *third*, "Quantity Survey"; *fourth*, "Form of Agreement Between Contractor and Owner." You get all these when you buy the complete building service offered by The Architects' Small House Service Bureau.

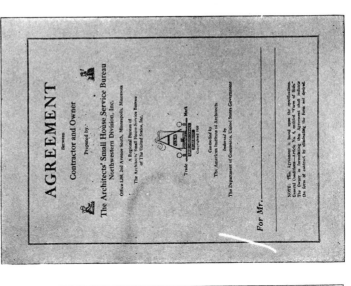

The "Specifications" tell the way in which your house is to be built and the materials that are to go into it. They provide an opportunity for you to indicate beforehand the manner of construction and the various materials you may prefer. *See Page 154.*

The "Quantity Survey" is an unusual and most helpful service. It lists the quantities and sizes of each of the different materials required. Its purpose is to make it possible for you to buy the amount of material needed. *See Page 155.*

The "Agreement Between Contractor and Owner" contains four pages covering general contract. It provides a clearly understood business-like agreement between your builder and yourself. *See Page 155.*

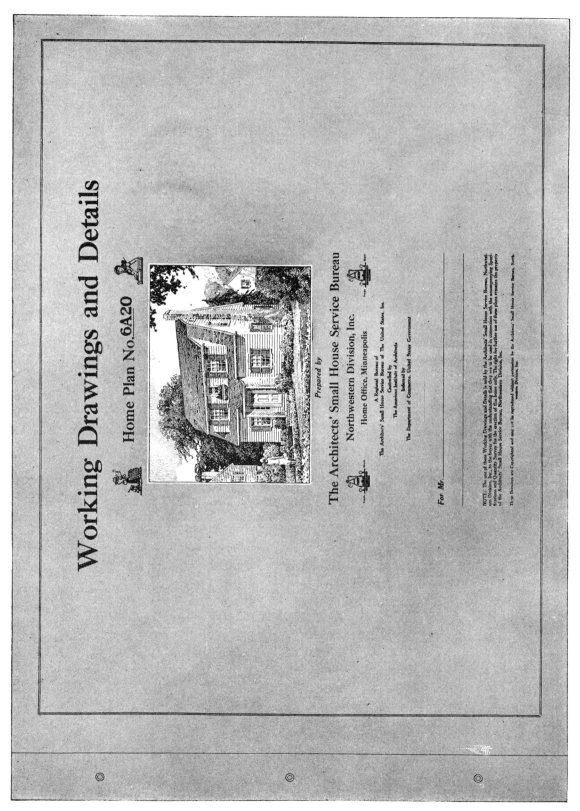

Working Drawings and Details

Home Plan No. 6A20

Prepared by

The Architects' Small House Service Bureau

Northwestern Division, Inc.
Home Office, Minneapolis

A Regional Bureau of
The Architects' Small House Service Bureau of The United States, Inc.

Controlled by
The American Institute of Architects

Indorsed by
The Department of Commerce, United States Government

For Mr. _____

NOTE: The use of these Working Drawings and Details is sold by the Architects' Small House Service Bureau, Northwestern Division, Inc. to the buyer with the understanding that they are to be used in connection with the accompanying Specifications and Quantity Survey for the erection of this home only. The right for further use of these plans remains the property of the Architects' Small House Service Bureau, Northwestern Division, Inc.

These Drawings are Copyrighted and may not be reproduced without permission by the Architects' Small House Service Bureau, Northwestern Division, Inc.

The "Working Drawings and Details" are blue prints bound with a cover of heavy brown kraft paper. These blue prints measure 17 inches x 24 inches. This document contains three to five complete sheets showing floor plans, elevations and details. The picture of your future home appears on the front cover. Your name is lettered on the cover and on all other documents supplied to you by The Architects' Small House Service Bureau. *See Page 154.*

These four documents are combined together and sent you by parcel post in a heavy pasteboard mailing tube, securely sealed.

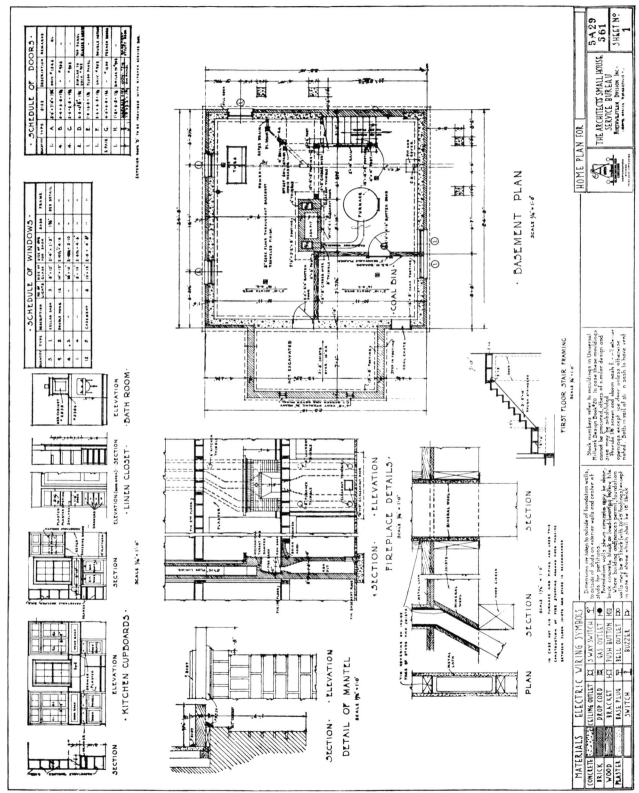

REPRODUCTION OF WORKING DRAWING—SHEET NO. 1

158

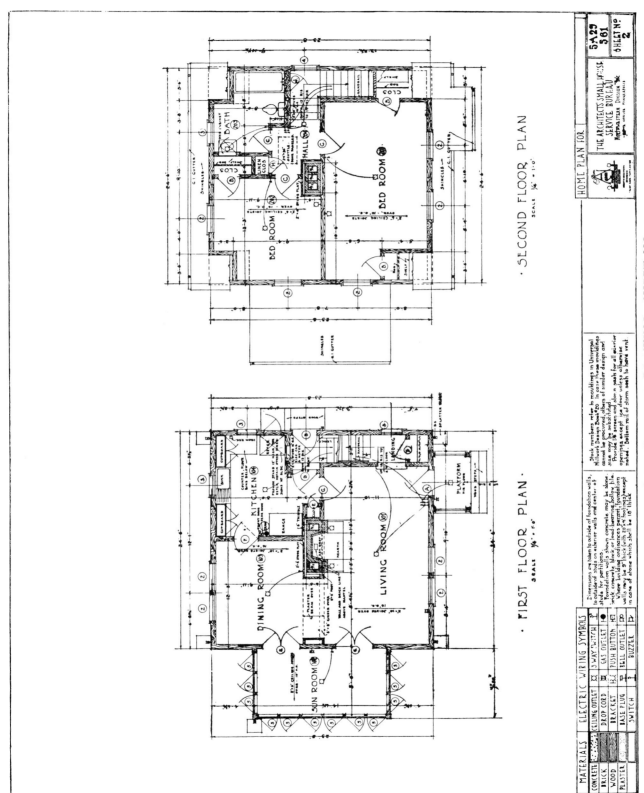

· SECOND FLOOR PLAN ·

SCALE ¼" = 1'0"

· FIRST FLOOR PLAN ·

SCALE ¼" = 1'0"

REPRODUCTION OF WORKING DRAWING—SHEET NO. 2

159

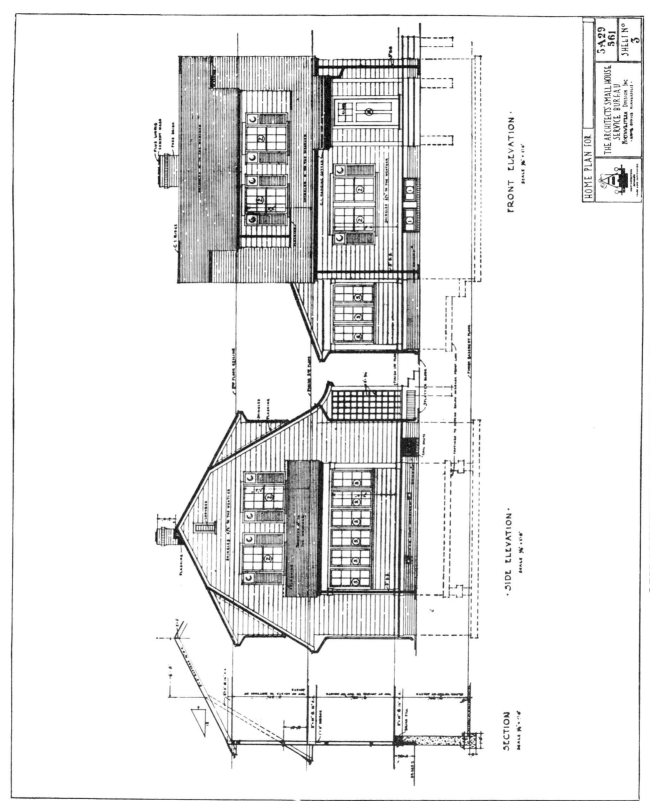

REPRODUCTION OF WORKING DRAWING—SHEET NO. 3

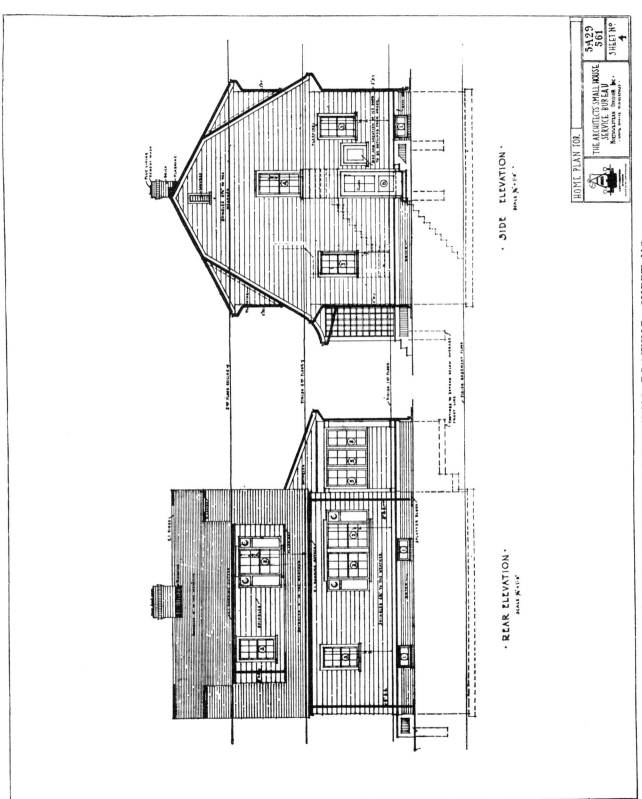

· SIDE ELEVATION ·
SCALE ¼"=1'-0"

· REAR ELEVATION ·
SCALE ¼"=1'-0"

HOME PLAN FOR.

THE ARCHITECTS SMALL HOUSE
SERVICE BUREAU
NORTHWESTERN DIVISION Inc.
MINNEAPOLIS MINNESOTA

5A29
561
SHEET N° 4

REPRODUCTION OF WORKING DRAWING—SHEET NO. 4

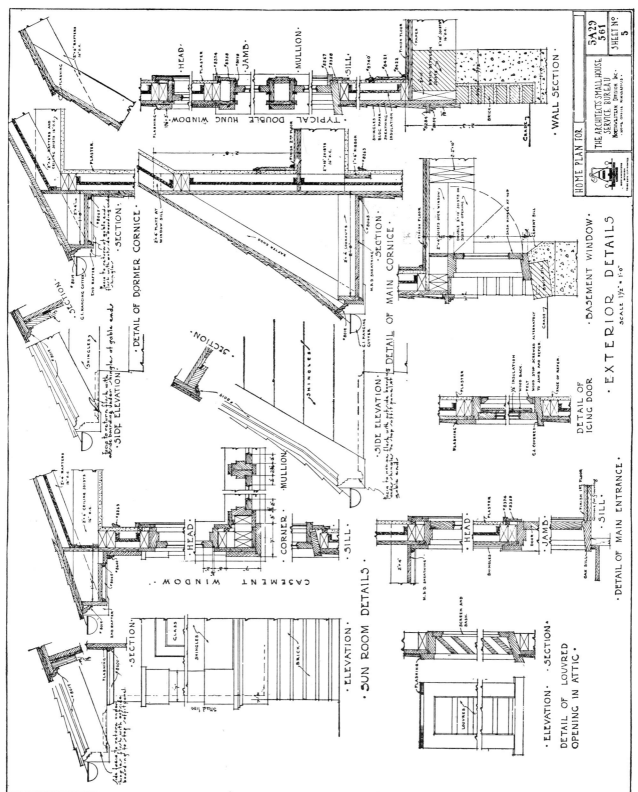

REPRODUCTION OF WORKING DRAWING—SHEET NO. 5